Other Ways of Growing Old

Other Ways of
GROWING OLD

Anthropological Perspectives

Edited by Pamela T. Amoss and Stevan Harrell

Stanford University Press, Stanford, California

Stanford University Press
Stanford, California
© 1981 by the Board of Trustees of the
Leland Stanford Junior University
Printed in the United States of America
Cloth ISBN 0-8047-1072-4
Paper ISBN 0-8047-1153-4
Original edition 1981
Last figure below indicates year of this printing:
91 90 89 88 87 86 85 84 83 82

Preface

In 1976, when Pamela Amoss was preparing to introduce a new course, Aging in Cross-Cultural Perspective, she discovered that there were few published ethnographic accounts of what old age is like. Knowing that many of her colleagues, like most anthropologists, had spent a lot of their time in the field with old people, she asked some of them to deliver guest lectures in her class, synthesizing their impressions of old people's roles in the societies they had studied. Stevan Harrell, Paul Hiebert, and James Nason, among others, each prepared a lecture highlighting a different aspect of old age, drawing on their experiences with old people in Taiwan, India, and Micronesia. But because Harrell had to be home with his children at the time the Aging class met, we had to videotape his lecture for the class. While preparing his script for this novel (to him) experience, Harrell suggested that perhaps all the guest lectures should be videotaped or, better still, written up for publication. This was the genesis of an idea that soon matured into a project. The original plan for the book was based on an ecological-evolutionary model used in the course. During the long process of soliciting, editing, accepting, rejecting, and introducing that is the work of volume editors, our own perspective shifted to the cost/contribution approach presented here. As the book developed, this took on the shape of an argument laid out in the Introduction and illustrated by the individual articles. The Introduction thus serves, we believe, as a preliminary formulation for the theoretical study of aging, one that we hope will provide enough insight into the aging process to allow others to build upon our approach and eventually supersede our initial general outline. Although the ethnographic contributions reinforce our theoretical argument, they remain what we wanted them to be in the first place: examples of what getting old is like in other places.

As a cooperative project, the book has been something of a paradox: we have worked it out primarily among ourselves and our contributors, spurred on by the editors at Stanford University Press and their reviewers. They all deserve our heartfelt thanks for their attention to detail, their patience with our slowness and inefficiency, and their persistent optimism that there would, indeed, be a book.

Outside the circle of contributors, editors, and critics, we want to thank two of our colleagues who helped us with advice and criticism at crucial junctures. In the early stages Robert Ekvall, professor emeritus, ethnographer, and writer of long experience, encouraged us to get the project under way by discussing and criticizing our ideas. In the final throes of manuscript preparation, Edgar Winans took time from his own work to read, criticize, and ultimately improve our Introduction.

P.T.A.

S.H.

Contents

Contributors

PAMELA T. AMOSS is Assistant Professor of Anthropology at the University of Washington, where she also earned her M.A. and Ph.D. degrees. She has done fieldwork among the Coast Salish Indians of Washington and British Columbia and among the Hazara of Afghanistan, and her publications include *Coast Salish Spirit Dancing* (1978).

MEGAN BIESELE has spent three years in Botswana living with the !Kung, first doing fieldwork on their mythology and ritual as part of the Harvard Kalahari Research Group, and later doing development work supported by the Kalahari Peoples Fund she helped to found. Now living in Woodville, Texas, she heads a descendant of that fund called the Center for the Study of Human Adaptation, studying the planning process in countries with hunter-gatherer minorities.

ELIZABETH COLSON is Professor of Anthropology at the University of California, Berkeley. She has carried out research among Native Americans in California, Washington, and Arizona; among Plateau and Gwembe Tonga in Zambia; in Darwin, Australia; and in a war relocation camp for Japanese and Japanese Americans. A major research involvement has been the longitudinal study of Gwembe District, Zambia, initiated in 1956.

CARL EISDORFER is Professor and Chairman of Psychiatry and Behavioral Science in the School of Medicine at the University of Washington. He received his Ph.D. from NYU in 1959 and his M.D. from Duke University in 1964. Author of over 150 articles and books in the field of gerontology, he is currently editor-in-chief of the *Annual Review of Gerontology* and president of the Western Gerontological Society.

STEVAN HARRELL is Assistant Professor of Anthropology at the University of Washington, where he teaches both anthropology and Chinese studies. His M.A. and Ph.D. degrees were taken at Stanford University, and he has conducted field research in Taiwan in 1970, 1972–73, and 1978. His research interests focus on Chinese society, family, and folk religion.

PAUL G. HIEBERT was born and raised in India. He received the Ph.D. from the University of Minnesota with a dissertation based on his field research in rural Andhra Pradesh. His publications include the village study *Konduru*, and he is currently Professor of Anthropology at Fuller Seminary in Los Angeles.

NANCY HOWELL is Professor of Sociology at the University of Toronto. Her demographic contributions to the article on the !Kung in this volume derive from two years of fieldwork in Botswana. Her publications include *Demography of the Dobe !Kung* (1979).

SARAH BLAFFER HRDY is a Research Associate at the Peabody Museum of Archaeology and Ethnology at Harvard University. She is the author of *The Black-Man of Zinacantan: A Central American Legend* (1972), *The Langurs of Abu: Female and Male Strategies of Reproduction* (1977), and *The Woman That Never Evolved: A Primatologist Examines Her Sex* (forthcoming). She is currently engaged in fieldwork on langur monkeys in Rajasthan, India.

JAMES D. NASON is Associate Professor of Anthropology at the University of Washington and Chairman of the Anthropology Division at the Thomas Burke Memorial Washington State Museum. He received his Ph.D. in 1970 from the University of Washington, after conducting field research in Micronesia in 1968–69 with funding from the National Institute of Mental Health.

THAYER SCUDDER is Professor of Anthropology at the California Institute of Technology. He has carried out research on the impact of resettlement in many parts of Africa and Asia, as well as among the Navajo in the United States. In the longitudinal study of Gwembe District, Zambia, initiated in 1956, he has focused on the effects of stress on relocated populations and the anthropology of development.

M. NAZIF SHAHRANI was born and raised in Afghanistan. He was educated in the United States, gaining a Ph.D. in anthropology from the University of Washington. He is currently a Visiting Assistant Professor of Anthropology at the University of California, Los Angeles, and he has published a book on the topic of his paper for this volume, *The Kirghiz and Wakhi of Afghanistan* (1979).

HENRY S. SHARP is Associate Professor of Anthropology at Simon Fraser University in British Columbia. He received his M.A. degree from Lehigh University and his Ph.D. from Duke University, the latter in 1973. He has done considerable fieldwork among the Chipewyan of Northern Canada, and is primarily interested in social anthropology and the cross-species study of social behavior.

PETER W. VAN ARSDALE is Research Anthropologist for PRC Engineering Consultants, Inc., of Denver, Colorado, and Research Anthropologist/Research Associate at the University of Denver's Institute of Gerontology and Center for Teaching International Relations. He was formerly an Assistant Professor of Anthropology at the University of Denver. He is the author or editor of three books and a number of articles based on his fieldwork in New Guinea, Sumatra, the Sudan, and the United States (the last involving Vietnamese refugees).

KENNETH M. WEISS is Associate Professor at the University of Texas Health Science Center at Houston. He received the B.A. degree in Mathematics and the M.A. and Ph.D. degrees in Biological Anthropology, the latter two from the University of Michigan. His major research activities currently center on the demography and genetics of disease patterns in the Rio Grande Valley. He is the author or editor of three books and many papers on topics in anthropological demography.

Foreword

CARL EISDORFER

This collection is designed to bring a cross-cultural perspective to the study of social gerontology. As such it may help to distinguish between aspects of old age that are fairly general and perhaps not easily changed and those that are shaped by the particular conditions of a given social and cultural system and presumably more readily manipulated. A number of comments are in order in discussing these observations.

First, it seems important to underscore the point made by Kenneth Weiss that contemporary demographic events should by now have demolished what seemed heretofore universally true—that the aged are only a small percentage of the population. This basic change in the relationship between the old and the rest of the population brings with it some profound consequences for one of the salient issues this volume addresses, that of the balance between the contributions of older persons and what different social groups are willing to expend to maintain them.

Second, although popular attention has focused on the "aging crisis" in the industrialized West, the massive increase in the numbers of the aged is a worldwide phenomenon. Because the developing nations have been experiencing a dramatic drop in mortality (from 20 per thousand in 1960 to 14 per thousand in 1975) while the developed countries have been holding steady at their more favorable rate of 9 per thousand, and because most of the lives saved in the developing countries have been those of infants and young children, the population profile in the Third World is still heavily weighted at the youthful end of the scale. However, while the increase in the proportion of the old among those countries does not look so impressive as in the industrialized world, the increase in actual numbers of old people will be greater in the developing world. In fact, the countries whose economies are least able to bear additional burdens—whose traditional social arrangements are experiencing the most rapid change—are precisely those that will very shortly have to bear the double burden of many more dependent elders as well as many more dependent young children (Beattie 1978; Myers 1977; Hauser 1976). In Africa, Latin America, and Asia, the number of people over 60 will more than double before the year 2000, putting a severe strain on existing social arrangements for meeting their needs. At the same time, as the papers in this volume and other sources note (e.g. Cowgill & Holmes 1972), social change is undermining the traditional opportunities and arrangements for old people in these areas to contribute to their own support.

In the West, particularly in the United States, this change in the age structure is leading to a redistribution of social, health, and financial resources. Traditionally, young children were the beneficiaries of the labors of adults, with the relatively small number of surviving aged supported by resources they had accumulated during their own or their families' years of productivity. A limited number of the aged were dependent upon society at large, particularly when resources were insufficient. The recent growth of this older group and the aging of the aged in relation to other segments of the population have begun to result in demands for more and more resources. This has come to affect lifelong distribution of income and to challenge our traditional system of education for the young, work for adults until age 65, and leisure for the aged.

It is well recognized that the aged are a population at heightened risk. With increasing age, people tend to have more physical, economic, and social problems, and are more likely to manifest specific types of disorders, e.g. the dementing illnesses (Kramer et al. 1973; Kay 1977). The risk that people will need long-term institutional care, in those cultures that provide it, also increases rapidly with age. It is thus important to note that the number of people aged 80 and over is growing, and that in North America from 1970 to 2000 this age group is predicted to increase by 96 percent (Beattie 1978: 6). Large as this percentage increase appears, it is small compared to the projected increases of 112 percent in Africa, 215 percent in Latin America, 176 percent in East Asia, and 134 percent in South Asia.

There has been a widespread popular American belief in a golden age of preliterate societies (Tobin 1978). The difficulties in which the old today find themselves are often attributed to the emergence of an industrial society that has devalued human in favor of technological contributions. It is presumed that in more labor-intensive cultures old people play more significant roles, that older people are always better valued in stable, preliterate or primitive societies, and that only in "westernized" or modernized cultures are they poorly treated.

The contributions to this volume challenge the accuracy of such simplistic ideas. Indeed, two other themes emerge from this instead: first, that the social rank of the old is determined by the balance between the cost of maintaining them and the contribution they are perceived as making; second, that family and kinship networks play an important role in protecting the old in all societies. Folk wisdom has always maintained that the most important investment a person can make for a secure old age is raising a family. Care and love lavished on children and grandchildren are almost always repaid, if not out of affection, then out of a sense of duty or fear of what the community will say. There are, however, limits to what families will do; in the case of the very demanding older persons (i.e. those with extraordinary needs), even family support systems may be overstressed, and there is a socially accepted transfer of responsibility from the family. These themes bring an important if troublesome message, both for our own society and for the developing world.

Under the manifest cost/benefit approach adopted by the editors, it would seem that many nonproductive elderly are the recipients of a society's largess. The challenge thus becomes, How can a society best create for the aged a role in which they can make a contribution that balances their cost? It would seem simple enough to resolve this dilemma by maintaining older persons in the labor force. But in the face of the problem of supporting more older people, society is caught in a dilemma. The pressure to remove older persons from the labor force is continuous and defended as necessary for the generation of new ideas, vitality, and leadership, as well as for the employment of the young and the channeling of their energies. There seems to be a pattern in union negotiations to press for a reduction in the retirement age and for a shortening of the work life. Associated with this theme is the belief that aging leads necessarily to physical and mental deterioration and that the aged are therefore poorer workers and not employable. The denial of access to employment and the resulting atrophy through disuse of many older persons' physical and cognitive capacities provides some reinforcement for this self-fulfilling hypothesis. As a consequence, we create policies that support retirement, thus helping society maintain the economic dignity of the individual while denying the same individual a relevant social role in the productive sector (except as a consumer).

When young adults and the middle-aged generate a sufficient surplus of resources, then the old may be subsidized. But if resources diminish in relation to needs, problems may emerge, including direct political conflict between the dependent and productive sectors or between separate groups of dependent people. Conflict between dependent groups for limited resources leads to attempts to acquire greater political power, as shown by the recent emergence of such groups as the Gray Panthers and the increases in the membership of organizations such as the American Association of Retired Persons, the National Retired Teachers Association, and the National Council of Senior Citizens, which now count members in the millions (Maddox 1978).

How are the anthropological perspectives in this collection likely to contribute to our making intelligent policy decisions? First, they may lead us to reassess the economic value of the old for the greater society. Given their greater marginal propensity to consume, the elderly may be viewed in Keynesian terms as a vehicle to stimulate the economy through creating increased demand for consumer goods. Unfortunately, this expedient tends to be interpreted as charity, whereas subsidy to industry is defined as a valuable investment in the economy. The labeling is crucial: support of the aged should be recognized as healthy for the economy and a return on the earlier work investment by the old. Second, anthropological perspectives may help us look beyond these purely economic considerations to the more complicated matter of how to assess the benefits to society of knowing one's heritage and better appreciation of the human life cycle through familiarity with one's grandparents (Mumford 1968). The stabilizing effect of several generations living in closer proximity is another yet-to-be-evaluated factor that merits attention. Indeed, such subjective variables may be as important to assessing the contribution of old people as are the more readily enumerable economic factors.

Certainly a desirable alternative would be to allow our elderly to follow the example of the most successful elders described in the articles in this collection—the old !Kung San who "own" resources, the Chinese matchmakers, the contemporary Coast Salish ritual leaders, the Kirghiz herd managers, and even the matriarchal macaques. They are all contributing valuable services and thus earning their respected social place. In our society maximizing the social utility and value of the old might include involving them in programs of retraining and education to avoid obsolescence; developing alternative social roles for them through a range of voluntary efforts and part-time employment; and identifying alternative ways to finance retirement, for example economic alternatives and supplements to Social Security that would provide a proportional "investment" in the economy as opposed to an eventual publicized depletion of general-fund revenue, which will be required to subsidize underfunded federal programs.

To improve the quality of life in old age, older persons must have a better self-image, must perceive that they have a range of options and that how they exercise those options will make a difference to the wider society. The concept of second, or perhaps multiple, careers might also be advanced. Individuals would no longer be placed in the "up or out" situation, but could move to alternative career options like the aged Brahman who is counseled to devote himself to spiritual fulfillment—a course thought to benefit not only him but his relatives as well. The entitlement to education for a new career could be accumulated as a social credit for years of work or social service, and support for the older student could be seen as a return for services rendered. The possibility of obligating older persons to provide services to the community could yield social benefits at least as valuable as military conscription for the young. An honorable discharge after a period of services to a community would entitle a person to a variety of educational and occupational benefits that could help reestablish him or her in a new program or at least increase the subsequent entitlement for a pension.

Turning to the role of the family in successful aging, the options seem more straightforward. The place of the family in supporting the old is an area where cultural consensus remains strong. The articles in this collection explore how family dynamics foster concern for aged parents and grandparents in a variety of cultural settings. Despite social and economic pressures that challenge the more traditional patterns of household composition and community structure, in the United States the preservation of family cohesiveness remains a strongly held belief. It would seem reasonable, therefore, that policymakers support the family's role in maintaining older people in the community. A policy that included support for families and a network of community-based services could probably do much to prevent, or at least postpone, institutionalization of some older people, and might reduce much of the stress coincident with helping dependent older relatives.

The developing countries, until recently overwhelmed by the burden of so many young children in need of food, education, and health care, have come to recognize that they are facing an unprecedented number of older people in need of services. As pointed out above, although the numbers will be large, the percentages will remain lower than in the West (for some time) because of the continuing high birth rate. Third World policymakers, concerned about this problem, have asked for a worldwide conference on aging to be held in 1982, the year following the third White House Conference on Aging planned for the United States.

The problems facing the developing countries, where all but three of the peoples described in this book live, are illustrated by what the authors tell us about the adaptation of older persons to the changes brought by modernization. Wherever medical care and food supplies are generally available, sources of wealth and influence are changing and the elderly are often unable to compete successfully for new avenues of affluence and power. Furthermore, children and grandchildren who traditionally support many older persons are being lured away to new jobs distant from the old village or camp. These are examples of changes that led Cowgill and Holmes (1972) to argue that modernization lowered the rank of the old.

Modernization not only is undermining many of the traditional supports of older people but is inexorably increasing the numbers of older people through improved medical services prolonging the lives of the old and middle-aged—not to mention children who will in their turn eventually be old. If the industrialized West is feeling the pressure of the old on limited resources, how much more may the developing countries, whose resources are already woefully inadequate, feel them? Though the problems of aging in the developing world are formidable, there are at least two factors that could make their situation more promising than that in the underdeveloped countries. First, most of the developing nations have not yet formulated or committed themselves to policies, and may still learn from the mistakes of the industrialized world. Second, and paradoxically, the poverty of the developing nations may force most of them to avoid the more expensive (and less desirable) institutional solutions that have proved so troublesome in the West. These nations may begin with the kind of arrangements that policymakers in United States are only now beginning to examine seriously, such as funding of supplementary care for the old through support of the family. Also, the very population pressures that are such a nightmare to Third World planners may affect the longer-term solutions to care for the old because with the high birth rate and much higher survival rate it is likely that the next several cohorts of old people will have surviving children and grandchildren. The Western experience has shown that filial piety, far from being a casualty of modernization, is perhaps one of the most tenacious of cultural values. Given the continued problems of unemployment in the developing countries, children and grandchildren may be happy to receive a modest government stipend for caring for older family members; then they could help with such care not only out of a sense of duty, but also out of economic necessity. McKain (1972: 156–57) has suggested that although respect for old age persists in the Soviet Union as a cultural value, the elderly are welcome in their children's homes because they make real economic contributions through their small pensions and the housekeeping and baby-sitting services they can provide.

The problem of "replacing" social roles for older people is monumental in the face of the great cultural and social diversity represented by the nations and peoples lumped together as "developing." Again, however, it looks as if at least some of the Third World countries are attempting to preserve traditional family relationships in the face of economic and political change. Whether they will be able to achieve a synthesis of economic modernization and traditional values is difficult to assess, but I would conjecture that they are most likely to succeed in their attempts to rally around the ideals of family cohesiveness. Certainly this has emerged in the longer term, even when governmental policy has attempted to minimize the integrity of the family.

It now seems clear that a national as well as an international program of social innovation is needed to address a number of issues stemming from the changes in world age demography. To continue to treat the problems of the old purely in terms of increased provision of services such as income, housing, nutrition, and the like is to risk serious economic difficulties some decades hence—unless we can guarantee a healthy economy capable of sustaining, in a welfare situation, twice or more times the present number of older people at a higher level of care. Even then, the emotional costs to the individual of being the recipient of society's munificence (i.e. being on the dole) may be too high. Being a drain on one's family without contributing to it may also be hard for many to accept.

The data from other cultures suggest that maximum participation of the elderly is the preferred route for policy. Research into illness prevention, maintenance of function, improved distribution of one's own resources throughout the life span, and different educational environments and elements is a necessary first step. The challenge of longevity should be to maximize a person's potential for contributing to himself and to society throughout life.

Other Ways of Growing Old

Introduction: An Anthropological Perspective on Aging

PAMELA T. AMOSS AND STEVAN HARRELL

As anthropologists, we offer this book about aging in a wide variety of human societies in the hope of its making three contributions. First, this book will help to remedy a massive neglect of old age by the discipline of anthropology. The pioneering work of Leo Simmons (1945) has remained a lonely monument since the 1940's, for despite recent interest in the subject of aging in modern Western societies on the part of social gerontologists and sociologists, little has been done by anthropologists on aging in non-Western societies. Where it has been treated at all, it has been in the form either of a few final paragraphs in the discussion of the life cycle or of a simple ethnographic fact among other facts about a certain social system. What has been missing has been any attempt to put aging in a cross-cultural or comparative perspective, to give this vital subject the same treatment that has been accorded marriage, for example, or death or inheritance or sex roles.

Second, this book will bring a needed cross-cultural perspective to the study of social gerontology. The recent explosion of interest in this field has been largely confined to the study of aging in North America and Europe. But we anthropologists feel that such a culturally limited study, though interesting and productive in its own right, is dangerously narrow if it does not consider what aging is like in other societies. What aspects of aging, for example, are human universals and have to be planned for as inevitable, and what aspects are cultural particulars and can be avoided, modified, or strengthened under certain social conditions? By presenting both a biological account of the universals of human aging (Weiss),

and specific ethnographic accounts of aging in a wide variety of societies, we believe we can help to put North American aging into
perspective.

Third, we hope this book will serve as an illustration of a particular anthropological approach to unity and diversity in human
societies and cultures. Perhaps the main task of sociocultural anthropology is a twofold one: the explanation of cross-cultural universals, somehow rooted either in the biological nature of the human species or in universal imperatives of social organization, and
the explanation of intercultural variations, rooted in a dialectical
interaction between culture and the material conditions (partially
created by culture) in which it exists. If unity and diversity can indeed be explained in this way, the cross-cultural study of aging can
serve as a paradigm. By first setting out what seem to be the universals determined by the biology of the human species, and by then
exploring the range of variation in cultural solutions, we ought to
be able to formulate a set of principles that will allow us to explain
why variations occur in a certain way. Nine ethnographic case studies are enough, we believe, to enable us to formulate some preliminary hypotheses about the nature and causes of variation in the social process of aging.

Human Universals

In his paper in this volume, Weiss posits that aging is a process
somehow genetically programmed into the human animal, that a
physiological maximum of somewhere between 90 and 100 years
represents the limits on human life except in quite unusual cases. In
the later part of this life span, certain processes of physiological deterioration are inevitable, so that people in the final decades of the
span are almost certain to experience certain kinds of physical and
mental disabilities. Both the length of the life span and the physical
deterioration characteristic of its final phases are universals that
any cultural pattern has to take into account.

The fact that our biological life span far exceeds our reproductive span is another universal—and one that calls for an explanation. Most higher mammals remain fertile throughout their life

spans, as do many nonhuman primates. But the females of some of our evolutionarily close relatives, the Old World Monkeys, appear to undergo menopause before the end of their life spans much as human females do. Why is this so? Hrdy suggests that for the langurs and macaques she discusses the survival of females beyond reproductive age enhances the prospects for survival of the kin-based groups to which the old female monkeys belong: among langurs, old females defend their daughters' children against infanticidal males; among macaques, old females lead the "matrilineages" that are the basic units of macaque social organization. In addition, survival beyond reproductive age allows animals to raise their offspring to adulthood before they themselves die. As Weiss points out in his article, however, such positive adaptive advantages may not be necessary to explain human survival beyond reproductive age, because our aging clock runs at about the expected speed for a mammal with our body size, metabolic rates, and degree of encephalization. From this point of view, maybe there is really nothing special about the *human* life span that requires particular explanation.

These biological universals contribute to certain cultural universals in the way human societies handle aging. Every known society has a named social category of people who are old—chronologically, physiologically, or generationally. In every case these people have different rights, duties, privileges, and burdens from those enjoyed or suffered by their juniors. This group is defined differently in different places, but it exists everywhere and is the group we refer to as "the old" or "the aged" when speaking of any human society.

It is also nearly universally true that societies divide the category of aged persons into two classes. The first consists of people who are no longer fully productive economically (and who must consequently depend on others for at least a portion of their livelihood) but who are still physically and mentally able to attend to their essential daily needs. The second consists of the totally dependent—people who require custodial care and supervision, whether for physical or mental reasons. There is of course a continuum here, but conceptually most societies distinguish two categories.

There seems to be little cultural variation in the plight of the incompetent aged; they are everywhere regarded as a burden. Some peoples make more elaborate provisions for their care than do others, and some, like the Chipewyan discussed in Sharp's paper, until recently simply abandoned them to die when the burden of supporting them endangered the existence of the family or band. Other societies, like the Chinese or Tonga, make grudging provision for their care, allowing them food, shelter, and sometimes a little company. Because their sad lot seems an intractable human universal, they are not a major focus of this book.

It is with the other category of the aged, those who are still physically and mentally competent, that this book is primarily concerned; here we encounter both human universals and cultural variation. One universal stands out as requiring particular comment: the biologically determined prolonged dependence of the human infant, which results in the young everywhere developing an intense identification with those who nurture, protect, and instruct them. These attachments are so strong that they persist throughout life, even when the former caretakers are old and have come to depend on those they once nurtured. Exactly who these caretakers are varies both among and within societies, but they always include mothers. For this reason, people everywhere have feelings of affection for and attachment to their mothers, feelings that translate into positions of respect in the family group. Such ties of affection and respect are often not enjoyed by fathers or other senior relatives. This can be particularly striking in societies like the Chinese, described by Harrell, where women rise from a low position in the family during their productive and reproductive years until as old women, because of the affection their children hold for them, they often enjoy more real esteem and attention than do their brothers and husbands. However tinged with ambivalence, affectionate feelings toward mothers can be seen in the role of old women everywhere.

Cultural Variation: Some Tools

The human universals set out above are rather few, and simple of conception and explanation. Though they set the parameters within which cultural variation must occur, they form in a sense only the background to the main task of our analysis, which is to explain the nature and extent of cultural variation and to uncover the factors that contribute to it. Before beginning our analysis, however, it is essential that we set out in full certain assumptions and hypotheses that we have adopted.

First, we assume that old people, like other human beings, are not passive actors in a system determined by outside influences but create the conditions of their own existence within the limits established by factors they cannot control. We believe that the aged in any society are constantly adapting to changing conditions, and constantly striving to shape events to serve their own goals.

Second, we assume that the conditions old people have to adapt to set limits on their adaptation. These conditions include the human universals described above, the demographic structure of particular populations, the nature of the natural environment and subsistence economy, and the wants, strategies, and powers of other groups in the population.

Third, we assume that there are certain universal goals toward which old people everywhere will strive. These include physical and emotional security, the respect of other members of the community, and an assurance that they are playing a useful part in the life of the family and the society. Insofar as these goals are met in a particular society, we describe the position of the aged there as "high" or "good"; insofar as they are not, we describe their position as "low" or "bad."

Given these assumptions, we hypothesize that two factors largely determine the relative success old people have in a particular society in achieving their goals. The first is the balance between the costs old people represent to the group and the contributions they make. The second is the degree of control old people maintain over resources necessary to the fulfillment of the needs or wants of younger members of the group. In some systems specific powers or privileges—political, juridical, ritual—inhere in old people as a collective. In others, old people do not automatically have power or privileges simply because they are old, but they nonetheless can

gain significant power as individuals. Thus we take it that the position of the aged in a given society can be expressed in terms of how
much old people contribute to the resources of the group, balanced
by the cost they exact, and compounded by the degree of control
they have over valuable resources.

Of course it is simplistic to attempt to generalize about *the* position of the aged in any society without taking into account differences between the sexes and class differences, or the impact of
social change. Even in the simplest societies the roles of old people
vary by sex, and all of our articles illustrate clearly the differences
between the position of old men and old women. In complex societies, sex differences are compounded by class differences, a fact
that comes out strongly in Hiebert's description of India and Harrell's account of the Chinese in Taiwan. Finally, social change everywhere makes the process of aging different for each new generation
of old people. This is pointed out clearly in the contributions on the
Chipewyan (Sharp), the Coast Salish (Amoss), the Asmat (Van
Arsdale), the Etalese (Nason), and the Gwembe Tonga (Colson and
Scudder). Nevertheless, we believe that variation within societies
can be explained in the same terms as variation between them—
i.e., in terms of the cost/contribution balance and the degree of
control the aged are able to retain. In the remainder of this Introduction we will test this hypothesis in several spheres of social activity, drawing on the ethnographic material provided in the articles that follow for examples.

Demographic Factors

We have seen that there is a theoretical maximum to the human
life span, which evidence indicates has not changed much throughout the course of human history. But there has been great variation
in the frequency with which people have actually lived out this life
span. Today, societies relatively untouched by modern developments in the realm of health and sanitation tend to have fewer old
people as a proportion of the population than do societies where
these developments have long been embraced. (Societies in the process of change represent a middle ground that we will leave aside

for the moment, since the introduction of modern medicines can often increase the life expectancy of the aging but paradoxically reduce their proportion in the population because of the concomitant decline in infant mortality.) Since a large part of the cost of maintaining old people in any given society depends upon the percentage of the population they constitute, we can see that where the aged are relatively few, the cost of maintaining them is light. Indeed, one of the reasons why aging has become such a subject of concern in the West today is the realization that the developed countries will soon have to deal with the cost of supporting an unprecedentedly high percentage of old people. In addition to the question of cost, however, is that of control over resources: as old people become more numerous, they may exercise greater control over the distribution of goods and services, at the expense of the young.

Another point about population structure bears particular mention here, both because it appears many times in the papers that follow and because it contradicts, to some degree, a popular stereotype that is based on the recent experience of modern industrial societies alone. This concerns the sex ratio among the aged. In modern industrial societies, women tend to outlive men by wide margins, but in the societies described in this book the sex ratio among the aged is generally near unity. In the cases of the Asmat (Van Arsdale) and the Kirghiz (Shahrani), as well as in some populations in India (Vatuk 1976), old men actually outnumber old women. Whether this disparity results from the loss of young women in childbirth or from other factors is a subject for further research. Another significant ethnographic fact—that there is almost universally a larger number of widows than of widowers—is in all likelihood a result of men's marrying later than women in nearly all societies, not of any difference in life expectancy.

Subsistence Economy

In societies where people make a living solely by hunting and gathering, where the basic social unit is the band of no more than a hundred people, where frequent mobility makes possessions necessarily few, and where productive resources are held in common, the balance between the subsistence cost and contribution of the aged is perhaps the most important factor in determining their position. Our collection contains ethnographic case studies of three such societies: the !Kung San of the Kalahari Desert in southwestern Africa (Biesele and Howell); the Chipewyan of subarctic Canada (Sharp); and the Asmat of coastal New Guinea (Van Arsdale). Since the subsistence activities of men in these societies differ from those of women, we must consider the costs and contributions of the aged in this sphere separately by sex.

For men in these three societies—and in all societies of this type—old age tends to be defined in terms of withdrawal from the major subsistence activity of hunting. But the position of retired hunters differs greatly among these groups. For the Chipewyan especially, subsistence means hunting, and the subsistence that hunting brings is often precarious. Since old men no longer able to hunt exact a great cost from the group while making no contribution, their position is low; old age is consequently despised and feared, and Chipewyan men unable to hunt feel useless, left out, and powerless. Indeed, as Sharp tells us in his paper, the Chipewyan, along with other Athapaskan groups (Van Stone 1974: 83), were sometimes even forced to abandon their old people when it came to a choice between the old people dying and everybody dying. The Eskimo of the Canadian Arctic (Guemple 1969 : 69), who led a similar mobile hunting existence, were also sometimes forced to abandon the old. But the sedentary Eskimo of St. Lawrence Island (Hughes 1960) did not leave old people to die, and the two Eskimo groups held similar attitudes toward the elderly, attitudes quite different from those of the Athapaskans. The Eskimo did not despise their old people; they honored them. When food supplies were very short it was the old people themselves who were expected to make the hard choice, not their younger kin (*ibid.*). It thus appears that the emotional cost may have been less for all concerned among the Eskimo, but the result was the same: the dictates of harsh subsistence realities won out, here as among the Chipewyan.

Among the !Kung San and the Asmat, by contrast, old men were often able to assert political leadership in kinship and local groups even after their hunting skills had deteriorated. This seems related to the fact that in neither of these societies was the subsistence economy so precarious as it was for the Chipewyan, so that the reduction of subsistence contributions was less crucial. To balance their subsistence cost, old men made social contributions in other spheres, which we will consider in a later section.

Women in these three societies managed to weather the aging process better than men. This is because women's tasks do not require the extreme physical vigor that is a prerequisite for successful hunting. As long as a woman can walk, she can gather; as long as she can see, she can do relatively light domestic chores. Particularly important in this regard is old women's continuing ability to care for small children, most often their grandchildren. In all these societies (as in many others) grandparents look after children, a responsibility that falls mainly upon the women, though not exclusively. In caring for grandchildren, an old woman is not only freeing a younger woman for productive labor, she is also helping to shape the important grandparent/grandchild emotional ties that so often provide comfort and solace for the aged.

For the rest of the societies in this book, the position of the aged depends much less on a simple balance between their subsistence contribution and the cost of maintaining them. Even in the more complex societies, however, subsistence needs and contributions cannot be overlooked. Harrell's article on Chinese workers and farmers in rural Taiwan shows, for example, that when old men become unable to bring in income from the farm or the coal mine, they gradually lose their managerial position in the family as well. Old women in Taiwan, like those among the hunter-gatherers, remain useful around the house and thus are more likely to maintain their respected position.

Property

Among hunter-gatherers, subsistence goods belong to those who acquire them, or to their family members, other kin, or fellow band members. Access to land and its products is free, and those who supply the labor necessary to acquire subsistence products "own" those products. Thus old people in such societies who can no longer produce for themselves are dependent on junior kin or on various sorts of economic partners for their livelihood. In agricultural and pastoral societies, however, the situation is more complex, because fields or herds are conceived of as being the property of someone, and that someone can be an old person, even one no longer able to supply the necessary labor to produce the means of his or her own livelihood. Old people are just as dependent on their juniors for the labor needed to produce subsistence goods, but the relationship is not conceived of as simply one person supplying the products of labor to another. Thus old people who control property (either as outright owners or, as among the Chinese, through trusteeship and managerial rights) can use their rights over it to compel others to support them or provide them goods and services. Thus the second dimension of our model of the position of the aged enters the picture: the dimension of control. Through control of access to resources, the old, though physically dependent on others, can make others legally dependent on them. So, when examining the way old people maneuver and plan for old age in agricultural and pastoral societies, we must look at the way they attempt to acquire and maintain rights over property—rights that will ensure their livelihood when they can no longer provide for themselves.

A graphic example of the importance of property in determining the position of the aged is given in the discussion by Colson and Scudder of the Gwembe Tonga of Zambia. Before the mass relocation resulting from the building of the Kariba Dam in the 1950's, Gwembe men could secure their position by accumulating property in land and small livestock. Property provided the wherewithal for men to pay the bridewealth necessary to accumulate several wives, whose labor (in due course together with that of their sons and their sons' wives, and occasionally of their matrilateral nephews) provided them with support. The heads of successful extended families of this sort were well supplied; those less successful had only the minimum of necessities and comforts. With relocation in 1958, control of lineage-held lands, now mostly under water, lost its meaning, and many old people became increasingly dependent on the good will of their sons and nephews for their sustenance. Colson and Scudder expect, however, that the position of the elderly will improve again when the men who were in early middle age at the time of relocation become elders. These men were in a position to gain control, through their own labor, of most of the best land in the new locations; when they grow old, they may well hold something resembling the power that their grandfathers once held.

In another paper describing an agricultural society, Nason shows how for the Etal Islanders of Micronesia, whose social norms condemn elders who attempt to keep all of their property at the expense of their grown children, the maintenance of some control over property is crucial to a successful and comfortable old age. Old people, rather than turning all their property over to children or other relatives, try to keep enough to ensure continued care on the part of those juniors who hope to inherit. If their own children do not care for them well, then there will be other young relatives, eager for a potential share of the inheritance, to pick up the slack. The success of this system requires striking a careful balance between the amount of property the old give over to their heirs and the amount they retain for themselves.

A somewhat different sort of relationship between property and aging is set forth in Shahrani's article on the Kirghiz of Afghanistan. In this community of about 2,000 high-altitude nomads, a few families own over 80 percent of the livestock. The senior members of such wealthy families have great advantages over their poorer kin; a man can take several wives to produce children who will provide all the labor necessary to support him. A wealthy family with little labor can let out stock to poorer families and gain some return from the arrangement. An impecunious family, on the other hand, is dependent on its own labor to herd the yaks, cattle, and sheep it rents from wealthier neighbors; and where such a family has little labor power, the senior members are condemned to an insecure, uncomfortable old age.

For a final example, we can look at Hiebert's study of aging in a village in south India, where the religious ideal of mendicancy and detachment in old age, theoretically available to any member of the "twice-born" higher castes, is in fact a realistic hope only for a man whose household economic affairs are secure enough that he can leave his wife in the care of grown sons or other relatives who can manage his property.

In all these societies, control of property stands out as a way for old people to ensure a reasonably secure livelihood for themselves. Without it, old people end up at the mercy of their children and other juniors. Moreover, unless elders have been successful in acquiring control over property, what their children and other juniors can provide is limited by the juniors' own lack of access to property. At the same time, the economic power of senior members of families and kinship groups in agricultural societies comes at the price of considerable emotional tension between generations. Younger people prevented from "coming of age" by parents' reluctance to yield control experience ambivalent feelings about their elders, a topic we shall consider more fully later.

Politics

In most societies, older people gain access to positions in which the laws and customs of society give them considerable political power. Within any society, it is useful to distinguish two kinds of politically powerful positions that older people may occupy. The first are those that are assigned automatically (or nearly so) to all people who reach a certain culturally defined age level. Perhaps the clearest example of this sort of position occurs in age-graded societies, where elders as a corporate group wield power in local communities.

Among East African groups like the Samburu (Spencer 1965) age grades can balance the divisive tendencies of lineage organization and permit the mobilization of all youth by all elders for certain kinds of jobs, e.g. defense and raiding. This kind of arrangement confers special authority on the senior men, legitimized by an ideology that imputes greater wisdom and supernatural power to the old. The price of this arrangement is perpetual tension between older and younger age sets and a lack of flexibility in responding to the needs of individual men who may fall at the older or younger extremes of their set (Foner & Kertzer 1978: 189–90).

But even outside formally age-graded societies there are politically powerful positions that fall to nearly everyone who attains the requisite stage in the life cycle. These are positions of leadership in family groups, which are illustrated in our volume by the headship of the *oey* among the Kirghiz of Afghanistan, or of the extended *jia* household among traditional Chinese. The preceding section made clear, however, that such political power in the family depends on the availability of resources, so that in economically stratified societies elders of wealthy households can generally command their adult children's labor and resources more effectively than elders from poor households, where income may primarily take the form of wages earned by the younger members. Both China and India provide examples of such class differences in the power of elders over their juniors, and also in the persistence, in the face of modernization, of the extended family structures that have traditionally conferred such power on senior members.

The second type of political positions older people may hold are not assigned to everyone who reaches a certain point in the life cycle but are held by particular people to the exclusion of others. Since in most societies the exercise of political power of this sort requires diplomatic skill, a wide network of contacts, and experience in "arranging things," and since these things take time, the old predominate in such political offices.

The clearest examples among the case studies in this book come from Shahrani's article on the Kirghiz and Van Arsdale's on the Asmat. Among the Kirghiz, Shahrani tells us, there is a hierarchy of three levels of political offices: camp head, lineage head, and Khan, or head of the whole society. Access to all these positions comes through a combination of wealth, ability, and seniority within the kinship group. Holders of these offices are usually among the oldest, as well as the wealthiest, of the household heads within the units they lead, and Kirghiz respect for the aged generally is magnified in the case of the political leaders, who are by definition elders.

Among the Asmat, before significant acculturation (which began not more than twenty years ago), political power in Asmat local groups was in the hands of *tesmaypits*, "men who could arrange things," who were both the military and the civil leaders of their bands. Through a combination of war prowess and ritual and artistic ability, these men became recognized leaders who arranged not only raiding and revenge, but ritual, trade, and the periodic relocation of villages. Supporting the general attitude of respect for elders as political leaders were myths celebrating old-man figures who were the creators and culture heroes of the Asmat world. But with intensive culture contact, the termination of head-hunting and raiding in the coast area, and the more or less permanent relocation of part of the population in villages near the coast, the abilities of prestigious old men to manipulate political factors in the traditional society very quickly became irrelevant, and their position suffered a dramatic decline. Both in the process of modernization and absorption into the Indonesian economy, and in the "cargo cult" new religions which, in typical New Guinea fashion, have arisen as responses to the pressures and frustrations of rapid social and cultural change, it is younger men who have taken the lead. The former *tesmaypits* are now, according to Van Arsdale, relatively powerless old men, no longer commanding nearly the respect they once had from their juniors. Their skills, the political and ritual skills of the old system, are no longer relevant to arranging things in the new order dominated by strange people and alien ideas.

Knowledge

Both the contributions made by old people and the control they exercise over valuable resources are perhaps seen most clearly in the case of knowledge. Though there is great variation in the degree to which old people control property or exercise political power, as well as great differences in the contributions old people make to the economy, there is much less variation in the way old people monopolize valuable knowledge. And though specialized technical information may be controlled by old people in some societies, it is through their control of ritual and religious knowledge, or the knowledge that contributes to the whole enterprise of "generating and sustaining meaningful forms" (Ortner 1974: 72), that the old gain a special measure of respect almost everywhere. Moreover, the central position of the elderly in this cultural enterprise is a consequence of dominant patterns of human development. The old have had the longest time to learn and practice the symbols and meanings of their cultural system. They are more fully enculturated, more fully socialized. To borrow a perspective from Levi-Strauss (1970), the old are to the young as culture is to nature. Levi-Strauss has proposed that a dichotomy between the humanly created world—"culture"—and the natural environment—"nature"—is present in the conceptual map of every human culture, represented in myths and religious ritual. Although nature is conceived of as powerful, it is also seen as disordered and dangerous and perhaps unpredictable in comparison with humanly created culture, which is predictable, controllable, and ordered. Origin myths that explain how humanity came to be as it is always tell how the first people learned the ways of culture—how to use fire to cook their food, to speak, to build houses, to regulate marriages, and the like. In this progression from a state of nature, like animals, to a state of culture, like people, culture is placed in a superior position to nature. Just so, the old are seen as superior to the very young. Whereas young children are unruly and unmannerly, without language, shame, instruction, or memory, the old are dignified, masters of their native language and its oral traditions, sensitive to honor, well versed in customary law, and able to remember periods of time unknown to younger adults. Old people are not only more individualized than young people, they are also more fully committed to their own cultural system, its modes of expression, its technology, its dominant themes, and its aesthetic values. So not only do the old represent culture in general as opposed to nature, they embody the culture of a particular group most fully.

Insofar as the activities of younger adults are seen as less cultural and more natural, less human and more animal, older adults will enjoy higher status than younger ones. The !Kung San (Biesele & Howell) and aboriginal Coast Salish (Amoss) offer interesting illus-

trations of this point. In these societies, as among many hunting
and gathering peoples, sexually active adults had to observe many
ritual restrictions on their contact with supernatural powers and
with important food resources. Pregnant and menstruating Coast
Salish women had to avoid hunters and their gear, berry patches,
fishing sites and clam beds, and shamans practicing their curing
arts. Men also had to refrain from any sexual contact before they
went hunting, fishing, or to war. All during their reproductive years
both men and women had to avoid certain foods and any contact
with certain kinds of supernatural power. Most of these restrictions
were lifted from people past the age of begetting or bearing children. The significance of this ritual freedom for the old has been
variously interpreted, but we suggest that insofar as human reproduction is "natural" because it resembles the general mammalian
pattern, those beyond the reproductive period were released from
the ritual disabilities and impurities it generated. Because under
premodern conditions women were necessarily more involved in
the process of bearing and nurturing children than men, the end of
their reproductive careers had a more dramatic effect on their status than the gradual waning of men's reproductive capacity. Both
sexes were released from some of the demands of nature, but for
women the change was more dramatic and the proportionate rise in
status greater.

Healing is a cultural specialization of the elderly in many societies, and in most the curer's art is a composite of spiritual power
and practical knowledge of medical skills. Among the !Kung San,
old people are dispensers of all kinds of ritual and supernatural
knowledge. But their specialization in the arts of healing is particularly noteworthy, since it consists primarily of trance perfor-
mances, in which spirit mediums attempt to cure by divine powers
they receive in their state of possession. Although people in their
30's and 40's can work as curers, it is much easier for those past active child-rearing years, released from food taboos and other ritual
restrictions, to acquire, keep, and use spirit powers. Along with
trance goes dance, and the purely aesthetic manifestations of music
and dance movement are also developed by old people, many of

whom spend a good part of a lifetime becoming more proficient in dancing and the associated curing rites.

Another example of the central importance of the aged in maintaining cultural values comes from Hiebert's work in India, where the traditional Hindu laws prescribe a four-stage life cycle for high-caste men: student, householder, ascetic, and mendicant. In the last two stages, religious men are enjoined to renounce worldly attachments to home, family, sex, and the sensual pleasures of life in favor of seeking enlightenment in the forest. In this way, the pursuit of the highest form of knowledge is limited to older men of higher castes. Not only the pursuit of knowledge, however, but also the dissemination of knowledge is the preserve of these learned elders. Although many are simply hermits, avoiding human contact of any sort, a considerable number become learned teachers, and draw crowds of followers eager to partake of their wisdom.

Ritual knowledge, of course, is not the only sort for which older people are valued: in many traditional societies wise elders are relied on for technical, social, and legal knowledge as well. The *tesmaypits* of the traditional Asmat was not just someone with ritual knowledge, he was someone whose organizational and political knowledge enabled him to arrange all sorts of things. Nason's description of a Micronesian atoll gives us examples of old people providing the legal knowledge necessary to settle disputes, as well as specialized technical know-how in navigation, canoe building, and divining. But on the whole, it seems that technical knowledge is not as likely to be the special preserve of the elderly as ritual knowledge, perhaps because technical knowledge is fairly simple and straightforward, and also because it is most valuable to those who use it directly—the young and middle-aged adults who are most active in economic production. By contrast, not only is ritual knowledge complex, secret or esoteric, and useful to everybody, it also embodies a plan for how people should live—a kind of prescriptive map of the social universe.

The contribution of ritual knowledge to the power and prestige of the aged is not, however, universal even in relatively stable societies. We can see this clearly in the Chipewyan, among whom the elderly are not held in esteem. The Chipewyan believe that power is based on magical knowledge independent of age. Since the source and nature of the magical knowledge can never be revealed without losing it, power can only be demonstrated by success in the most important pursuits of Chipewyan life—which for men means hunting. So in this society, when a man can no longer hunt he is assumed to have lost his magical power.

We have spoken thus far of the value of knowledge in relatively traditional societies, where knowledge, at least in the ritual sphere, has remained comparatively stable for a long time. South Indian villagers still hold closely to the teachings of centuries, and the free-living !Kung San in the late 1960's and early 1970's were not yet severely threatened by the ideas and religion of those bent on settling and civilizing them. But in order to make our survey of the intellectual role of the elderly more complete, we must also examine societies in which the belief and idea systems have been severely challenged by the presence of competing systems, usually promoted by agencies and governments more powerful than the people they have come to "civilize." It would seem reasonable that for people bent on a course of adaptation to modern society, traditional knowledge would become less useful. And indeed, we have seen this happening with the Asmat, whose *tesmaypits* today possess little of what the younger generation sees as really important knowledge— the abilities to read, to speak Indonesian, and to deal with powerful government agencies. Other examples of the declining relevance of traditional knowledge are provided by the Tonga, whose leaders were partly left behind by the beginnings of rural education in Zambia; the Taiwanese, many of whose younger men and women are beginning to participate in a semi-Westernized, urban-oriented society based at least partly on Western technological and scientific knowledge; and the Etalese, who are beginning to value Western education over learning of traditional skills.

This general trend of the declining relevance of traditional knowledge with rapid social change brings us to one of the most interesting cases of the intellectual place of the elderly, that of the Coast Salish Indians of Washington, described by Amoss. In this society, as in so many other native North American groups, there has been something of a nativist revival in the past decade; many people of all ages are turning away from the values and structures of the dominant white society and attempting to reassert their identity as Indians. One of the most important aspects of this return to Indian identity is the survival and revival of the traditional religious spirit dancing (Amoss 1978). Because it is the elders who have traditionally held the greatest spirit powers and who best remember the forms and details of the rituals, the esteem in which they are held has risen considerably with this most recent social change, a change that has once again made their ritual knowledge valuable. This case should serve to warn us against simplistic assumptions about the nature of social change and its effect on the elderly. Most social change that we observe today is change away from tribal or peasant forms and values toward the forms of industrial society and secular values based at least partly on the Western example. Cowgill and Holmes (1972: 9) are probably right to generalize that in such cases rapid change means a decline in the position of the elderly. But there are also cases like the one Amoss describes, in which the direction of change is toward a conscious restoration of old forms. Amoss's description of what happens to old people in such cases is probably typical: their position improves because their contribution increases.

The Experience of Aging

Finally, we turn from questions about costs, contributions, and control to a more subjective topic: how do people experience old age? How do old people feel about themselves in particular societies, and how do others feel about them? It seems to us that there are two primary aspects to this subject. The first concerns how people perceive the life course. What cultural timetables do they have, and how do they adjust to the discrepancies that may arise between their own lives and the models society offers them? The second concerns the emotional costs or gains incurred by old people as a result of their position in society generally, the importance of emotions both as a determinant of the position of old people and as a result of that position.

In our society, at least, people develop a kind of generalized life script or mental map of the life cycle, tailored to their own perceptions of themselves, sex, social class, family background, etc., and they monitor their own progress against this standard (Neugarten & Hagestad 1976: 35). It seems more than likely that this process, or something very like it, is a human universal (Levine 1978: 2). Part of the task of old age is a kind of final assessment of one's life against the culturally constituted goals provided by society, internalized in youth and reinforced and reinterpreted during the course of adult life (Butler 1975: 412). Unfortunately, most of our authors give us relatively little information about the insiders' perspective on their own life courses. The notable exception is India, where Hiebert offers us some insight into the life review and reinterpretation of the rules practiced by at least one innovative old man. Much of the material in the volume suggests similar processes going on in the minds of many old people. The Coast Salish elders who are becoming active in old-style rituals had learned in their youth to disavow any interest in such things, at least when communicating with non-Indians, and many had even committed themselves to other forms of religion. Looking back on it now, they can tell when at an early period in life they had an encounter with a spirit power, not recognized as such at the time. Many of them are already at work reevaluating experiences and reinterpreting beliefs from an earlier period in their lives so that the final story will be all of a piece with their present commitment to the "Indian Way." It would be particularly interesting to have a wide sample of the kinds of adjustments made by people caught in the middle of changing maps of what a "good" life should be. We already know from our own society that being forced to change life-plans in mid-course is very hard on people. We need to know more about how people who are forced to do it try to make sense of it all.

We also need to understand, or at least encounter, the emotional experience of old age. It seems ironic that despite the fact that anthropologists spend so much time with old people, they so seldom communicate the "passion of aging" from the perspective of their informants. In this collection, the article by Colson and Scudder on the Gwembe Tonga gives a poignant sense of what it feels like to be old on the shores of Lake Kariba, missing the valley of the Zambezi River, the fields, and the homesteads all drowned by the rising waters of the dam.

Most of what this collection has to tell us about the emotional aspects of aging is taken from the outsider's perspective and concentrates on the psychodynamics of family organization. As with so many other aspects of aging, people can plan and manipulate the emotional dependencies of others in order to gain affection, companionship, and security in old age. Chinese society provides a clear example of sex differences in the emotional relationships between old people and their children. Harrell tells us, following Wolf (1972) and others, that there is a fundamental difference between the attachments children have to fathers and to mothers in Chinese society. Fathers train and discipline children primarily by fear and distant sternness; the filial obedience taught Chinese children usually does not generate warmth or emotional closeness to the father. As a consequence, the position of the aging father depends almost entirely on his political and economic power within the family; when this goes he may be supported out of duty, but not out of devotion. Mothers, on the other hand, discipline with a mixture of fear and kindness, and generally manage to raise sons who feel close emotional bonds to them. So aging mothers, many of whom never had a strong economic or political hold on their sons, nearly always manage to bind them with ties of real affection, and the loss of what little power they once had is not disastrous to their position.

Emotional ties between mother and child buttress the position of old women in many societies, but grandparent/grandchild ties are also a powerful factor in determining the lot of elderly people. This is brought out particularly clearly in Biesele and Howell's paper on the !Kung San. Grandparents, here as elsewhere, tend to pamper their grandchildren; the little ones are not afraid to ask for a handout or to sit down to listen to another story. The myth of the Elephant Girl related at the beginning of the paper shows how the emotional tie between grandparents and grandchildren can come to symbolize the very gift of life.

The other aspect of the emotional experience of aging is not so uniformly positive, however. On the one hand, we have argued that there is solace and security for the aging to be derived from the roles they play as religious specialists. This is illustrated in Hiebert's account of a south Indian village. On the other hand, we see emotional results of aging that are not always so comforting to either the old or the young. The conviction that the old have special supernatural connections generates two kinds of negative judgments on old people in general, sometimes closely related to each other. One of these is that there is an allotted human life span (different in most cases from the physiologically "allotted" life span discussed earlier) beyond which it is improper, or at least unusual, to live. Sometimes people living beyond this ideal span are felt to do so by some sort of magical power. The Tonga, for example, believe that very old people survive and remain vigorous only through powerful medicine paid for by human sacrifice. Old people may be blamed for the untimely deaths of younger people—as if there were only a certain amount of life around and the old people were somehow improperly appropriating some that rightfully belonged to their juniors. This same kind of belief made young Apache fear and distrust the old (Opler 1936: 473).

This seems to be an example of the idea that there are limited resources and that it is unfair for certain people (in this case the older generation) to monopolize them. This idea has other manifestations as well, typically in the psychodynamics of intergenerational relationships within the family, particularly in cases where the political and/or economic power of the aged is constricting or stifling to the younger generation. In societies where people gain control over productive resources only by inheritance, this can become particularly acute. The Tallensi of West Africa are a good example. Oldest sons, who stand to inherit much of the father's control over the family economy, are said to hate their fathers, and much of the malevolent character of Tallensi ancestors can be laid to the guilt sons feel over having wished their aging fathers dead. Fortes suggests that these guilt feelings appear in the hostility attributed to the ancestors (1949: 173, 234). Similar tensions are evident in Chinese society (Ahern 1973) and among Irish countrymen who fear the "old man's curse" (Arensberg & Kimball 1940).

Implications — The Position of the Aged in Human Societies

Having examined the cost/contribution balance and control over resources, we encounter the questions of what, after all, determines whether the aged will be able to make a substantial contribution to the group and of what allows them to control resources or prevents them from doing so? Here we find ourselves on more difficult terrain. It is obvious that there are constraints set by the natural environment, or by the larger human environment of rapid social change. The decline of the position of Asmat elders was an inevitable consequence of the beginning of the incorporation of the Asmat into Indonesian society, in the same way that the decline in the position of Tonga elders derived naturally from the washing away of their lands. But other differences arise not out of some inevitability beyond society's means to control, but rather out of the particular solutions that a society has created to its own natural and human environmental setting. That Tonga elders traditionally exercised fuller control over land than did their Etalese counterparts is probably not a function of the difference between alluvial valleys and coral atolls. That Indian elders are enjoined to go begging in the forest as part of a search for wisdom, whereas Chinese elders ideally remain at home surrounded by crowds of grandchildren, reflects not environmental conditions but the different religious ideals of the two great Asian civilizations. Given the constraints of the natural and human environments, cultures can adapt in different ways; many of the differences between the positions of the aged in the societies described in this book reflect just such cultural choices, which have themselves become parts of the human environment to which old people have to adapt. At our stage of knowledge of the problems of aging, at least, we must acknowledge the value of cultural relativity in formulating explanations. Not only must the cultures within which old people operate be seen in their own terms, but we must recognize the ability of the aged, like anyone else, to manipulate their environments, and to continue to shape circumstances to their own best advantage.

These considerations lead us to the other major implication of this cross-cultural comparison. Knowing the constraints set by the environment, and knowing at the same time that the position of the elderly in any society is also partly determined by cultural choices, we must examine both the environmental limits, natural and social, and the possible cultural choices affecting the position of the aged in North American society. Is the current position of old people here explicable in terms of the cost/contribution and control dimensions we have discussed? How might these dimensions be changed in order to ensure the best possible position for the aged in our future society? And finally, what sort of cultural attitudes should we seek to teach and promote if we wish to make the final years of life pleasant and useful ones in the coming decades? We believe that our cross-cultural analysis is relevant to the understanding of all these questions.

Evolutionary Perspectives
on Human Aging

KENNETH M. WEISS

Most people who read this book will generally have associated aging with physical deterioration or diseases, with discrete points in the life cycle (such as menopause, retirement, age 75, or becoming a grandparent), or with death. We have given far too little thought to aging as a process that is always with us, and to what determines it, how it comes about, and what factors shape our thinking about it. In this paper I want to take an evolutionary perspective on aging, by seeing first how aging affects the individual human being, and then how the events in the lives of individuals relate to the population as a whole.

The deterioration of the human body with age is so systematic and predictable that there is surely an evolutionary biological basis for it; yet the specific pattern to be found in any individual can be predicted only in terms of probabilities, and then only vaguely. Sorting out the commonality in a set of observations on individuals who are all different is the central problem of the evolutionary biologist, who wants to know how much differentiation there is among individuals and how this reflects the factors that control aging and that brought about the pattern we observe. Much of the differentiation we see among individuals can be explained biologically, but much is simply the result of random, or "stochastic," factors.

This paper was written with financial support from the National Institute of Aging, grant AG-01028, National Cancer Institute, grant CA-19311, and the U.S. National Institute of General Medical Sciences, grants GM-19513, 1K04GM00230-01, and CA-19311, which are gratefully acknowledged. Dr. L. L. Cavalli-Sforza also very kindly made the facilities of the Department of Genetics, Stanford University, available to me during a research leave when much of this was written, for which I offer thanks. This is Demographic Epidemiology of Aging and Disease, paper no. 8.

We will first look at the evidence for a built-in, or *intrinsic*, aging pattern that is fundamental to our biological nature. This will be based on studies of the average experience of individuals, using evidence from diverse biomedical sciences. Then we will look at how various environmental, or *extrinsic*, factors affect the expression of the intrinsic process. Combining these lines of inquiry, we will attempt to view the subject of biological aging as the product of millions of years of biological evolution.

We will then examine how a collection of individuals, that is a *population*, would be structured by the combination of extrinsic and intrinsic factors in operation. This is one way of assessing the interplay of human culture and human biology in the aging process as it relates to the length of life—an interplay that greatly affects our interpretation of the biological evolution of aging.

Culture also evolves, so that it is important to take a cultural evolutionary perspective on aging. This is because our view of any matter, and certainly one so important as aging, is fundamentally affected by the cultural conditions of the viewer. We will see that the way in which the intrinsic and extrinsic factors in biological aging operate in a given cultural setting will determine our thinking on the subject even at the scientific level.

Thus, beginning with the individual and ending with the population, I hope to show that aging can be viewed in diverse ways, that these ways are related to one another, and that our concepts of aging are related directly to all of them.

The Evolution of the Human Life Span: Intrinsic Factors in Aging

It is obvious that we have within us patterns of biological decay and increased dysfunction that come from the nature of our constitution rather than from specific external factors. The process these patterns give rise to is what scientists call *senescence*, a term often equated with "aging." Here we shall consider these patterns—the evidence for them, the way they relate to human evolution, and their biological basis.

Length of life and maximum life span

The *life expectancy* at any age x is defined as the average number of years individuals now age x will have from their present age until they die. Life expectancy at birth is the average age those born into a population at any given time (called a *cohort*) will live to be. These values relate to collections of individuals, with which we shall deal later, and are summary measures of the mortality risks that the x-year-olds must face in the future. But let us consider the experience of the individual—after all, aging and death occur individually and not as collective processes.

Perhaps the best way to understand aging is to examine what would occur if aging did not take place—to imagine that the risk of death for any given person were independent of age. For example, let the probability that an individual will die within the next calendar year be equal to q, and let q not change with age. Then the chance of surviving a year is $1 - q$, and the chance of surviving for x more years is $(1 - q)^x$. Under these conditions, one would expect to live an additional $1/q$ years. This life expectancy would be the same at birth as at any other age. Thus, if $q = 0.01$, a newborn child would expect, on average, to live 100 years before death; however, on its 100th birthday, it would look forward with equal confidence to an additional 100 years.

Only under special circumstances could a cause of death in the real world operate in this way. What we actually observe of course is that the major identifiable causes of death have very characteristic age patterns. In fact, we are so conditioned to view death as an age-related phenomenon that, for example, we would not consider the death of a child to be due to "natural causes" but would instead make great efforts to find a precise disease "cause," since children do not, in our view of things, die of "natural causes."

Aging is actually a well-tuned process that does not differ in general quality among closely related species of higher organisms such as mammals. It is not a process that involves only one or a few species-specific organ deteriorations, but rather is a constellation of changes affecting virtually every physiological function and organ system; it is the overall *rate* at which these changes take place that is characteristic of a species. In fact, if the rate of deterioration of a species is calibrated in terms of its *maximum life span potential* (MLP), or that age beyond which no member could survive even in a protected environment such as a laboratory, then the pattern of decay among the mammal species is remarkably similar. This constellation of deteriorating processes has been detailed by a number of investigators (Shock 1960, 1961; Comfort 1979; Strehler 1977; Kohn 1971; Cutler 1972, 1976a, 1979, Burnet 1974; Hershey 1974; Rosenberg et al. 1973).

Students of the aging process naturally wish to know what underlying biological factors could be responsible for, or at least be indicators of, the time-calibration of a species' aging rate and the determination of its MLP. Recent work by Sacher (1975, 1976) and by Cutler (1975, 1979) has been of much interest in clarifying this at least to some extent. If one plots the MLP of various diverse mammal species on one axis of a graph, and on the other axis plots a value that is a combination of information about the species' body size, metabolic rate, body temperature, and brain size, one finds that the points for most mammal species fall very close to a straight line. This is called a *regression* of MLP on these physiological variables, and the particular way in which the variables must be weighted for the relationship to hold is determined by well-known statistical procedures. It has also been shown that an adequate, if less precise, relationship can be drawn between MLP and an index that is based only on body size and brain capacity (because, among other reasons, body size itself is a good indicator of development rates, metabolism, and so on). Such relationships can account, statistically, for over 80 percent of the observed variation in mammal life-span values. It is thus a useful way of measuring the results of whatever evolutionary changes may have occurred during the millions of years leading from apelike ancestors to modern human beings.

To illustrate both the MLP changes and the nature of the life span–body size relationship, Table 1 provides values for various primate species (although the relationship can also be shown for

TABLE I. The Relationship Between Body Weight, Cranial Capacity, and Life Span in Living Primate Species

Superfamily and genus/species	Average body weight (g)	Average cranial capacity (cc)	Life span (yrs) Observed	Life span (yrs) Predicted
TUPAIOIDEA				
Urogale everetti	275	4.28	7	7.7
LORISOIDEA				
Perodicticus potto	1,150	14.0	12	12
Galago crassicandatus (greater galago)	850	10.3	14	11
Galago senegalensis (lesser galago)	186	2.8	25	9
LEMUROIDEA				
Hepalemur griseus	1,300	9.5	12	9
Lemur macaco fulvus	1,400	23.3	31	16
TARSIOIDEA				
Tarsius syrichta (tarsier)	87.5	3.63	12	9
CEBOIDEA				
Saguinus oedipus	413	9.8	15	12
Saimiri sciureus	630	24.8	21	20
Cebus apella	2,400	75	40	29
Cebus capucinus (capuchin)	3,765	74	40	26
CERCOPITHECOIDEA				
Presbytis entellus (langor)	21,319	119	22	24
Macaca mulatta (rhesus)	8,719	106	29	27
Papio hamadryas (baboon)	16,000	179	36	33
HOMINOIDEA				
S. syndactylus (siamang)	11,100	126	16	29
Hylobates lar (gibbon)	5,500	104	32	30
Gorilla gorilla (gorilla)	140,000	550	40	42
Pan troglodytes (chimpanzee)	49,000	410	45	43
Pan t. paniscus (pygmy chimpanzee)	38,500	356	40+	42
Pongo pygmaeus (orangutan)	69,000	415	50	41
Homo sapiens modern	65,000	1,446	95	92

SOURCE: Cutler 1976b.

NOTE: Based on the regression, due to Sacher: life span = 10.839(cranial capacity)$^{0.636}$ × (body weight)$^{-0.225}$. *Galago senegalensis*, *Lemur macaco fulvus*, *Cebus apella*, and *Cebus capucinus* have life spans significantly longer than predicted, attributed by Cutler to metabolic traits.

mammals ranging in size from mice to elephants). It is clear that the predicted MLP is close to that observed. It is fortunate that one's index need not include measurements of body metabolism (such as temperature) directly, for then it could not be related to fossil mammal species. Since it requires only an estimate of body size and cranial capacity, we can apply it to such fossils and assess the MLP of fossil human ancestral species, if we can assume that the relationship would have been as valid in the past few million years as it is today among living mammals (which is almost surely true, because the diverse mammals used to derive the pattern separated evolutionarily about 80 million years ago).

Table 2 presents some data on the evolution of MLP in human ancestors as based on the available fossil specimens, from material about 14 million years old to the present. Though there is debate about these fossils in terms of their lineal relationships to present species and in terms even of how many hominid species may have coexisted at some times past, and though there are ambiguities inherent in estimating average cranial capacity and body size for ancestral species based on fragmentary fossils, it seems clear that the MLP for our ancestors prior to about one million years ago (i.e., prior to *Homo erectus*) was about 50 years.

Australopithecines are the first generally recognized hominid (i.e., clearly not apes and clearly on the road to modern humans). Compare their MLP estimates with those for contemporary apes (values probably attained by the time of Australopithecines). There was about a 10-year increase in MLP in 10 (or less) million years. The evolution of the Australopithecines themselves into *Homo erectus* (which took place from about 4 to about 1 million years ago) produced most of the changes in MLP that have occurred to the present.*

---

* It is proper to note here that Mann (1975) has argued from X-ray studies of Australopithecine jaws that these earliest hominid ancestors matured at a rate comparable to our own. If this is so, the stages of life in the much smaller Australopithecine would have to be calibrated on our own time scale, and the relationship of body size to age would be somewhat in error for human evolution. Further, sexual dimorphism may have been very much greater among Australopithecines than among ourselves, which the relationship does not adequately take into account. Our general conclusions do not change, however.

TABLE 2. Life Span and Stages in Hominid Evolution

Genus/species	Est. avg. body wt. (kg)	Est. avg. cranial cap. (cc)	Predicted life span (yrs)	Time of appearance (yr × 10⁻⁶)
Ramapithecus punjabicus	32	300	42	14
Australopithecus africanus	32	450	51	3
Australopithecus robustus	40.5	500	52	2.5
Australopithecus boisei	47.5	530	52	2
Homo habilis	43	660	61	1.5
Homo erectus javanicus	53	860	69	0.7
Homo erectus pekinensis	53	1,040	78	0.25
Homo europaeus pre-Wurm	—	1,310	89	0.1
Homo neanderthalensis europaeus	—	1,460	93	0.045
Homo sapiens europaeus Wurm	—	1,460	94	0.015
Homo sapiens recens	—	1,460	94	0.01
Homo sapiens modern	63.5	1,410	91	present

SOURCE: Cutler 1975.
NOTE: This table is taken directly from Cutler to illustrate the trend; no claim is made that taxonomic assignment, weight, or cranial capacity estimates are exact. This area is somewhat controversial at the moment; however, the trend is in general not affected. Cutler's data are from various primary sources

These figures mean two things to us: (1) the changes in MLP have been fairly rapid as evolutionary changes go, and (2) there has been virtually no change in MLP since the origin of *Homo sapiens*, 100,000 years or more ago. This second point means that all of the cultural evolution observed, from the simplest of hunter-gatherer societies to the most industrialized and complex ones, has taken place in populations whose individual members have the same average life-span potential. Any significant variation we observe in what we call aging must hence be attributed to cultural or ecological factors. As evolutionary ethnologists from Tylor to White have pointed out, the human being is the constant relative to cultural evolution. There is no useful evidence for meaningful biological life-span differences between any living human races.

One may well ask whether the reputed longevous populations of the Caucasus parts of the Soviet Union, of Ecuador, or of the Himalayas may not reflect true genetic differences within the human species in MLP. It has not yet been satisfactorily demonstrated that longevity in these remote and isolated populations is genuinely greater than in other human groups, and there are many sources of potential bias and misinterpretation of the data. But even if we accept for argument's sake that there are pockets of genetically more long-lived peoples, the fact remains that (1) these are only trivially small subsets of our species, and (2) cultural evolution as observed in the ethnographic present and in the archeological record took place in normally longevous populations. Aging differences in the overwhelmingly larger human populations of the rest of the world must still rest on the interplay of cultural variables and a relatively uniform biological substrate. Even yogurt eaters usually die before they reach 100!

At this point we must stop to discuss the philosophical meaning of the concept of a maximum life span. Certainly we have some idea of what this means and that it is important in the study of comparative aging rates. But what exactly *does* it mean, and how is it determined? It must be recognized first that, although we have an idea of the life-span potential of members of a species, there are certain obvious members of the species who do not at all possess that life span (for example, bearers of genes that produce lethal diseases at unusually young ages, such as Huntington's disease). Second, we would like to consider MLP in a way that does not allow it to be affected by certain causes of death that we feel are not related to biological potential longevity (e.g. spider bites). Thus, we generally estimate MLP from animals observed in protected laboratory or zoo environments. We should, it seems clear, acknowledge that there is some arbitrariness in the kinds of things from which these animals are protected by us.

These facts show a certain slipperiness in the concept of a maximum life span, but there is a very much more important way in which we must recognize that it is a statistical concept only. We would all agree that a single death does not inform us of a species' life-span potential. But we should recognize that the life-span esti-mates for all species are based on a finite number of individuals ob-served—and for some of the species from whose life-span estimates the body size—brain size relationship was drawn the number has been *very* finite (how many elephants' protected life spans have been observed?).

One of the reasons that brain size had to be included in the re-gression equation for mammalian life spans is that human beings, for their body size, have too high a life span. If our life span were, say, 60 rather than 90 years, we would fit much closer to the line. But the value of 90 years has been derived from observations on *millions* of human beings. Were we restricted to an estimate based on observing a few tribal villages, we would be most unlikely to ob-serve anyone dying much older than 60 or 70. Similarly, were we to observe the lives of millions of mice or elephants we might raise their life-span estimates, because we would then see the rare very long-lived individuals.

Because of these problems, we must recognize maximum life span as a statistical concept. Perhaps it would be better to use the average age at death of protected populations as our estimate of the species' aging characteristics, a measure far less sensitive to sample size than the maximum. If this led to our no longer needing to con-sider brain as a major indicator, it might significantly change the in-terpretation we make of the reasons for the evolution of the long human life span, namely, that it relates to our intelligence and the accumulation of wisdom over the years of a long life. Let us not put undue emphasis on relationships that tend to satisfy what might be preconceptions about our own evolutionary nature, especially when those relationships are derived from very limited (and hetero-geneous) sample sizes.

Evidence for a programmed aging pattern

To clarify further the fact that our aging rate is not solely the re-sult of external environmental factors but is in some manner intrin-sic to our biology, it is of value to show some of the evidence for a programmed species-specific aging pattern. There is a wealth of laboratory evidence. Cells from mammalian connective tissue, grown *in vitro*, seem to have a finite lifetime, or a finite number of cell divisions that can occur (Hayflick 1975, 1976) before the cell culture dies, even if kept in a fresh medium free of waste products and pathogens. For humans, this number of cell divisions depends to some extent on the age of the cell donor, as one might expect, and the maximum is about 50–60 divisions. This "Hayflick limit" is controversial in detail, and may not apply as widely in *in vivo* systems (Cutler 1972), but many authors take it as significant evidence for the presence of some process that programs death into cells at a certain age or that (if based on a probabilistic decay pattern) leads to very slight odds of surviving beyond the "limit."

Other biochemical/physiological evidence for intrinsic aging includes increased production of defective protein with age (Cutler 1973); a life-span-related increase in redundancy in genes coding for messenger RNA molecules; age-dependent changes in the types of RNA present in mice (Cutler 1972, 1973); lowered cell proliferation rates and cell numbers, increased lag time in enzymatic reaction induction rates, loss of function in the immune system with age, increased amounts of DNA breaks and increased dysfunction in DNA repair systems (Burnet 1974); and increased rigidity in the body's collagen, which constitutes a very large percentage of total body protein (Kohn 1971).*

One view of aging that fits this evidence goes somewhat as follows. Living systems are constructed and maintained by gene products, that is by molecules that derive from the nuclear chromosomes and their DNA. The forces of the environment, both internal and external, tend to degrade structural organization including that of biological molecules. Therefore, there must be effective means by which cells protect themselves, and the integrity of their chromosomal DNA, and by which molecular damage is repaired or damaged cells eliminated. We know of many such systems. There are DNA repair systems, there is the nuclear membrane itself and

---

* These factors are reviewed by Kohn 1971; Burnet 1974; Hershey 1974; Hayflick 1975, 1976; and by detailed textbooks such as Strehler 1977 or Comfort 1979.

other cell membrane protection, there are immunological defenses, and there are other means of eliminating cells that do not behave as cells in their specific tissues ought to behave. There is also a redundancy in the genes, i.e., repeated genes coding for the same protein, so that if one copy is damaged (by radiation, say) other copies remain to produce the needed protein.

Even with a complex defense system, however, there eventually will accumulate enough undetected, uncured, or uncurable molecular errors and mistakes that an organ or organism can no longer function. This degradation is not of a positively programmed nature, but is an accumulation of basically stochastic, or random, errors due to the chance factors of exposure of specific cells to degrading elements of their environment. When, for example, the defense mechanisms in a specific vital organ are overwhelmed, or themselves suffer error, the whole organism dies. The probability that this will happen would be simply determined by the rate of exposure to such random degradative effects (and there will always be the chance, however small, that breakdown does not occur and life continues).

What kinds of factors can cause such degradation of genes and biochemical molecules? Prime suspects would include the instability of many of these molecules themselves (for example, there is a small probability that whenever a cell divides, any given gene on a chromosome will suffer a mutational change due to improper replication of the DNA molecule), the denaturing effect of heat including body heat itself, radioactive and other ionizing or otherwise bioactive molecules taken in in the food, and so on. Tissues with more rapid cell turnover tend to suffer mutational disruptions with age, and thus organs composed of these tissues show an increased risk of disease with age. All of this can occur strictly because of stochastic disruptional forces. The number of vulnerable cells, however, can be so large that although the process is basically stochastic it gives the appearance of a deterministic internal clock for aging.

This view of aging, as basically a mutational or biochemical-

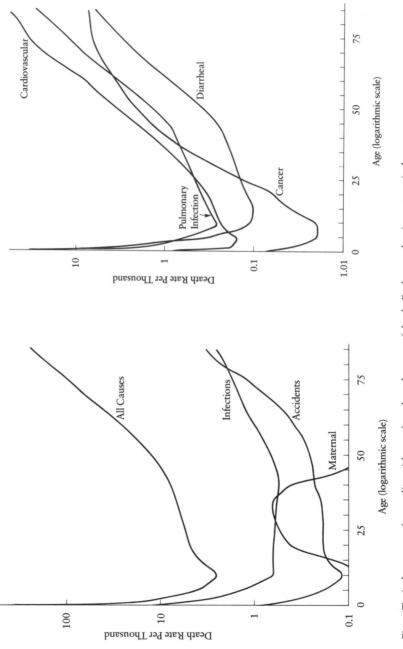

Fig. 1. Typical patterns of mortality with age, for selected causes of death. Each cause has its own typical pattern. Data are averages for over 160 populations. Based on data from Preston 1976.

error process, is probably the most widely accepted one at present. It certainly has application to the pattern of fatal degenerative diseases of major organ systems. It may or may not apply as well to general degeneration in such systems as bone, muscle, or nerves. Organs lined with cells that have high turnover rates, such as the gut, lung, stomach, or the interior of arteries, are subject to mutational forces which, more and more frequently as one grows older, lead to small foci of cells that are incorrectly differentiated for those specific tissues. These foci occasionally are neither eliminated nor well-behaved, and they can grow in an uncontrolled way. This is the process that leads to cancer and to much obstructive blood vessel disease.

Even though based on random events, the regularity of aging and its consistency with statistical models of decay can be seen from demographic and epidemiological evidence in humans and in other animals. A typical curve of mortality rates with age shows a high rate among the newborn dropping to a minimum at the age of puberty. After this, there is an exponential increase in risk with age until the age is reached at which there are no longer any individuals left to die. This pattern is observed so widely in different species and populations that, in its general shape, there can be no doubt that it is a fundamental reflection of biology and aging. We can illustrate some of the details of this with Figure 1. The pattern for all causes of mortality combined is given, as are those for several selected causes. The individual causes reflect the nature of the causal agent and its interaction with the biological host. Maternal mortality, obviously, reflects the reproductive ages. Accidents reflect the exuberance of young adults and the frailty of the old. Infectious diseases often cause death because there is no immunity in the host or because the host, due to his/her general health, was overwhelmed by the pathogen; such deaths will only mildly reflect immunological deterioration, which is slow with age, so the risk curve does not rise very rapidly (Burnet & White 1972). Most of the other causes reflect the vulnerability of infants and the very systematic deterioration of adults as they age. In fact, it is remarkable how similar in pattern are the diverse chronic, degenerative diseases that largely reflect cellular errors accumulating in high-turnover cells of different organs.*

Given these very similar disease risk patterns (which are similar in other mammals), it has often been concluded that each species is programmed to die at a certain age, that an underlying vulnerability pattern effects the coordinated deterioration of diverse organs at the same age, so that by the time of death due to old age most of our organs are simply worn, or programmed, out. This is incorrect. Even though a vast array of diseases strikes with the same *relative* pattern regarding age, the *absolute risks* among different organs vary by factors of 100 or more. Lung cancer and diabetes, for example, are both much more common in those age 75 than in those age 50, but most 75-year-olds do *not* have either lung cancer or diabetes. If we were to project the death rates of each human tissue into the future life of the individual that would exist if no other causes of death were acting, the age at which basically everyone would be dead would vary from just about 150 to over 18,000 years depending on the tissue! This is illustrated in Figure 2. We show the loss to death by age of various cancers selected to illustrate this point (the curves are schematic, and represent the experience of many nations around the world). There is very little disease at age 25, and there is the typical increase with age of the different causes shown. However, note that by age 90 the disease rates are still far below 100 percent, and that the projection into the future shows very different patterns for different diseases. It is only the restricted window of observation of disease, from ages between about 50 and 80 or 90, that produces the *appearance* of similar risk, because after that age there is no one left to die. You can see this illusion if you cover this graph everywhere except in the window shown between the dotted lines.

Thus, all of our organs do not wear out at the same age, and the reason that the average age at death from most chronic diseases is

---

* It is possible to construct models of mutational errors that fit the chronic, or aging, diseases, very well (Armitage & Doll 1961; Doll 1971; Burnet 1974; Cook et al. 1969; Weiss et al. 1980; Ward et al. 1980). This is generally taken to support the random-error viewpoint.

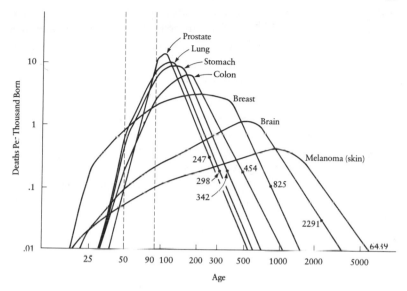

Fig. 2. Representation of typical age patterns of death for degenerative disorders. Data are given for seven cancer sites. The death curves after age 90 are based on theoretical considerations and assume that only that cause was acting in the population. Small figures indicate the age at which 99 percent of the population would have died if only that cause were acting. The restricted window of observations through which we view these processes, between approximately ages 50 and 90, is indicated between the dotted lines. The human life span, determined by the multiple action of many causes of death, gives an artificial impression of similarity in death rates, as can be seen. Plotted on logarithmic scales.

Note that these are the probability density functions for deaths due to the causes given, under the stated assumptions, and *not* the death rates themselves. The two are very similar in the human range of ages. Later, the death rate curve becomes asymptotic at a nonzero value while, as shown, the density, or loss due to death per person born, declines asymptotically to zero. From Weiss et al. 1980.

about the same is that there are so many different diseases competing that by about age 80 some one tissue is likely to have gone bad. Thus, in relation to disease evidence, it is not correct to say that we die at age 90 or less because our organs are predestined to self-destruct at that time.

Yet, there must be some underlying calibrating cause of the rate at which tissue decay and error accumulation takes place. If this were not so, then the evolutionary relationships of body size and longevity, or the regular pattern of aging, would not occur. A slight upward or downward adjustment in the rate at which all tissues age can change the age beyond which virtually no individual will survive. In fact, the particular history of human evolution is the strongest evidence that the underlying calibration mechanism is simple (Sacher 1975; Cutler 1975, 1976a, 1976b). In a few short years (evolutionarily speaking) all of our body systems have come to decay at a much different rate from that of our ancestors. There has not been enough time for there to have evolved separate rate patterns for each of our organ systems—some common factor must have changed. Perhaps it is just the genetic system for controlling growth and development rates or body temperature, but whatever it is it is likely to be simple.

Perhaps an analogy would be useful here. If one watches a sidewalk as it begins to rain, one can see the gradual reduction of the dry area with time until none remains. How long this takes will depend on the intensity of the rain. Although one can set a limit on the time there is likely to be any dry area remaining with some accuracy, no intrinsic characteristic of the sidewalk is involved. The species calibrator, in effect, might only be the overall intensity of the rain.

Evolutionary theory: Is the program an active or a passive one?

The above view is somewhat in conflict with prevailing views among biologists about the evolution of the mammalian life span drawn *a priori* by argument from evolutionary and population genetics theory. Such views hold that the aging process is probably a complex one involving many genes, and is probably specifically progammed rather than a random process (Medawar 1952; Williams 1957; Hamilton 1966; Emlen 1970). Senescence may be an evolutionarily produced final stage in the normal growth and development cycle of a mammal, just as puberty is an earlier stage.

These views are based on considering how it would be most advantageous for evolution to allocate reproductive fitness by allocating susceptibility to death to various ages in the normal life and reproductive cycle. Perhaps, it is argued, evolution for longevity worked by producing very *healthy* individuals at the age of puberty; a side effect of this might be the observed decay pattern or vulnerability to degradative forces in the environment. This latter phenomenon may be programmed into the developmental cycle or merely an indirect, *passive* result of evolution for a healthy young adulthood: the mortality results would be the same.

There has been one major general argument put forth to advocate an *active* programmed elimination of older individuals on evolutionary grounds. It is that the species is better off in the long run if it programs its individuals to be eliminated from the population after a certain time so that young individuals, with new combinations of genes and unsullied by the mechanical scars of a long life, can confront the ever-changing environment. This is an argument for species adaptability rather than individual adaptation. However, genes for such prescience have not been identified (this would be called "group" selection). Furthermore, we can ask how long it should be before replacement ideally would take place: why should it be advantageous to rats to replace themselves every 3 years but to elephants every 50? Do their respective environments change at different rates?

That evolutionary argument relates aging to mortality. Another, used in the case of humans, relates aging to evolution for long *survival*. Should there not be an evolutionary/adaptive reason for the postreproductive survival of human beings (i.e., living after menopause)? (Why does a woman have a menopause in the first place?) For this phenomenon, we must find arguments not to eliminate the old, but to preserve them.

Several such arguments have been put forth (Hrdy's paper in this volume is a good example of this kind of reasoning applied to monkeys). The reasoning centers on the valuable role of grandparents in general child care and of parents in rearing their lastborn offspring: elders may not be producing any more young, but their evolutionary biological fitness is increased by helping close kin (their children and grandchildren) to survive. Grandparents are also useful "living libraries," people who can remember what to do in the case of rare events such as floods or droughts. The selective advantage of having such elders around accrues to the whole group.

Unfortunately, I do not see the need or the validity of such arguments in explaining the delay of human senescence. Our aging clock is calibrated, as has been shown, generally along the lines of our body size and metabolism. We are not, in that sense, anomalous as regards longevity. Furthermore, survival to old age is rare among "primitive" peoples, and I know of no convincing evidence that the benefits from these unusual "living libraries" produce sufficient selective advantage to produce delayed aging in humans. If it did, why did not more elderly survive? In fact, it seems to me that the "artificial" protective effects of the simple possession of culture—the use of weapons to fend off predators and of tools to make food available (and chewable) to the elderly—are sufficient explanations for our long survival. It is an epiphenomenon of the existence of culture. Without culture we, like the wildebeest, would be caught by predators when we slowed down sufficiently. Living to 90 is a fluke in the wild.

The difference between the view of senescence as a program for death or as the result of the program for life (body size, etc.) is more than semantic, though the results in terms of ages at death will be the same under either viewpoint. In the program-for-life view, senescence is the random by-product of our general constitution, and neither evolutionary biologist nor biomedical scientist need search for self-destruction genes. In the program-for-death view, one should be able to find the offending chemical. I personally favor the random-error view. There is no need to see aging as the result of some genetic alarm clock that, at its appointed hour, rends the sleeping humors with a biochemical tocsin!

Causes of Mortality: Extrinsic Factors in Aging

Although aging is largely a pattern of intrinsic physiological changes, the differences in mortality rates between populations depend on the relationship between these changes and certain extrinsic, environmental characteristics such as climate, food supplies, and biological pathogens. The connection between extrinsic and intrinsic factors determines the specific demographic structure of a population. We will now look at some of these extrinsic factors and their relationship to the intrinsic aging factors that give rise to the complex dynamics determining demographic structure.

One major extrinsic factor consists of biological pathogens, including protozoans, worms, bacteria, viruses, and so on. The result of exposure to these pathogens has to do with the (intrinsic) life history of the immunological system: in general, one's immunological defense powers are related to age, but exposure to diseases is itself somewhat age dependent and serves to produce a natural immunization against many diseases. Such natural immunization requires both an extrinsic cause of disease and the biological capacity to produce the proper antibodies. (An extensive discussion of the natural history of infectious disease can be found in Burnet & White 1972.)

We have already seen that degenerative diseases such as cancer are age dependent, and that this has largely to do with the development of mutations of some sort. This is, in general, an intrinsic phenomenon; however, exposure to environmental mutagens—such as certain industrial products and pollutants—can serve to speed up the onset of the mutations. Again, this is a combination of an extrinsic factor and an intrinsic biological characteristic.

The causes of death are the same in most societies: it is their relative importance that differs and that accounts for the mortality difference between populations. In the main, the observed difference is the result of environmental factors. We know that in primitive societies exposure to parasitic organisms is common, and that gamma globulin levels are high, indicating a high prevalence of foreign antigens. Trauma and attack by poisonous or dangerous animals are also major causes of death. Accounts in ethnographies generally indicate the presence of intestinal or other acute visceral disorders leading to fever and death. It is not likely that acute infectious communicable diseases were too important before contact with Europeans (Black 1966, 1975; Black et al. 1970), because such diseases generally infect a pool of susceptibles and die out unless another

pool of susceptibles is present nearby to carry the infection. In precontact times it is not likely that many such diseases existed as we
know them; we have evidence that some, such as malaria, may have
resulted directly from cultural conditions (Livingstone 1958). Infections in which the infectious agent persists in the victim for a long
time, and whose effects are generally chronic or of long duration,
may persist in small groups. However, these may not have been lethal very often. Though certainly more important than they are at
present in industrial nations, infectious epidemics were probably
not as serious a cause of death in primitive populations as they
were in the last 2,000 years in Europe. However, we have no good
experience with populations unaffected by contact.

Though we cannot speak in detail about death and disease in the
uncontacted tribal populations of our species history, we do know
that the relative importance of different causes of death depends
greatly on culture, and that certain causes of death are related to
each other. These facts offer a clue to understanding the relationship between the historical change in the relative importance of different causes of death and the change in overall life expectancy. Extensive studies (Preston et al. 1972; Preston & Nelson 1974) of
causes of death in 165 national populations during the past century
relate to this question better than any other available information.
Table 3 shows the correlations between the rates of various identified diseases and the overall death rate in the 165 populations.
From this it can be seen that the infectious diseases are positively
correlated with the overall crude death rate (the number who die
each year per 1,000 in the population), but that the degenerative
diseases such as cancer and cardiovascular ones are negatively correlated. This means that the increase in life expectancy since the beginning of the Industrial Revolution has resulted from the reduction of infection as a cause of death at relatively early ages. The
remaining disorders now accounting for the vast majority of mortality are of the intrinsic type: degenerative diseases of later life. If
this pattern were to be extrapolated to the very low life expectancies of "primitive" populations, infections would be by far the primary culprits. As one might expect, accidents and violence do not

TABLE 3. Correlation Between Rates of Specific Causes of Death and
the Rate for All Causes for 165 Populations
(Number per year, per person in the population)

Cause of death	Coefficient of correlation with death rate, all causes combined	
	Females	Males
Respiratory tuberculosis	0.860	0.866
Other infectious and parasitic diseases	0.905	0.880
Neoplasms	−0.477	−0.664
Cardiovascular diseases	0.113	−0.153
Influenza/pneumonia/bronchitis	0.926	0.938
Diarrhoeal diseases	0.804	0.782
Certain chronic diseases	0.291	0.308
Maternal complications	0.890	—
Certain diseases of infancy	0.765	0.733
Violence	0.224	0.404
Other and unknown (residual)	0.892	0.872

SOURCE: Preston & Nelson 1974.

explain much of the change in death rates by comparison with the other diseases more directly related to hygiene and the rise of modern medicine.

We can see more of the dynamics of mortality causes by looking at how they relate to each other (with the effect of overall mortality level removed). Again Preston and Nelson (1974) have shown that degenerative disorders are negatively correlated with the incidence of other diseases. It is impossible to evaluate the incidence of many degenerative diseases in the past, since they were not recognized, diagnosed, or classified in a satisfactory way. But by all means of accounting it is obvious that intrinsic causes of mortality—the degenerative disorders—are more important now that the more predominantly extrinsic causes such as infection have been removed, reduced, or shifted to older ages. Even predominantly extrinsic diseases like infections are expressing themselves through intrinsic aspects of human biology now—they strike when the immunological system is ebbing and when medicine can no longer support the inherent immunological defenses sufficiently to prevent death (though often the elderly victim of infectious diseases such as pneumonia has been weakened by many nonimmunological things as well). On the other hand, the largely intrinsic disorders may now be increasingly affected by extrinsic factors such as cigarette smoking and over-rich diets. In the past, when insults to the system from available causes were too often overwhelming, the degenerative aspects of human biology were usually not expressed. This can be seen to relate to the nature of intrinsic aging and its evolution; in humans as in other animals, few lived long enough for the degenerative processes to manifest themselves in such a way as to enable natural selection to make effective changes. Unlike the situation today, degeneration of the muscle-bone-tooth-joint systems may well have been important in early human mortality, as it is in other animal mortality. But chronic degenerative diseases of circulation or of epithelial/secretory organ systems (lung, liver, gut, bladder, pancreas, breast, stomach) were not so often manifest.

A further indication that we are now existing at the "intrinsic" level comes from examining Table 4, which illustrates the impact of various causes of death in terms of the number of years of life expectancy at birth removed by them. I have given data from New Zealand in 1881 to illustrate populations of the nineteenth century, El Salvador in 1950 to illustrate contemporary "Third World" mortality, and the Netherlands in 1964 to illustrate one of the lowest mortality rates in human history.

In 1881, the life expectancy of New Zealand males was only 53 years, infant mortality was 10 percent, and only 64 percent of those born lived to age 50 or more (the end of reproduction). But note that the elimination of neoplasms would only have increased life expectancy by one-half year, and that the elimination of other degenerative disorders (not including cardiovascular ones) would have had even less impact than that. On the other hand, infectious diseases accounted for a little over 10 years. In El Salvador in 1950, the life expectancy at birth was just under 50 years, and infant mortality was over 10 percent. Fifty-eight percent survived to age 50. As in New Zealand the elimination of infectious diseases would have had an enormous effect, whereas the elimination of neoplasms and

TABLE 4. Competing Causes of Death in Selected Populations

Statistical measure	New Zealand, 1881	El Salvador, 1950	Netherlands, 1964
Infant mortality	9.8%	10.4%	1.3%
Survival probability to age 50	63.7%	57.7%	94.6%
Life expectancy at birth (*years*)	53.3	49.9	76.4
Addition to life expectancy (*years*) if the following cause of death were eliminated:			
Infections	10.02	12.87	0.50
Cardiovascular diseases	3.09	0.90	8.86
Neoplasms	0.49	0.34	3.25
Other degenerative diseases	0.28	0.44	0.50
Accidents	2.58	2.87	0.73

SOURCE: Preston et al. 1972.

degenerative diseases would have mattered little in extending life expectancy. In the Netherlands one might expect to find neoplasms (which are felt to be a great problem today largely owing to industrial pollutants and so on) to be very important determinants of life expectancy. Yet although the Netherlands life expectancy is 76 years and infant mortality is only 1 percent, and although the elimination of infectious diseases completely could produce only one-half more year of life (since they are virtually eliminated already), the elimination of cancer would only add about 3 years of life expectancy. And in the United States today that figure would only be 1.5 years.

Even with all of the culturally produced disease inducers (radiation, pollution, cigarette smoke, and auto exhaust), cancer is basically an intrinsic aging disease. It strikes at such a late age, in general, that if one is cured of it some other degenerative disease is likely to strike anyway. In a sense, we are living a more fundamentally "biological" life than ever before in our history.

The history of human life expectancy

Given an unchanging biological aging rate, but changing extrinsic levels of mortality, what has the average person had to look forward to in terms of his own longevity through the course of human
history? Although we cannot identify in detail the causes of death,
and data are scanty, we can make some attempts to assess average
length of life in most typical human cultures. The past decade has
seen a lot of work in this direction, so that in recent years we have
gotten a better idea of our longevity history (Swedlund & Armelagos 1975; Acsadi & Nemeskeri 1970; Ubelaker 1974; Weiss 1973).

In any effort to summarize so complex a subject, it is inevitable
that some oversimplifications will be made, as well as some assumptions we really are not in a position to test. These include (1)
the categorization of cultures into various stages or levels, following the general, standard groupings (Service 1975); (2) the assumption that where archeological evidence at a site seems similar to the
material aspects of some culture in the "ethnographic present," the
past culture was in fact similar (this assumption, a kind of "uni-
formitarianism," is usually made by anthropologists, but I think
should be made explicit [Howell 1976]); and (3) various technical
assumptions of demographic theory that must be made in order
to extract life expectancy estimates from very fragmentary data,
mostly concerning the stability of the underlying demographic rates
in particular populations and the representativeness of the data.

Table 5 provides a summary of this work. The very fragmentary
nature of the earlier materials leaves much to be desired, but it
seems, based on considerable evidence, that from very early hominid times even through early agricultural populations, life expectancy at birth was only about 20–30 years. There was, typically,
heavy infant mortality, so that those surviving infancy would have
somewhat higher life expectancies (they would, on average, live
through their thirties at least).

We can conclude from the table (1) that the intrinsic aging factors
were relatively little expressed in terms of mortality; and (2) that
the "neolithic revolution," the major advance in human culture

TABLE 5. History of Human Life Expectancy
(*Approximate values in years*)

Cultural group	General range of life expectancy
Australopithecines	±15
Neanderthals	±18
"Hunters" through the Neolithic	19–25
Early agriculturalists and horticulturalists	20–27
Westerners of the classical and medieval periods	22–29
Living primates	22–29
Sweden 1780	38
United Kingdom 1861	43
Sweden 1905	55
Sweden 1965	76
Guatemala 1893	24

SOURCE: Weiss 1973.

(as agriculture was discovered) that produced much population growth, did not greatly improve life expectancy. The latter point is quite important, because there is a general impression among most anthropologists that the population expansion that always took place when agriculture was invented somewhere was the result of better living conditions leading to healthier, longer lives. The evidence is that simply more people were allowed to live, but not to live longer. How this came about, in terms of age-specific demographic rates, is not known.

The vast majority of longevity increase has taken place since industrialization. Why is this? The answer is not known. However, it is clear that although there were several forces which should have led to increased mortality (pollution from factories, overwork and danger in the workplace, and urban crowding), it actually decreased rather systematically. Medical science had very little to do with this until the first third of the present century. The major factors probably were better nutrition and public hygiene measures of various sorts.

Much of the change in life expectancy has to do with the reduction in infant mortality. This is probably due to several factors, including nutrition, although again we know little about it. Table 6

TABLE 6. Age-Specific Life Expectancy for Selected Human Populations
(*Additional years of life at a given age*)

Population	Age		
	0	15	50
1. Average hunter-gatherers[a]	22.0	22.5	13.3
2. Average primitive agriculturalists[a]	26.1	30.0	17.5
3. North American Indian ossuary	23.0	20.4	5.2
4. Roman Egypt[b]	28.7	25.3	16.0
5. 11th century Hungary[b]	28.7	30.4	10.7
6. Sweden 1780, females	38.5	44.7	20.3
7. United Kingdom 1861, females	43.0	44.9	21.1
8. Sweden 1905, females	56.8	51.4	24.8
9. El Salvador 1950, males	49.9	48.7	23.7
10. Sweden 1965, females	76.1	62.4	28.9

SOURCES: Rows 1 and 2, Weiss 1973; row 3, Ubelaker 1974; row 4, Russell 1958; row 5, Acsadi & Nemeskeri 1970; rows 6, 7, 8, and 10, Keyfitz & Flieger 1968; row 9, Preston et al. 1972.
[a] A representative series of values.
[b] Juveniles unreliable.

illustrates the point, however, with values of life expectancy for 10 populations at three critical points in the life span: birth, puberty, and older age. (It should be remembered that life expectancy is *not* the age at death, except for infants, but the number of years *remaining* from the given age. Although there has been change in life expectancy at all ages, the point to note from this table is that by far the greatest change has been in life expectancy at birth. The number of years added since primitive times to an infant's life has been about 50, to a 15-year-old's life has been about 30, and to a 50-year-old's has been only about 12 years. In fact, by the time one reaches age 65 very little change in longevity has occurred even since the year 1900. We have been able to relieve the burdens of extrinsic diseases, but have been able to do little at all about the degenerative, or aging, diseases.

The Age Structure of Populations

Equality in the face of death: Yes or no?

The discussion just concluded relates average experiences at various cultural levels to each other. We have seen, however, that these depend on the age being used for comparison, which provides us with the motivation to look at the details of the pattern of mortality rather than just its summaries. In fact, it is easy to show that though the life expectancy, or average age at death, of a member of a cohort might be x years, very few will actually die at that age. To take an example, the life expectancy value for Japanese males in 1964 was 67.72 years (67 years, 263 days). Yet of the 847,592 boys born that year, only about 58 will die on their appointed day if mortality rates do not change. This is only 7 thousandths of one percent dying at the average age at death; the other 99.993 percent will die at some other age! Clearly, the average is not the whole story.

In fact, if everyone died at the same age there would be no aging and no demography as we know it (and there would be no argument about a programmed life span). But since there is great variation in age, although we might learn about aging biology and biochemistry from the study of the individual, an understanding of the aging phenomenon must be sought rather through the study of the *population*.

Exactly how is mortality spread among the biologically variable members of a population? In fact, we know very little about the fraction of deaths that may meaningfully be attributed to the biological nature of the victim except in certain rare and extreme cases. However, we do know that if we begin an experiment with a cohort of genetically identical animals (fruit flies, mice, etc.) and subject them to identical conditions, there will be substantial variation in their ages at death. This supports what surely must be our common perception: the vast majority of deaths are accidental, or stochastic, in regard to biological constitution. Even with identical genes there is differentiation among individuals in the face of death, and in that sense death can never be the great equalizer, but instead is the great differentiator.

We are led to ask whether in the course of human cultural evolution we have become more or less differentiated in facing the ultimate experience. Has the increase in social stratification accompanying the transition from tribe to chiefdom to state made our lives more, or less, equal in length? Data on this point are given in Table 7 for three populations: a typical tribal one, Sweden in 1780 (to represent preindustrial civilization), and Sweden in 1965 (to represent modern states). The table presents the risk of death in the next 5 years that a member must face at three critical ages, 0, 15, and 65. The average 5-year risk that a member of these populations must face is also given.

Clearly there have been dramatic changes both in the mortality risks themselves and in their average—with the greatest change, as we have seen before, taking place since industrialization. Individuals now face smaller risks, and those risks vary less with age than they did previously. Can this not be expected to have pervasive effects, both subtle and deep, on our attitudes toward aging?

Looking at the risks of death at selected ages tells us something of the varying intensity of mortality, but looking at the distribution of the actual ages of death will be far more revealing. Table 7 provides data on the average age at death in the three selected populations. It also provides the statistical *variance* in the age at death; the variance measures the dispersion about the mean, and a higher variance means that individuals died at more dispersed, or different, ages relative to the mean than does a lower variance. Table 7 clearly shows that modern nations have far less variation in the age at death than previously occurred; but, interestingly, preindustrial civilization may have had a higher variance than tribal populations. This would primarily be the result of low mortality in the main adult years, relative to tribal times, with still high death rates among the very young and very old resulting probably from the impact of infectious epidemics.

Though we have become socially less and less equal, we seem to have become more and more equal in our experience of death. Nutrition, medicine, and hygiene make even biologically different individuals more and more alike in their ages at death; but at the same time, stochastic factors in the occurrence of mortality make even genetically identical individuals unequal. One impact all of

TABLE 7. Mortality Patterns with Age in Selected Cultural
Circumstances

5-year risk of death	Tribal	Sweden 1780	Sweden 1965
Age			
0	.384	.307	.014
15	.115	.029	.002
65	.297	.275	.089
Average	.1998	.1353	.0421
Age at Death			
Average	26.1	38.9	76.1
Variance	633	967	234

SOURCES: Tribal, Weiss 1973, table MT: 30-50; Sweden, Keyfitz & Flieger 1968.

this has is to reduce greatly the way in which natural selection can operate in regard to any genes that may have to do with the aging rate: whether cancer strikes at age 75 or 90 makes no difference to natural selection. Modern culture allows the rather complete expression of the aging process, which has removed some of its mask, if not its mystery.

Cultural evolution: The age distribution and perceptions of aging

We cannot yet lay this subject to rest. What we think about aging will be based on our subjective perceptions of it as much as it will on the technical biology of the matter (if not more so). One key factor in determining our perceptions of aging is the frequency with which aging individuals are seen in a population. If they are rare, then aging will seem exotic and mysterious, but somewhat removed from our own experience; if common, it will become prosaic, an economic burden, and probably an object of dread.

The frequency with which we see aging individuals depends on the *age distribution* of the population, that is, the proportion of people of various ages. The age distribution is determined by the ways in which death strikes at different ages and in which individuals replace themselves through reproduction. This can be envi-

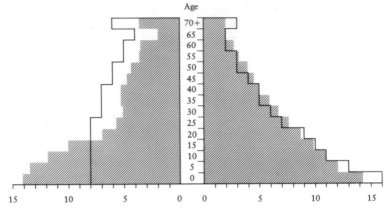

Fig. 3. Examples of population pyramids showing the effects of changes in mortality and fertility on the age distribution. On the right, a typical tribal population before (shaded) and after (solid line) a 50-percent reduction in mortality rates at all ages (Weiss 1973, table MT:30-50). On the left, the 1965 U.S. nonwhite population structure (shaded), then growing at about 2 percent per year (a fairly rapid rate), and the same population if growth were reduced to zero solely by a reduction in fertility (data from Keyfitz & Flieger 1968). The top bar includes everyone over age 70, so is larger than a single 5-year age class would be at those ages.

sioned by way of the *population pyramid*, examples of which are given in Figure 3. Each bar in this diagram represents the proportion of people who are in the respective 5-year age class, beginning with zero-to-four-year-olds at the bottom and ending with the oldest individuals alive at the top of the diagram.

The population pyramid is a direct representation of a census count and the rates of mortality and growth that prevail: a pyramid with a wider base reflects either higher mortality or higher fertility rates in the population. The slope from one bar to the next, moving upward, reflects the mortality experience between those age classes. Fertility is reflected directly only by the lowest bar, the infants', because that is where everyone's children will appear first.

Let us look at the way the age distribution is determined by birth and death rates. Suppose first that we hold mortality constant, but allow fertility rates to change. If fertility increases, this will lengthen the lowest bar of the population and, if the change persists, will in general widen the whole base of the population pyramid producing what is known as a "younger" population. A decrease in fertility rates would have the opposite effect, narrowing the base of the pyramid and producing an "older" population. For example, Figure 3 (left side) shows what would happen to the nonwhite population in the United States if, using 1965 mortality rates, we shifted from 2 percent growth to zero growth. This large difference in the age structure of a population will affect the social phenomena associated with aging. The recent reduction of fertility in the industrialized world is producing a markedly older population, which is reflected among other things by much worry over the economic support of the aged, their institutional care, and their social well-being. There is a resulting great interest in gerontological research (as shown, probably, by the existence of this book). All of these changes have occurred with virtually no change in mortality or life expectancy, and hence with the same amount of "aging" in the biological sense.

What would be the effect of changes in mortality on a population if fertility remained constant? Figure 3 provides an example based on tribal data. The situation can be complex, because mortality changes directly affect each age class. A reduction in death rates, for example, will allow more people to live or live longer, and this will produce an older population structure; however, these people by living longer can reproduce more, and that will produce a younger population. Each case must be worked out separately to find out the net effect (Keyfitz 1968; Coale 1972). It can easily be seen, however, that changes in fertility affect a population far more than comparable changes in mortality (Coale 1957, 1972). Thus, the proportion of a population that is "aged" has to do less with the mortality process that permits the aged to exist than with the behavior of those who are not aged!

Until the Industrial Revolution human populations had been young ones, with wide-based population pyramids reflecting both high mortality and fertility rates. A typical tribal cultural condition, whether hunter-gatherer or swidden-agriculturalist, allows only about 10 percent of those born to survive beyond age 60, and these will make up only about 3 percent of the population. Many bands or villages will have few or no individuals of that age. Those who do survive consequently become a rare social asset because of their knowledge and seniority, without presenting a serious economic burden to the group.

The rise of civilization from kin-based cultures probably saw a small increase in the proportion of the population at older ages, but we have no evidence that this was more than small. Even in Sweden in 1780 only about 25 percent survived past age 65, and these were only 5 percent of the whole population.

Contrast this with circumstances in recent years in the industrialized world. We are having to deal with what must be a very unusual situation: 75–85 percent of us survive to age 65. Our age distributions are becoming very narrow-based and vertically steep, with high proportions of the population at older ages. Because these people must be economically, and medically, supported, there survival in conjunction with our reduced fertility rates has profound social effects. They must compete for space and resources, and a print-based world has little need for their wisdom and experience (in fact we are forcing them out of work at ever earlier ages).

Until this century, through a million years of human history, there has been no reason for people to make the strong connection between aging and death that is made today. Most people died of infection, trauma, animal bites, childbirth, and the like; very few died of diseases specific to old people. Tribal peoples commonly look for an external cause, such as a religious hex, to explain any adult death, and do not recognize death as due to old age or natural causes. It should not surprise us that the inevitability of death as a consequence of growing old, and the associated dread and avoidance we now have for the subject, would not have been a strong element of one's perspective on aging in times past (see Pollack 1980).

Conclusion

Although they share underlying rate determinants, our different organs age at different rates, and we can ask whether enough diseases of individual organs could become treatable for a meaningful lengthening of life expectancy to result. Recent developments in molecular genetics have opened up the possibility that the major degenerative diseases might in fact be dealt with at the level of their actual pathology. By special gene-isolation and culturing techniques we are rapidly gaining a detailed knowledge of the regulation and functioning of genes in cells, to the extent that we might actually be able to isolate and replace genes gone awry. Such genes are very probably the proximate offending factors in many types of cancer and other aging disease. This new biomedical frontier is unlike any that has been available to us since the discovery of immunization, and there is no doubt that many diseases will become curable as a result of it.

Yet I believe it is incorrect to think of diseases as specific entities and to try to approach the problems of biological aging by fighting a series of clinical crises, one by one, as they arise in the body. This will be a losing battle, because there are too many organs and too many ways for them to malfunction. Although they may be vastly important on an individual basis, medical cures will not lead to a serious lengthening of the average life.

The other approach to increasing longevity would be to attempt to modify the biological clock that underlies the clinical states of disease. Some experiments with laboratory mammals have shown that reducing caloric consumption in the diet or body temperature can make a noticeable difference in average length of life (Sacher 1977). Whether such measures (or others we may discover) could be attempted on a large scale in human beings, whether they would work, or whether we would care to take them—all remain to be seen. If we will not give up cigarettes, with their very high and well-known risks, or slow down our industries sufficiently to improve our air and water, it is doubtful that we are, at present, serious enough about increasing our life spans. In any case, there must be rather strong constraints on how much tinkering we could do in this regard without basically disrupting fundamental human physiology.

We must also recognize that the pervasive physical scars that result from a long life of wear and tear are not in the generally avoidable category, and that increased longevity will not make the elderly spry. Mental attitudes, largely formed in the biologically determined process of early learning and experience, cannot be expected to be made markedly more flexible by any medical measures we can forsee at present. The "generation gap" will, if anything, lengthen if lives are much extended and our culture continues its pattern of very rapid change. Adding years to the end of the life span will not be a medical victory or an improvement in public health if the result is the trading of one disease for more intractable ones, or for increased periods of institutional care and medical expense, burdens our young may in any case be unwilling to bear. Modern culture continues to put us into circumstances for which we have not had, either biologically or culturally, a long time to adapt. They are profoundly different from the conditions of our evolution. We cannot see at all clearly into the future in regard to aging, but of one thing we can be sure: that evolution will continue.

"Nepotists" and "Altruists": The Behavior of Old Females Among Macaques and Langur Monkeys

SARAH BLAFFER HRDY

If one were to ask a primatologist how old animals behave in the wild the answer might well be "They don't," for it has long been thought that very few primates in natural habitats could evade predators and disease long enough to grow old. As a consequence, little attention has been given to old animals in the vast literature on primate behavior. Nevertheless, recent observations on several species reveal that some wild primates are surviving to old age and suggest that in the case of females menopause—or its analogue— may terminate reproduction prior to death. This latter notion is noteworthy because heretofore it has generally been held that only human females undergo menopause.

In this paper I examine the behavior of old females among two groups of primates—macaques and langurs—that have been widely studied. Some of the ideas I present are frankly speculative, and argument shuttles back and forth between what we would expect to

This article, originally written by Dr. Hrdy in 1976, has been updated and revised by Pamela Amoss. Dr. Hrdy has developed the ideas in this article in new directions in her forthcoming book *The Woman That Never Evolved: A Primatologist Examines Her Sex.*

Dr. Hrdy would like to thank Diane Chepko-Sade, Peter Ellison, Daniel Hrdy, S. M. Mohnot, and M. L. Roonwal for assistance in the field and for helpful discussions about macaques and langurs. She is particularly grateful to Donald Sade and John Herbert, who made it possible for her to watch old female macaques on Cayo Santiago and La Parguera islands off Puerto Rico. Her former student Jeff Moley introduced her to the growing body of literature on the subject of senescence and led her to share his enthusiasm for the topic. Her thanks also to Wolfgang Dittus, Martin Etter, Jim Moore, Jennifer Partch, Jon Seger, and Ken Weiss for their comments on the manuscript, and to Peter Waser for permission to cite his work in advance of publication.

be true based on evolutionary theory and what we know to be true. I believe this mixture of theory and fact to be a fruitful approach for an emerging field.

It is a common error to regard nonhuman primate societies as "simple" models of our own, near biological relatives unconfounded by culture. But primate societies display enormous variation both between and within species, and this should warn us never to assume that the behavior of one group of primates typifies the biologically "normal," or that what we find among one undisturbed group of primates is what necessarily should exist—the commonplace "naturalistic fallacy." Seemingly small shifts in a group's social or genetic composition, or ecological circumstances, may generate very different biological responses that are nonetheless entirely natural. By the same token, we should also be on our guard against the notion that because variation in behaviors exists among members of the same species, those behaviors must be learned or nonbiological—what might be termed the "culturalistic fallacy."

The Evidence for Aging Among Primates

Field primatologists are increasingly aware of the presence of old primates in the wild; and of the differences in appearance and behavior between such animals and younger ones. Still, it is difficult to be certain about the ages of wild primates. A close approximation can be gained by examining a wild primate and comparing its dentition and appearance with those of captive congeners of known age, usually zoo animals. Monkeys and prosimians in zoos often live 20 years or more; some apes, and an occasional monkey, survive into their forties.

Many of the traits exhibited by old primates in different species are similar, and in some respects are analogous to characteristics of old people in our own species. Such traits include erosion and tartarization of the teeth, deepening creases in facial skin, balding, changes in skin pigmentation or hair color (but not necessarily graying), and weight loss. Recent psychological studies of seven 18- to 26-year-old rhesus macaques (*Macaca mulatta*) (Davis 1978,

Fitts 1976) revealed that they had slower reaction times and poorer memories and were significantly less likely than middle-aged monkeys to profit from mistakes in a test situation (see also Cohen et al. 1979). In addition, females in a number of primate species have a decreased probability of reproduction with age. Although it has been commonly thought that menopause is unique to human primates, accumulating physiological evidence for caged primates and demographic data from wild ones indicate that women are not the only primates who cease to reproduce with age. Reproductive histories of lab-dwelling animals have established that rhesus macaque females cease to menstruate at around 25 years of age (van Wagenen 1970, 1972). Patterns of vaginal bleeding and serum hormone profiles of macaques in the third decade of life are similar to those described for peri- and postmenopausal women (Hodgen et al. 1977). Flint (1976) reported that among female chimpanzees over 40 years of age there was sporadic amenorrhea accompanied by a lack of primary follicles in the ovary.* Graham (1979), however, has reported a continued high frequency of menstrual cycles in caged chimpanzees between 35 and 48 years, although actual conception for such females was greatly reduced (3.85 percent, compared with 20 percent in the same animals aged 15 to 25). Of five old female chimpanzees exposed to males, only two conceived: one pregnancy in a mother of 38 resulted in a live birth; the other in a mother of 40, resulted in a stillbirth. Reduced fertility and longer birth spacing for old females accords with observations of wild chimpanzees in the Gombe Stream Reserve in Tanzania.

In a recent study of two troops of mangabeys (*Cercocebus albigena*) in the Kibale forest of Uganda, Waser (in press) assumed that one of eight adult females in the two troops was postreproductive. According to Waser, she looked old and she was never seen to cycle or give birth, although it was clear from her elongated nipples that she had given birth in the past (i.e. she was not sterile). (This

---

* There are no comparable data for male primates, although Engle (1938:23) presented results of a postmortem examination of the genital organs of a 31-year-old male gibbon showing a "general picture [of] advanced senile involution [of the testes] similar to the case in aged man."

female was the only one in the course of the study who disappeared, which probably meant she died.)

Documented cases of decreased reproductive capacity with age
for wild primates include Dittus's (1975) study of toque macaques
(*Macaca sinica*) in Sri Lanka, and my own study of hanuman langurs in Mount Abu, in northwestern India. A toque macaque female in the peak of her reproductive career, between the ages of 15
and 25, produces an average .86 infants per year. After the age of
25, her productivity declines to .29 infants per year. A langur female apparently peaks in reproductive fitness in her youth, between
five and about twelve years of age, when she produces an average of
.67 infants per year. Productivity declines thereafter to .38 infants
per year in middle age, and to .18 infants per year in old age.* The
typical reproductive careers of females in different primate species
are related to the social roles old females play. To illustrate, I will
compare the behaviors of old females in the best-studied species belonging to two widespread genera of Asian primates: the macaques
and langurs. I have chosen macaques and langurs because information for these two groups is available from a number of study sites,
and because they illustrate how the patterning of behaviors in old
animals responds to different social conditions. I focus on females
for two reasons. First, unlike most aging males, they remain with
the group and continue to play a vital role in troop life. Second, because old females do stay with the group they can be easily observed and we know more about them than about their male age-
mates.

The "Nepotistic" Macaques

Free-ranging Japanese macaques (*Macaca fuscata*) and rhesus
macaques (*M. mulatta*) have been studied for many years at the
Japanese Primate Center and on Cayo Santiago and La Parguera islands off the coast of Puerto Rico, respectively. From studies of
these provisioned colonies we have longitudinal data that include

---

* The low productivity of old females was the result of longer and longer intervals
between births. (See Blaffer Hrdy 1977).

exact ages of animals and genealogical relations among them. In both species, female hierarchies have been shown to be extremely stable over time (Kawai 1958; Sade 1972). With extraordinary regularity and few exceptions these hierarchies conform to two rules: daughters fit into the hierarchy just below their mothers, and younger sisters rank above older sisters. As a result, troops tend to consist of ranked matrilines (Kawai 1958).

There are long-range advantages conferred by high rank. For example, data from the rhesus troops on La Parguera indicate that inheritance of rank may be crucial for reproductive success. Population statistics collected there over a ten-year period (summarized in Drickamer 1974) indicate that (1) a larger percentage of high-ranking than of low-ranking females breed each year; (2) offspring of high-ranking females have a better survival rate than offspring of low-ranking females; and (3) the daughters of high- and middle-ranking females in turn produce offspring at a significantly earlier age (3.85 years) than do daughters of low-ranking females (4.4 years). A female's rank, then, has a great potential effect on her genetic contribution to subsequent generations. A mother's rank may also affect the status of her sons (Koford 1963), but the reproductive consequences of this influence are not well documented.

This strong correlation between a macaque female's rank and her reproductive success may explain the risks that females sometimes take in dominance struggles. Although rank relations are typically stable, occasionally hierarchies are disturbed by either external or internal events (e.g. death). At such times, both males and females may engage in fierce and sometimes deadly fights that are resolved when a new hierarchy is established (Marsden 1968; Bernstein 1969; Lindburg 1971). In short-range terms, high rank may mean access to such priorities of survival and reproduction as preferred or limited food resources, or position near the dominant male; it may also provide such species-specific perquisites as being groomed. In long-range evolutionary terms such advantages are translated into the production of offspring.

Consistent with the findings that dominant matrilines are able to monopolize certain resources and that females in higher-ranking lines may be more fertile, Sade has reported that on Cayo Santiago, the highest-ranking matrilines in a given troop appear to have a faster rate of growth than lower-ranking ones (Sade et al. 1975). Among macaques, then, the distribution of benefits is determined by genealogy and benefits are transmitted to successive generations. This is why I have called them "nepotistic." Both a female's individual fitness and her inclusive fitness are linked to those of close female matrikin.* Females in the same line thus have a powerful incentive to cooperate. A female belonging to the high-ranking matriline will benefit from cooperating with and defending relatives so as to maintain the rank of her own matriline relative to other lines in the same troop. Partch (1978) found, for example, that post-reproductive females defended infants in their own family lines in preference to infants of other lines. Furthermore, postreproductive females who belonged to high-ranking lines were significantly more likely to engage in such caretaking than were old females who belonged to low-ranking lines.

This mutual dependence of individuals in the same matriline may explain the prominent position reported for old families in macaque troops. Despite increasing feebleness with age, old females in high- and middle-ranking lines are still deferred to by their younger and more vigorous descendants. It is not uncommon on Cayo Santiago to see a stiff-legged, humpbacked, and balding old matriarch displace a muscular young adult male from a choice food item. The advantages to the younger animal of preserving the matriarch's rank, as well as his alliance with her, apparently outweigh the immediate small benefit to be derived from displacing her.

Thus the continued high status of an old macaque female is linked to the high rank of her descendants. But not all monkeys follow the macaque pattern: among hanuman langurs, for example, the position of old females is quite different.

* Biologists use "fitness" to refer to the genetic contribution an individual makes to the next generation. The more offspring, the greater fitness. "Inclusive fitness" denotes not only the individual's own genetic contribution but also any contribution the individual's behavior makes to the reproductive success of his or her close relatives.

The "Altruistic" Langurs

Troops of hanuman langurs (*Presbytis entellus*) are composed of overlapping generations of matrilineally related females accompanied by one or more adult males who have entered the troop from outside. Females remain in the same troop in the same home range throughout their lives, but males typically leave their natal troop or are driven out before maturity. Free males join nomadic all-male bands and do not return again to troop life unless as adults they succeed in invading a largely female troop and deposing the resident males.

Langur troops are generally smaller than troops of Japanese or rhesus macaques. Whereas in a macaque troop there are usually several reproductively active males present at once, in a langur troop there is often only a single male fathering infants at any one time. An important consequence of the different breeding systems is that females in a langur troop are, on average, more closely related to one another than females in a macaque troop are. Female langurs of the same age not only share the same father but are born to closely related mothers. It has been calculated that females in a langur troop thus share a minimum of one-eighth to one-quarter of their genes by common descent.* Langur troops do not appear to be segmented into matrilines, and it is very rare for one set of females to form an alliance against another set within the same troop. Most dominance interactions involve individuals, not alliances. There is little evidence, for example, that mothers and daughters or sisters support one another against less closely related females, as is the case among macaque females.

In a typical langur interaction, one female approaches another and either threatens her or pinches or slaps her, whereupon the animal approached moves away. At Abu, the direction of such displacements was consistent over short periods. Within a three-month span, for example, the outcome of a displacement interaction could

---

* Hypothetical minimum degrees of relatedness were calculated by following a typical troop through a number of generations. (See the results of computer simulation of the langur breeding system in Blaffer Hrdy 1977, appendix 3.)

be correctly predicted in advance about 97 percent of the time. Over year-to-year periods, however, there were marked changes in the female hierarchy.

Although langur dominance relations are not yet completely understood, in general juvenile and young-adult females rise in the hierarchy at the expense of older animals (Blaffer Hrdy & Hrdy 1976). In three troops, young females in or just entering their reproductive prime occupied the top half of the hierarchy, and older females and very young, immature females the lower half of the hierarchy. Since a langur does not reach her full weight until several years after she achieves reproductive maturity, this meant that young adults displaced substantially larger and older females.

Whereas in the macaque system a female's rank is determined at birth and is more or less fixed for life, in the langur system a female's rank changes. In a rhesus macaque troop, the highest-ranking female is usually an old one; in a hanuman langur troop, however, old females are usually among the lowest-ranking adults. In each of the three troops observed at Abu, the oldest females could be displaced by most other adults and even by some immature langurs. These old females were thus at a competitive disadvantage in their access to preferred or limited food sources.

There are also important differences between the behavior of old and young langur females. Whereas young females intrepidly initiate contacts with troop members—approaching, grooming, or embracing them, or competing with them—old females avoid close contact with their fellows. One old female I observed fed only on the outskirts of her troop, or else absented herself from the troop entirely. If the troop was feeding at the main food source, this female would wait to forage until other troop members were dozing or grooming each other. When she did attempt to feed with others, she fared poorly: on three occasions she was threatened away from an advantageous position at a palm tree oozing sap (an important food source for langurs during the dry season); on five occasions she was attacked by another female bent on usurping the food; and on two occasions other females attempted to remove food that was hanging from her mouth.

In her pioneering study of langurs at Kaukori, in north-central India, Jay (1963) found a similar peripheralization of old females (although the hierarchy itself was less strongly expressed). Younger females almost never left the troop, but old ones often did—whether because of the routine displacement they suffered at the hands of other animals or (as has been suggested for humans) because of "social disengagement" (Cummings & Henry 1961). Studies of other primates confirm this tendency of old animals to withdraw (see Fitts 1976 for a discussion of peer preferences among monkeys; Riopelle & Rogers 1965 on chimpanzees; Waser in press on African mangabeys; and Ohsawa 1979 on gelada baboons). It is noteworthy that among macaques, unlike langurs, reduced social involvement of old females is not necessarily accompanied by a fall in rank.

Old langur females—despite both their apparent disinclination to compete with other troop members and their disadvantaged position within the troop—nonetheless participate vigorously in defending the troop, advancing troop interests, and protecting troop infants. Among langurs, males who have recently usurped control of a troop sometimes attack infants. Curiously, infants thus attacked may be more vigorously defended by old, low-ranking females than by their own higher-ranking mothers. From an evolutionary perspective postreproductive females have more to gain defending their genetic investment, grandchildren. The still reproductively active female would be ill advised to endanger her own life defending her infants since she can still partially recoup her loss by bearing more infants (see Blaffer Hrdy & Hrdy 1976). The concept of inclusive fitness offers an explanation for a ranking system that favors youthful females of high reproductive value combined with a defense system in which old females take great risks (Hamilton 1964). Under these conditions there will be selection in favor of the genes of a postreproductive female who "altruistically" invests in the preservation of close relatives. The situation is reversed for young females at or approaching their reproductive prime: in their case, natural selection favors those who selfishly leave troop defense to other animals. It is important to note here that I assume no conscious intent on the part of the animal; I need only assume that on the average the genes of animals who respond to certain situations in a manner beneficial to the fitness of kin are going to be disproportionately represented in subsequent generations. That is, if the relatives of old females who defer to younger troop members are at a selective advantage compared to the relatives of old females who continue to compete, then over evolutionary time the relatives of deferring old animals—other things being equal—will prevail in the population. Such descendants will behave as if they were pursuing a conscious strategy. In fact, natural selection alone is sufficient to explain the complex of behaviors.

An Evolutionary Theory for the Behavior of Old Primates

The findings that primates, like other animals, grow old, and that female primates appear to go through menopause come as no surprise to evolutionary biologists. In the later part of the nineteenth century, the first evolutionary theory to explain the origin of physical decay and death was proposed independently by Alfred Russel Wallace and August Weismann. According to this theory, death was a preprogrammed event that evolved so that worn-out or more vulnerable members of the population might be replaced by younger, more vigorous ones. In the words of Wallace: ". . . it is evident that when one or more individuals have provided a sufficient number of successors they themselves . . . are an injury to those successors. Natural selection therefore weeds them out. . . . Many moths and other insects are in this condition, living only to propagate their kind and then immediately dying" (cited in Weismann 1889: 23).

The early theory fell short of explaining why the older generation was less viable, that is, how physical decay arose in the first place and how it could be selected for in a world where evolutionary rewards (i.e. disproportionate representation in the next generation's gene pool) fall to the individuals who best survive and reproduce. As George Williams (1957) put it in a critique of Weismann's theory of a built-in "death mechanism": "It is indeed remarkable that after a seemingly miraculous feat of morphogenesis, a complex metazoan [multicellular animal] should be unable to perform the much simpler task of merely maintaining what is formed." Furthermore, the theory relied on individual self-sacrifice for the benefit of a larger population, not all of whom would be close relatives. Except among humans, no instance of pure altruism (i.e. altruism that does not have a high likelihood of specific enhancement of the benefactor's own genetic representation) has ever been documented. Williams, drawing on ideas presented by Haldane (1941), Medawar (1952), and Comfort (1956), went on to propose his pleiotropic theory of aging (1957). It should be clear from Weiss's comprehensive review of the biological bases of aging elsewhere in this volume that Williams's is but one of many theories purporting to explain why there is physical decay with age. But because Williams's arguments have a direct bearing on my approach to explaining the behavior of old female primates, I will elaborate on them here.

Pleiotropy refers to the capacity of a gene to affect several aspects of character, and to affect them at different stages of the life cycle. Williams postulated a type of gene that had beneficial effects early in life, but detrimental effects later. Since many animals would not in any case survive life's hazards to reach old age, any trait that conferred benefits early in life would be selected for in spite of detrimental consequences later. Williams also suggested that whenever a conflict arose, natural selection would favor youth over age. Once aging became a fact of life, reproductive value (the extent to which an individual of a given age is likely to contribute to the gene pool of succeeding generations) would begin to decline shortly after first reproduction and would decline steadily thereafter.* The bias in favor of youth would take on broader significance: the implicit assumption of Wallace's model—that older animals are "worth" less —would be borne out. In the case of organisms living in groups composed of close relatives and offspring, aging individuals might increase their inclusive fitness by altruistically contributing to the

---

* See Stearns 1976 for an excellent discussion of reproductive value and its importance for life history tactics.

survival of relatives (Hamilton 1964, 1966), or, as Wallace suggested nearly a century ago, by opting out of competition—even to the point of dying.

That kin selection might shape creatures to die sooner rather than later, or vice versa, is no longer merely speculation. In an elegant study of New World saturnid moths, Blest (1963) divided his subjects into two groups: cryptic species, which rely on camouflage to escape the detection of predators; and aposematic species, which rely on their terrible taste to discourage predators from ever eating a member of that species a second time. Postreproductive survival of the tasty moths is detrimental to conspecifics because a predator's discovery of any member of a cryptic species would establish a search image in the mind of the predator. By contrast, a predator's unpleasant experience with an aposematic individual would benefit its kin and other conspecifics. Adults of both kinds subsist on stored reserves and do not feed after hatching, so they do not compete with conspecifics for food. But postreproductive individuals from the foul-tasting varieties may still serve the community whereas old cryptics are nothing but a liability. As might be expected, cryptic moths at the end of their life spans begin to fly wildly and erratically, quickly exhausting their food reserves and dying, whereas the aposematic moths conserve stored energy and live on. The importance of Blest's study extends beyond kin-selected altruism, for it also documents the existence of genetically based behaviors that occur at one stage of an organism's life cycle but not at any other. Although the situation is more complex among mammals and particularly among primates, my evidence suggests that an analogous situation exists among primates where there has been selective pressure favoring the development of special behavior patterns in old animals.

Aging in Primates

There is some evidence to suggest a preponderance of females among those few primates reaching old age. At a site in Sri Lanka, Dittus (1975) found that "senile" females constituted 3 percent of the toque macaque population (10 percent of the adult female cohorts). Of the females classified as "senile," 60 percent had failed to reproduce for two or more successive years (Dittus 1975:132).* At Abu, I found 5 percent of the troop-dwelling langurs to be old females (7 percent of the adult female cohorts); indeed, all old individuals at Abu were females, and I never observed a male comparable in age to them. There are several possible interpretations for this. (1) that males do not show their age; (2) that my criteria apply only to females; (3) that old males do not spend time in the vicinity of the troops where most of my observations were carried out; or, (4) that males at Abu die at a younger age than females do. I am inclined to favor the last interpretation, because Dittus's data on wild toque macaques in Sri Lanka show that females generally outlive males (1975: table 7; and Dittus, personal communication).

If macaque and langur females do in fact outlive males, this finding would be in the direction predicted by Williams's theory of aging. Like many male animals, langur and macaque males fight more fiercely than females and are exposed to higher mortality risks. Hence one would expect the decline in reproductive value with age to be even more rapid in this more vulnerable sex, and, as a consequence, "the balance of selective forces [to] result in more rapid senescence in males of species in which these conditions are found" (Williams 1957:406). Nevertheless, it is clear that under protected conditions males also have a capacity for very long lives.

A typical pattern for males in a number of birds (see for example Lill 1974) and mammals, including such primates as baboons, macaques, and langurs, is for the male to remain more or less peripheral to the breeding system in youth and young adulthood, when he is relatively low-ranking; then to obtain higher rank and greater access to fertile females during his prime (at around 10-plus years for monkeys); and last to suffer declining rank and reduced access to females in old age. Bernstein (1968:2) reports, for example, that one old male lutong (*Presbytis cristata*) "designated senile on the basis of skin, teeth, locomotor patterns, and general behavior" remained in the troop in addition to a younger adult male. According

---

* Dittus uses the term "senile" to mean "old."

to Bernstein (personal communication), this male adopted several "female-like" behavioral patterns, including the female squeal vocalization. In other species, such as gelada baboons (*Theropithecus gelada*), an old male may remain with his harem in addition to a younger male, but the old male becomes subordinate to the younger one and leads a peripheralized existence (Dunbar & Dunbar 1975:56). The Dunbars have suggested that the bands of males that sometimes invade gelada harems in an attempt to usurp them may purposely seek out harems with aged leaders (personal communication cited in Moley 1976). Even after his harem is usurped, however, the old patriarch may remain and continue to protect his own offspring. Among hanuman langurs, old males are often excluded altogether.

Investment in Kin by Postreproductives

The example of Blest's moths raises an interesting issue concerning long-lived primates. Williams suggested that among humans it might have become advantageous for women of 45 to 50 to stop producing new offspring and concentrate on the promotion of extant ones (1957:406; see also Hamilton 1966, Alexander 1974). Given the large amount of maternal investment necessary for the survival of primate infants, Williams's theory applies to nonhuman primates as well. A possible illustration is Jane Goodall's story concerning the last two offspring of the old female chimpanzee Flo. At an advanced age Flo gave birth to one last child, called Flame, who died in infancy. This late birth attenuated Flo's investment in her next-to-last offspring, Flint; but after Flame's death, Flo resumed caring for him. Goodall suggests that because his upbringing was interrupted, Flint never became properly independent. Unable to fend for himself, he died within a month of his mother.* It is impossible to know for sure if the birth of that extra sibling affected Flint's survival, but I believe the example illustrates the potential

---

* Flo never cycled again after Flame's birth, and researchers at Gombe suspected she was menopausal (B. Smuts and R. Wrangham personal communication). I am grateful to N. Nicolson for the exact sequence of events concerning the Flo anecdote.

value of menopause for a species whose young are dependent for long periods.

Aging animals may invest directly in offspring, or they may contribute to the well-being of the troop, which typically contains many related individuals. Itani (1959) reported the adoption by an older Japanese macaque female of one infant from twins born to her daughter—presumably because two infants were more than the daughter could cope with alone. In emergencies such as severe droughts, old animals may serve as important repositories of information, leading the troop to a water hole outside the normal boundaries of troop movement (Kummer 1971; see also Chalmers & Rowell 1971, Alexander 1974). On a day-to-day basis, as well as during crises, old animals may play a part in directing troop movements—as they apparently do among mangabeys (Waser in press) and langurs—or in defending troop members. When a troop of langurs is threatened by dogs or humans, or by encroachments upon its territory by other langurs, it is typically the adult male or the oldest females who leave the rest of the troop to charge and slap at the offenders (Blaffer Hrdy 1977). I have already discussed the daring of old females in defending infants against assaults by infanticidal langur males. Similar courageous and persistent defense of younger relatives by old females has been documented for Japanese and rhesus macaques (personal communication from J. Kurland; Kurland 1977; and Partch 1978).

Partch's research on five troops of rhesus macaques at the La Parguera colony is the only long-term study to date specifically on how postreproductive females contribute to infant survival. Partch recorded 572 instances of protection or defense of infants by postreproductive females; 71 percent of these interventions were in defense of infants belonging to the old female's own matriline. During conflicts between troops, postreproductive females were more likely than breeding ones to chase or attack intruders. Furthermore, during the birth season, old females without infants of their own gave considerable care and attention to yearlings whose mothers were preoccupied with new infants (Partch 1978).

As I have shown, the lower reproductive value of aging primates has important implications for the evolution of age-specific behaviors such as altruistic defense of relatives (see, for example, the general models in Pianka & Parker 1975). But the total pattern of behaviors old animals display and the roles they play in troop life are also adaptive in the larger social contexts in which these animals have evolved; that is, the behaviors of old animals will vary between species and between individuals of the same species existing under different environmental or social conditions.

To show how such variation works, I return to the examples of macaque and langur social organization. Macaques and langurs represent two different systems of dominance hierarchies among females: among rhesus and Japanese macaques, rank is genealogically determined and close relatives support one another, old females generally retain their rank, and old matriarchs of high-ranking matrilines are deferred to throughout life; among langurs, by contrast, old females cease competing with younger females and fall in rank. It does not follow, however, that the differences described for the two groups are absolute. They may be two extremes on a continuum of behavioral possibilities. This concept of behavioral scaling has been proposed by Wilson (1975) to describe variation in the expression of genetically determined behavior patterns. Although the genotype of an organism remains the same, its phenotypic expression may vary with time or with changes in the social or physical environment. Crowded animals, for example, may behave more aggressively than conspecifics living at lower population densities. The concept of behavioral scaling is crucial to understanding variation in behavior that occurs at different stages of the life cycle in response to varying conditions.

Even with the Japanese and rhesus macaques, the two species for which the "macaque model" was originally constructed, there is variation between lineages and among individuals. Iwamoto (1974) presents evidence to suggest that some old Japanese macaque females may cease competing with younger females much as langurs do. Peter Ellison and I observed old rhesus females from low-ranking lines at Cayo Santiago and La Parguera apparently falling in rank with age and being displaced by younger females from their own matrilines. It would seem that there is little advantage in cooperation among low-ranking females merely to maintain a status that is already worth little.

To what extent, then, do the two patterns of dominance described represent species-specific behaviors, and to what extent are they simply opportunistic adaptations to circumstances? A broader look at the macaques, and a closer examination of idiosyncratic cases within the rhesus and Japanese macaques, suggest that the "macaque pattern" may simply be one extreme on a behavioral scale.

The first line of evidence suggesting a behavioral scale is variation in the patterning of dominance relations among macaques under different conditions. Among crab-eating macaques (*M. fascicularis*) in the Basel Zoo, Angst found that daughters fit into the dominance hierarchy below their mothers only about half the time; in the remaining cases mothers ranked below their daughters. Nor did the "rule" that younger daughters rank above older ones apply in all cases (Angst 1975). Furthermore, in three cases Angst noted decline in rank and peripheralization of very old females (described as "sterile" and approximately 30 years old). Such crab-eating macaque females are not clearly distinguishable in their dominance relations from langurs.

Conclusion

If the hypotheses I have developed here are correct, old age among at least some primate species is the product of evolutionary forces that favor the genes of animals who survive past their own reproductive periods to foster, support, and protect their younger kin. How they support the younger animals seems to vary with the sex of the animal and the situation of the group. Males generally bow out, leaving females to intervene actively in the fate of their descendants. Although high rank in mothers generally translates into better life chances for offspring, high rank throughout a female's lifetime may not be uniformly advantageous to her descendants. This observed range of behaviors argues strongly for the existence of a genetically determined behavioral scale rather than inherited species-specific patterns of dominance and submission in old animals. In some instances (e.g. among langurs or macaques from low-ranking matrilines), a deferential old animal's inclusive fitness may be greater than that of an animal who maintains her own status. In other instances (e.g. high-ranking macaque lines), high rank may be uniformly advantageous to the extent that a matriline encompasses members of all age-grades, that the rank of all members of the line is the same, and that inclusive fitness is cumulative for all members of that line.

Implied in the discussion of aging among primates is a comparison with human aging. What do my conclusions about the evolutionary significance of old age in primates suggest about the same phenomena among humans? It is clear from what little we know about the complex patterns of behavior among aging nonhuman primates that no simple pattern of species-specific aging behavior can be postulated for humans. At the same time I would urge anthropologists at least to consider the possibility that there is a genetic basis for the observed range of variation in patterns of behavior among old human beings. My review of aging among nonhuman primates strongly suggests that it would be rewarding for us to test the hypothesis that there exists in the human genetic endowment some kind of programming for a behavioral scale—obviously much more complex and sensitive than what I have suggested for monkeys. Such an approach need not jeopardize the traditional emphasis on learned and culturally transmitted adaptations, but should instead contribute to a better understanding of the complex relationship between culture and biology.

"The Old People Give You Life": Aging Among !Kung Hunter-Gatherers

MEGAN BIESELE AND NANCY HOWELL

Now the Elephant Girl had already warned her grandmother that some thing might happen to her. She had said "Watch well: a little wind will come to you. The little wind will come to you with something in it. It will bring you some droplets of blood. The blood will come to lodge inside your groin. Take that bit of blood and put it into a container. Don't let on what you're doing—just take it and put it into something. Something like a little dish or a little bottle." It happened just as the girl had said. A little wind came back to her grandmother. The bit of blood came to lodge in her groin. The grandmother saw it and said "Didn't the child tell me something like this would happen?" She didn't speak aloud, she just said this in her heart. She took the drops of blood and put them in a bottle. Then she sat and thought, and asked herself "Should I go to see what has happened to my granddaughter? No, it has already happened just as she said it would, so he must have killed her already and there's no help for it." She turned it over and over in her mind; meanwhile the bit of blood was grow- ing. It grew and grew until it was too big for the bottle. Then the grand- mother took it out and put it in a skin bag. It grew again and burst the bag, so the grandmother put it into something bigger. Then it grew some more and broke that. Only the grandmother knew about it. No one else knew that she had the Elephant Girl and was restoring her to life. She kept it a secret. She had the bit of blood and it grew, and she fixed it, and it grew some more and she fixed it. When it had grown completely it was a woman again! She looked just like she had before.

One morning when the camp awoke, the women decided to go gather- ing n/n. They got up and went off picking n/n. The Elephant Girl's little daughter went with them, saying "Today I'll accompany my aunts and eat n/n." The old grandmother said "Go ahead, go with them." So the Ele- phant Girl's mother and all the other women went gathering. The old woman stayed home alone. She spent the day quietly. In the afternoon she took a skin and spread it in the shade, spread it in the late afternoon shadows. Then she took out the Elephant Girl and sat her upon the skin. She ground ocher and spread it upon the young woman's face. She replaced her old rags with soft new skin clothing and hung her all over with ornaments. Then the old woman tied copper rings in her granddaughter's hair the way people used to tie them long ago. She fixed her up so that she was the beautiful Elephant Girl again.

Later the women came back from gathering. Toward sunset they returned. The old woman was telling funny stories and the Elephant Girl was laughing "/eh-/eh-/eh-/eh-o!" As the women came near the village, the Elephant Girl's little daughter said to the others "Who's that laughing just like my mother in the village?"

Her aunt said "How can you be so crazy? My older sister died a long time ago. Don't go saying you hear her laughing someplace."

Another girl said "My aunt is certainly dead: this child is crazy."

So they came closer, listening. The Elephant Girl laughed again. This time they said "Can it be? Whose laughter is this? When we left there was nobody but the old woman in the camp; we had all gone gathering. What young girl can that be whose laughter sounds just like our sister's?" When they came into the camp they saw the Elephant Girl sitting there with her grandmother. Her daughter cried "Mother, mother, mother!" and ran to her, flopped down, and began to nurse. The others cried out and said "Yo! Who has accomplished this?"

The Elephant Girl answered softly "Granny, of course. Granny lifted me up. Granny spoke the word and I sat up and was alive. If it had been up to you others alone, I wouldn't be here. Long ago Granny took me and sheltered me in a skin pouch and now I am alive again. That's how it was. The old people give you life."

This extract from a !Kung San folktale told in 1972 provides a fitting introduction to the consideration of the place of old people in !Kung life.* As the story from the Elephant Girl heroine cycle suggests, old people are highly valued and respected among these

---

* The story of the Elephant Girl was collected by Megan Biesele from !Kun/obe n!a at Kauri, Botswana, in 1972. The language of the !Kung San ("San" is increasingly being used by scholars in place of the term "Bushmen," which has negative connotations in Southern Africa) is a tonal one, with four distinct "click" sounds that serve as consonants: /, the dental click, is produced by pulling the tongue off the back of the top front teeth; ≠, the alveolar click, is produced by "popping" the tongue off the middle of the roof of the mouth; !, the palatal or alveopalatal click, is produced by "popping" the tongue off the back of the roof of the mouth; //, the lateral click, is produced by pulling the side of the tongue from the teeth on one or both sides. For the nonlinguist, the first two symbols may be approximated by "t," the second two by "k." The symbol ", as in k"xau (owner), is a glottal flap.

hunter-gatherers of the Kalahari Desert of southern Africa. In this paper we will consider, first, the demographic patterns that determine survival into old age, and the proportion of the population that can be called "old"; second, the household, family, and kinship patterns of !Kung society, which determine to such a large extent the conditions of day-to-day life for the old; and third, the economic patterns of subsistence work and the "ownership" of valued items in !Kung culture. All these factors contribute to the honored position of old people we have observed among the !Kung.

The Aging Process: How Old Is "Old"?

The !Kung people have little interest in numbers not of immediate practical value, and do not know their own ages or year of birth. They do, however, show a great concern with relative age in their relationships, which is reflected in the terms of address and reference used in conversation between any two people: no matter how close in age two people are, they always determine who is the elder and who is the younger, and the elder has small but real prerogatives in the relationship. Hence the older one becomes, the greater the number of relationships in which one is the elder and the more respect one is accorded. The !Kung also distinguish linguistically the stages of life, which are basically (with some differences between the sexes) infancy, childhood, young adulthood, full adulthood (with parenthood), old adulthood (when childbearing has ended and the work of childrearing is slowing down), and old age. The respectful suffix *n!a*, which can be translated as "big" or "old," is added to the names of people in their forties or fifties who are no longer bearing or begetting children, but who may still be at the height of their abilities. There is a special description for the extremely old, ≠ *da !i*, which means "nearly dead." This is sometimes used to describe people who seem indeed to be near death; but it is also used to emphasize the great age of people who are still vigorous, and it may be used in a joking, self-deprecating way by middle-aged people to describe themselves when they are tired or unwell.

To single out the people who are old in !Kung society, then, we might choose to talk about all those who are *n!a* (which would include some people as young as 45), we might focus on the *≠da !i* (most of whom are over 70), or we might go outside !Kung linguistic categories to talk about those whom we have estimated as being over a particular chronological age, such as 60. In the demographic sections of this paper it will be most convenient to use the last of these means of distinguishing "the old," whereas elsewhere we will follow the less precise but more appropriate !Kung categories.

One of the possibilities considered when demographic studies of the !Kung were first undertaken was that the !Kung might age more quickly than other people, attaining the status and physical appearance of "old age" at a younger chronological age than in other societies (see Howell 1976). But careful studies of absolute and relative age in the population have demonstrated that this is not true. Although the rigors of the hunting and gathering life and the continual exposure to the Kalahari sun and wind have some tendency to dry the skin prematurely and make people look older, this is balanced by the absence of obesity among the !Kung, which is often an indication of aging in other societies. All in all, guesses of age made on the basis of appearance were rarely as much as ten years off the ages arrived at by the use of careful and systematic procedures (see Howell 1979).

The oldest person in the group of about 500 !Kung San in the Dobe area of northwest Botswana in 1967 was a woman estimated to be about 81 years old. By 1972 she had died, and the oldest person was a man slightly younger than she had been, who was then about 86. These extreme ages, however, are those most insecure in the estimation process, since there is very little basis for corroboration of dates of birth from other people.

Surviving into old age

The probability of surviving into old age can only be known approximately for the !Kung, among whom no records of births and deaths are kept. From the analysis of deaths within the past decade, however, and from the study of the survival of children born to living adult women, we can obtain some idea of the probability of dying over the life span. The life table calculated for the !Kung for the period 1920–50 can be matched by the Coale-Demeny model life table (1966) with an expectation of life at birth of 30 years (MW5). For the period 1950–70, a table with an expectation of life of 40 years provides a closer fit to the data (MW9), which suggests that the effects of contact with the BaTswana, Herero, and European peoples have eased the conditions of life somewhat in recent decades. The public health service of Botswana incorporated the Dobe area into its inoculation and treatment programs in the mid-1970's, which is likely to improve the probabilities of survival still more.

A life expectancy at birth of 30 years, which seems to have characterized the !Kung before 1950, may be judged very low by Western standards. Yet the !Kung have established a secure basis for the continuation of their people, despite the obvious hardships involved in living in a harsh desert environment in small, undifferentiated groups dependent upon wild animals and uncultivated vegetables for food, in moving often, and in being without access to modern medical care or even to stored supplies of food to tide them over difficult periods of bad weather, epidemics, or bad luck. The !Kung have not been forced to engage either in a continuous struggle for survival or in the exhausting production of babies in order to keep their groups alive. Fertility levels needed to compensate for their level of mortality are not particularly high (an average of about 4.6 children per woman who survives to the end of the childbearing period), and the !Kung pattern of fertility tends to start relatively late (around age 19 for women), and to be characterized by long intervals between one birth and another (an average of more than three years between surviving children).

Of every 100 babies born, only about 54 will survive to age 15; about 45 will survive to age 30; about 33 will survive to age 45; and about 21 will survive to age 60. These probabilities suggest several implications about old age among the !Kung. First, though a 21 percent survival rate to age 60 is low in comparison to modern societies (in which 75–80 percent of those born are likely to survive to 60), it is high enough to guarantee a steady supply of old people to fill the roles associated with old age in the society: old age is and has always been a regular and unremarkable phenomenon in !Kung life. Second, the fact that some 79 percent of people die before reaching 60 means that death is not particularly associated with the old alone; and indeed, we found that people who reached 60 could expect to live about another ten years.

The Proportion of Old People

The proportion of the population over age 60 at a point in time is a function not only of the probabilities of survival but also of the balance of births and immigration with deaths and emigration. When the population is growing, the proportion of young people increases more rapidly than that of older people, so the proportion of persons 60 and over will decline even if the probability of surviving to 60 is increasing at the same time. Among the !Kung, who had a very slow rate of population growth until the 1960's, about 8 percent of the population overall would be expected to be 60 years old and older owing to the balance of births and deaths. Censuses taken on several occasions during the late 1960's indicated that migration of adults out of the area had increased the proportion of persons over age 60 to approximately 10 percent of the total population.

Health and handicaps of the aged

Many old people among the !Kung are vigorous and independent. Howell arrived unexpectedly at a !Kung camp one day to find four females playing jump rope. Their ages were 8, 11, 15, and 66, and the old woman was at least as active and enthusiastic as the children. Playfulness and exertion are commonly seen among !Kung old people in good health. Old women run and play games with children and adolescents, and old people of both sexes engage in bawdy joking and teasing with young people while middle-aged adults are busy with tasks.

When old people are hurt or sick, however, they often require special care and consideration from the younger members of their group. In a survey of health and handicaps taken in 1968, Howell estimated that about 6 percent of the population under 15 had a physical problem that required special help from others, that about 15 percent of those between 15 and 60 had some sort of a physical limitation, and that about 60 percent of those over 60 were similarly limited. Vision problems were the most common handicap. Four of 40 old people were totally blind and required constant assistance from others, and another twelve were blind in one eye or had some loss of vision. Eleven old people walked with difficulty or used a stick. Other handicaps recorded among the old included respiratory diseases (tuberculosis, chronic bronchitis, and emphysema). Truswell and Hansen (1976) reported that "some degree of lens opacity (cataract) is the rule in older San," that "teeth rarely show caries or fluorosis but with age become worn down to the gums" (no doubt owing to the abrasion of the !Kung diet and the continuous effects of small amounts of sand in the food), and that "mild osteoarthritis" afflicted many elderly San. Most remarkable, however, were the physical debilities they did not observe: they found hearing well preserved even into extreme old age; they found that mean blood pressures did not rise with age; and they did not observe anyone, at any age, with hypertension or with coronary heart disease. Some common degenerative diseases of industrial society, then, play a small role among the !Kung, whereas infectious diseases and accidents play a much larger role.

The !Kung treat illness by an elaborate and interesting method of medical care involving trance dances (Katz 1976; Lee 1967). When a person of any age is ill or injured, family members provide food, water, and psychological support, and relatives and nonrelatives alike provide dramatic psychological support through the trance dance. Senilicide has not been observed among the Dobe !Kung. In principle all !Kung support the efforts of old and sick people to recover from temporary illnesses, yet it is probably true that there are significant differences in the quality and quantity of care provided for those temporarily incapacitated. Old people who have close family members present probably are given more solicitous care in crises, have more allowances made for them in group moves, and enjoy a better diet when they can no longer provide for themselves. The death of a spouse and the lack of children or other close relatives to provide care may make it unlikely for a person to survive into old age.

!Kung Social Structure and the Old

Group structure and the management of resources

!Kung hunter-gatherers live in camps of individuals bound together by close bilateral kinship ties. Each camp has a "core" composed of older men and women, cousins and siblings of one another who through long tenure at a particular water hole are seen as its owners, or k"xausi. The oldest man or woman, the k"xau n!a, or "big owner," represents the core group as host to visitors who want to use the water. Similarly, the old maintain stewardlike control over specific food resources in the subsistence region (n!ore) around the water hole—again through long tenure in the area (see Lee 1972a, 1979; and Marshall 1960, 1976).

Familiarity with the local seasonal resources as they have fluctuated over the years is the real criterion for membership in the "core." As part of their stewardship of gathering locales and hunting grounds, the old pass on their accumulated knowledge on how best to use them. For this reason, the status of the old can be seen as directly related to their economic contribution. To exploit this environment with the technology available to them, the San need the detailed knowledge of local flora and fauna possessed fully only by the old.

The core system organizes camp membership and resource rights, and it also organizes sharing patterns within camps. It keeps conflict over scarce resources from arising both between and within camps. The old people know from years of experience how best to maintain community life: they are repositories of genealogical information and interpreters of the kinship system. Also, the large part they play in resource management is another indication of their economic importance.

A case in point is the "hosting" of the local water source by the oldest person. The !Kung live in an area where water sources can and do run dry, and where contingency plans must exist. It is important that some one person know *all* demands on the water source likely to occur in a given period so that available water can be fairly apportioned to all who have rights in it. The !Kung do not like to be caught unawares, without time to plan for emergencies.

The old *k"xausi* and their spouses provide genealogical stability over time to each water hole and resource area. Kin ties to these older people—as their siblings, offspring, or cousins—are the basis for younger people's camp membership. Younger members are expected to respect the old peoples' decisions regarding the food and water resources of the *n!ore*. The old people do not, however, act without regard for the opinions of the younger men and women. The vigorous hunters and gatherers participate along with the old in the process of arriving at group consensus, the !Kung way of making decisions.

Household composition

Among the !Kung, the smallest social unit is the nuclear family household, those who build a common hut to mark their place in the group, and eat and sleep together at the same fire. Groups of such households make up the "camp" or "village" (*chu/o*), which functions as the principal economic unit of production and consumption. The largest households among the !Kung are made up of mature adults in their thirties and forties and their dependent children. As the children reach puberty and set up their own households with marriage partners or temporarily with friends, the parents' household size is reduced, until only the couple remains.

The ideal household arrangement for older adults is probably that of living in couples, and about 60 percent of people over age 60 live with their spouses. When the death of one partner ends the marriage, the surviving spouse may live alone, as 30 percent of those over 60 do. Although the mean household size for the whole population is about four persons, only 6 percent of people over age 60 live in households with more than two members. These exceptional households may be made up of the partners of a polygamous marriage, of several persons of the same sex, or of an old woman with one or more of her teenage grandchildren (those who have reached the age when they should leave their parents' hearth).

Marriage

Rates of marriage dissolution and remarriage are high for the !Kung at all ages, as divorce is common and a spouse may die at any age. It is rare for a !Kung to have been married only once over a long lifetime, although most !Kung adults have had the experience of a long-term marriage at some point in their lives. Up to the age of about 50, widowed and divorced people almost inevitably re-marry within a year or so of the end of the previous marriage. After this age, it seems to be a matter of personal preference and con-venience whether the surviving spouse remarries. In some cases, the widowed person prefers to remain alone, taking advantage of the freedom of the single state to go wherever his or her closest relative (usually an adult child) is living. Others, and particularly those who happen to have no surviving children, are anxious to remarry. Old people sometimes seem to lower their standards in selection of a spouse; for example, a woman may be glad to enter a polygamous marriage, perhaps joining one of her sisters as a "junior wife," even if she was one of those who would have been too jealous and pos-sessive for polygamy in her younger days.

The !Kung custom that the husband is usually five to fifteen years older than the wife makes it likely that the husband will die first. About 40 percent of !Kung women but only 13 percent of !Kung men over 60 are unmarried widows or widowers.

Although the continuation of marriage into old age may have an important psychological effect in providing old people with a sense of security, more important is the presence of surviving children and other close kin, as an aged spouse may not be able to provide food on a regular basis. Old people are supported by the group in which they are members, but the presence of particular close kin who can be called upon to meet specific needs for food or care increases their security. Unfortunately, it can easily happen that the relatively high rates of mortality at all ages leave old people isolated, with no surviving spouse or children: about 5 percent of the men, and about 20 percent of the women, are expected to be isolated in their old age in this way, under the probabilities of birth and death among the !Kung.

Kinship connections

Old people find that their inventory of living kin changes as they get older, in ways that may be either advantageous or difficult for them. Despite the fact that they are the ones who formulate the answers to the question "*Msa re o kuri?*" ("Where—what—are we to each other?"), this inventory is finally not under their control. As their children marry and have families, some old people find themselves becoming the focal point of large groups of related people—in some cases far too many for all to live in the same camp at the same time. Other old people, through no fault of their own, may find that their children, if any, have few or no surviving children, so that their kin ties to younger generations are impaired. (In such cases, however, old people use the !Kung knack for plugging into the kinship system wherever they can [Richard Lee, personal communication].) Although three surviving lineal generations are commonly seen among the !Kung (and four generations, as illustrated in the story of the Elephant Girl, may occur), probably the majority of the !Kung at any point in time are not members of a group that has three surviving generations, because the grandparents have died prematurely or because the offspring failed to have children.

An important link for the old to future generations is forged through the custom of namesakes. Children are never named for their parents; rather, they are named for their grandparents or others in the first or second ascending generation above the parents. The !Kung feel that if one person is named for another, their identities mingle in important ways. For an old person, this seems to bring a feeling of continuity, whereas for the young, it gives a sense of unquestioned belonging to a line of forebears. Kinship terms used between old and young to indicate this relationship ("my big-name" and "my little-name") contain much implicit affection and a sense of special connectedness between the two persons.

Contributions from the Aged

Gathering for women and hunting for men may persist as regular activities throughout the life span, though they usually taper off in the older years. Because gathering demands none of the dramatic spurts of energy that hunting does, more old women gather regularly late into their lives than old men hunt (except for such mild forms as snaring birds). There is no restriction on men of any age gathering plant foods, and some older men may gradually substitute it for strenuous hunting. But past age 60, old people contribute relatively little to the subsistence of the group as a whole (Lee in preparation, chap. 3).

As the work load is lightened, however, other activities begin to absorb the energies of the old and account for the respect they continue to receive. Never do they really become "useless" (though some old people may talk of themselves this way), because, for one thing, as they age they are seen as the repositories of knowledge—both practical information and lore—accumulated over a lifetime.

Special activities of the old

Storytelling, for instance, is in large part the province of the old. Most men and women over about age 45 (i.e., those whose names have come to have the suffix *n!a* appended to them), are reasonable if not expert storytellers. Older people seem to take as great delight in hearing the stories as in telling them, and younger people, even if they are able to tell the stories themselves, tend to defer politely to older people when they are present. So it is with other items of cultural lore as well: "Ask /asa n!a," someone will say; "she is an old person and knows everything." The satisfaction older people derive from knowing and retelling the familiar tales—by turns bawdy, ridiculous, and amazing—is evident. They have heard these stories in all their myriad variations so often and for so long that they know them in the marrow of their bones and are proud of it. They delight in telling the stories again to make a new generation laugh. Storytelling is gladly undertaken as a valued skill to be exercised with interest and pride when one is old.

Old people form important parts of some of the various multiage groups with which children spend their time. Caring for small children while their mothers are off gathering is one function of such groups, which typically include older people, especially women. The companionable time grandparents spend with the young contributes to children's warm and relaxed feelings toward them. Young children easily and confidently demand food from their grandparents; they seem to regard them as a secure resource that they unquestionably possess. Also much important learning of skills, traditions, and social attitudes takes place as the children— who among the !Kung begin subsistence work rather late in life, between fourteen and sixteen—spend time with the old people. From interviews and observation, as well as from projective forms such as the folktale quoted earlier, it is evident that in children's minds the grandparental generation is pictured as loving, educative, and nurturant.

The tapering off of their work load enables old people to begin to spend more time in spiritual exploration. They also have more time for healing—though people in their thirties and forties can also be very active in this way. Healing is seen as an extremely important contribution to group life, and younger members are grateful to those elders who can draw upon supernatural resources to cure. Furthermore, released from prohibitions that constrain younger people, the old can control and manipulate ritual substances and powers thought to be dangerous earlier in life. In the exercise of this ritual power the old serve as the initiators of younger people into the successive stages of life. The verb used for what the old do to the young in several such initiation rites is *n≠um*, "to create" (see Biesele 1972 for further discussion of this many-faceted verb). The old are seen as symbolically responsible for the "creation" of new adults out of what were once children. They are seen as old

enough and strong enough to handle the powerful *n/um*, or spiritual energy, generated at such times.

Food avoidances that apply to younger people in the various
stages of reproductive life are often relaxed after the childbearing years. Young adults, for instance, must not eat steenbok meat.
There is also a prohibition concerning ostrich eggs: these must not
be eaten by men or women from the age of puberty until they are
old enough to have had five children. Believed to make these reproductively active people crazy if they eat them, the eggs are rel-
ished by children and by older people, who are felt to be past the
danger of having their minds affected by the rich food.*

Since some food avoidances do not apply either to children below the age of puberty or to elders past childbearing, freedom from
ritual constraints applying to the reproductively active is one link
between the very young and the very old in !Kung society. There is
another link in that passing childbearing age appears to be an
achievement that prepares both older men and older women to take
an active part in the transitional rituals involving the young. The
grandparent for whom a child is named gives him a handsome gift
at the rite of the child's first haircut (Marshall 1976: 309). Old men
serve as the initiators of the boys in the *tshoma*, a month-long male
initiation ritual held in a bush camp far from other people, where
young men endure cold, hunger, thirst, and prolonged dancing.
During this month, the old men impart to the young secrets about
the animals (Blurton-Jones & Konner 1976). Old women beat axes
together for sound and bare their buttocks as they dance for a girl's
first menstruation. It is an old woman, generally her grandmother,
who is with the girl in her seclusion hut and who teaches her the
things she must learn at that time. Old people may handle ritual
substances and the powerful ritual fires burned at the hunting and
initiation rites accompanying the entry of boys and girls into adult

---

* Though the !Kung in general observe these precautions, they are not above playing with their system of food avoidances. An old woman, having fun at the expense
of her husband one day, said that he was too old to be chasing young women. With a
straight face he responded by saying to a third party that one should not take seriously anything his wife said, because she was only "an old woman who eats ostrich
eggs."

life. The ritual division in !Kung society between childrearers and those past the reproductive years, which confers on the latter a special access to the young at their time of transition to maturity, is a strong factor in the social position of the elderly.

Partly because of their privileged position as handlers of ritual power, and partly because of their freedom from subsistence duties, older !Kung men and women are able to concentrate upon trance medicine and develop their healing powers. In his paper "Education for Transcendence," Richard Katz (1976) described the careers of trance healers as they worked through the years to gain control of this powerful psychic resource in order to be able to use it for curing others. In the Dobe area of Botswana today, just under half the adult men in !Kung society and perhaps a third of the women become *n/um k"xausi*, or owners of *n/um* (psychic power), during their lives. (Among precontact !Kung in Namibia in the 1950's, however, women healers were not a highly developed feature of the culture: the later Botswana figures may reflect changing times [Lorna Marshall, personal communication].) Even leaving the number of women healers aside, however, we see that this expertise is found in a substantial portion of the population. The interest of women in making music by singing and clapping, and of men in dancing, appears to be sustained into old age. Dancing is a serious pursuit of mature people and may become increasingly important in very advanced age.

Some old curers, of course, say that the *n/um* they had in strength in their mature lives has weakened or been taken from them by God in their infirm old age. They lament that they have become too thin, or feeble, or blind to go on curing. But there are others whose involvement with *n/um* seems to increase greatly in intensity with their advancing age. One old woman described by Katz (1976 and in press) had become so powerful and so completely taken up with the opportunity of healing and of altering her consciousness that she was in and out of trance continually. People came and sang and danced with her every day to accompany her trances, and she was known and respected far and wide for her power to heal. Sometimes such persons receive payment (clothing, tobacco, a goat) from the neighboring Bantu and even from San for curing, unlike the traditional *n/um k"xausi.**

Another old person, a man this time, was also a dance specialist in his old age. But it was as an artist of fun and a specially zany, gifted clown that he excelled, rather than as a curer (though he did curing as well). People came from all over to make a dance so that they could watch him hunch his shoulders and warble like a besotted bird on a branch, all the while shooting his legs forward at unexpected but somehow perfectly hilarious angles and shaking his dance rattles in joyful mock ferocity. He lived for dancing and for entertaining people, did practically no subsistence work, and was provided for as a matter of course by his amused relatives. There is great tolerance for individuals' differing relationships to the *n/um* of the trance dance: these propensities are considered God-given.

Similarly, there is tolerance in !Kung society toward idiosyncrasies and quirks in general, especially in old people. Like leisure, this tolerance is another manifestation of a kind of "surplus" these people have. The way subsistence is organized by the !Kung provides a degree of "fat" in their economic system, one of whose uses is to support playfulness, individualism, and "noneconomic" behavior among the old. The outspokenness and sense of self of many of the old people is a delight to the young.

Of course, it is readily admitted by !Kung that with old age sometimes comes not inspired madness but real foolishness and lack of sense. But they mention this frankly and kindly, just as they speak of other kinds of remarkable behavior.

Economic leveling and the old

Economic accumulation as we know it is not a source of power for aging !Kung. This egalitarian society keeps individuals of all ages from hoarding goods, largely through the rules of generalized reciprocity and the *hxaro*, or gift-giving, system, which militate against accumulation of wealth. Older people do not generally own

---

* Bantus like to use San medicine in addition to their own, and most often can pay for it—far more often than the San can.

more goods than people in other age groups. If they have become dependent upon few or improvident offspring, they may often own less. Also, as we have seen, though they form "cores" around which group membership and water rights are organized, the old also derive their authority from their roles as controllers of knowledge, skill, and ritual power.

Furthermore, restraints against individual self-aggrandizement discourage the assumption of "political" power over the course of a lifetime. Thus older people are not likely to have accumulated power in this way either, except in terms of mutual-help relationships and gift-giving relationships they may have built up. All his life a !Kung remains dependent on the web of mutual kin obligations expressed by reciprocal visiting and gift-giving (*hxaro*). In this system, kinship itself must be looked upon as a resource. Older people who have carefully tended their kin-based webs of trading and mutual-aid relationships have ensured that favors and gifts are owed to them as they grow old and can no longer provide for themselves.

Hxaro itself decreases with old age (Wiessner 1977). As a person matures and settles his or her children in secure marriages, he or she may pass on *hxaro* relationships to them or may let them drop. Some relationships become unnecessary as a person's needs lessen with age; others become hard to sustain as failing eyesight or infirmity make craftwork on items to be given as gifts difficult. Old people do keep up some old and strong relationships, but they also begin new *hxaro* ties with grandchildren and nieces and nephews. If old people become incapacitated and cannot make or procure *hxaro* goods for themselves, children and grandchildren may supply them.

Grandparents play a key role in the instruction of very young children with regard to *hxaro*. Periodically, they cut off and redistribute gift beads they have given the child, thus introducing the concept of continuous passing on of goods. For older young people, adolescents, and young adults, *hxaro* ties with the aged are connected with access to land and resources. If young people are using an area frequently, they seem to feel more secure in their claims if they can maintain *hxaro* ties to the aged of the area. Most often, however, these ties are with their own grandparents: it is not fruitful for young people to begin very many relationships with old people, because they will necessarily be short-lived.

Do the !Kung become more acquisitive as they grow older? There does exist a certain material standard accepted as right for mature people. "I'm an old (big) person, and I have things," is an expression often heard. Younger people, say those just starting a marriage, do not have all the implements they need, and must often borrow. Gradually, through receiving gifts, they accumulate what is necessary. Beyond a certain point, however, accumulation stops. Partly it is the necessity of carrying all one's belongings on the frequent moves in traditional life that keeps the inventory low. But it is also the desire not to stand out from others or to appear stingy. Few can resist the constant requests from kin for any items that appear to be surplus, or the life-long admonitions to be generous in sharing. "Share today and you will be shared with when you are in need tomorrow" is a way to phrase an adaptation that has stood these people in good stead in the sparse Kalahari environment. Unlike their neighbors, the BaTswana, who marry so as to keep the cows in the family and who accumulate wealth with age, the !Kung have organized their subsistence around the systematic avoidance of accumulation. The environment itself (instead of a granary or kraal) is their storehouse. Reaping food from it is reliable when the group of sharing individuals is taken as a whole, but is unreliable for any individual. Variations in rainfall, fires, animal migrations, the energies and inclinations of group members, and a wealth of other factors dictate the necessity of reliance on different individuals in turn as they chance to bring in food. For this privilege, one must also be relied *upon*, in turn. Old people have paid for the consideration they receive in their time of infirmity by a lifetime of gifts and services to others.

A Typical Day in the Life of an Old Couple

//Koka n!a (77 years old in 1972) and ╪Toma //gwe (70) are a core couple at Dobe, Botswana. They have been married over fifty years.* Their three married sons and married daughter built their huts in a cluster around the old people's hut, and this group of families, with occasional visitors, constitutes a camp. From time to time this extended family moves camp to another site within the Dobe area. //Koka n!a is feeble and rarely gathers anymore, but she is recognized as having rights, through her age and long residence in the Dobe area, over certain /*tosi*, or gathering locations. Permission to gather in them is asked of her. Her continued good appetite is satisfied, now that she rarely goes gathering herself, by a more or less steady stream of mongongo nuts, marula nuts and fruit, morethlwa berries, and many other plant foods gathered in the various /*tosi* by her daughter, her son's wives, and their offspring. //Koka n!a sits by her fire with her fire paddle for roasting nuts, a stone for cracking them, and a pot or two. Her small wooden mortar and pestle are there also, and with them she pounds for herself and her husband any food that is brought to them. (Their teeth are worn down and the mortar has become their constant companion.) The old woman and her husband snack on and off all day as foodstuffs come in, constantly muttering that their offspring never bring them anything. (Generally these mutterings surprise no one and create no special resentment. People of all ages voice such moment-to-moment pique in what seems to outsiders high relish for hyperbole.)

≠Toma //gwe, a man of fewer words than his wife, sits on his side of the fire and smokes, when he has a supply of tobacco. Sometimes he will peg out and scrape the skin of an antelope one of the younger men has killed. A young boy may be alternately watching and helping him, or perhaps only eating the scrapings. At other times the old man will disappear from the family circle abruptly, to reappear a few hours later with a guinea fowl or korhaan he has snared. When he snares a bird his eyes sparkle. In his youth he so loved sour plums that he was named for them, ≠Toma //gwe, "≠Toma Sour Plum." Now people often call him "//gwe n!a," "The Old Sour Plum." He says to his sons often that he is old and cannot help himself, and that he should therefore be given things.

* The ages of this couple are somewhat unusual, since as we noted earlier !Kung custom is for the husband to be five to fifteen years older than the wife.

He and his wife are well provided for. Children are sent from their parents' fires with dishes of nuts, a double handful of small fruits, several big tubers, or a joint of fresh or strips of dried meat for the old couple. Once or twice a day a child will be asked by its parents, or by the grandparents themselves, to bring the old people a bucket of water from the water hole. Though some children refuse, and are not pressed, most of the time the water arrives with fairly little fuss, with leafy branches stuck in it to keep it from splashing out of the bucket and being lost.

Even if their parents are in the camp, children often sit and share what their grandparents are cooking. Older children, approaching puberty, spend more and more time at their grandparents' fires and less at their parents'. It is clear that the role of the older generation in bringing boys and girls through the transition into adulthood has everyday as well as specifically ritual implications.

During the morning and afternoon, //Koka n!a and ≠Toma //gwe nap intermittently, in the shade of their small grass hut or of a nearby tree if it is hot, or in the sun next to the fire if it is cold. //Koka n!a often gets out her little skin bag containing the beads she is working on and strings glass trade beads she has received as *hxaro* presents from her trading partners on twisted threads made from the long back muscles of a kudu or gemsbok. If she runs out of sinew, she will send a child to its mother for some more. She sits and sews, and fusses that no one ever gives her any beads. People fuss back conversationally, barely needing to raise their voices to be heard from where they sit at their own fires.

//Koka n!a reaches into her bag for one of a few copper ornaments her husband has given her, takes it out, and ties it into her hair. Copper hair rings are worn only by women beyond "a certain age" and are signs of that age and of status. //Koka n!a enjoys the rings and feels she ought to have more, to tie all over her head.

As the sun begins to tilt toward the horizon, the sons of the old couple visit with their father at his fire, discussing plans and gossiping about local events. //Koka n!a gets up and goes into the bush. She is gone for perhaps half an hour. When the sun has just slipped down she appears, walking slowly, a tiny, bent figure under an enor-

mous load of firewood. Arrived at the fire, she dumps the wood un-
ceremoniously. She complains "/eh, /eh, /eh, my back!" as she low-
ers herself to the ground and begins to build up the fire for the
night.

If people are lively, there will be an evening's visiting by the fire,
perhaps with other people coming to talk from the nearby Dobe
camps. A welcome gift of fresh meat may unexpectedly arrive in the
dark. //Koka n!a or her husband will take it from the giver word-
lessly and cook and consume it, sharing it with anyone sitting at
their fire. There may be stories told, or news of a hunt, or a marriage to discuss. In the middle of the talk, //Koka n!a may decide
she is ready to bed down for the night. She curls up under blankets
next to the fire, her head covered too, and is soon asleep, though
//gwe goes on talking right next to her. The conversation may be
uproarious or very low and quiet, depending on who is there.
Gradually, the old man's sons and the other visitors go back to
their own fires. ≠Toma //gwe sits smoking and watches the moon
rise from behind an enormous white termite mound. Some nights
he may play his musical hunting bow for hours; he is a *n/um k"xau*
and can talk in this way to those who are gone. Some nights he will
feel old and weary, and will just go to sleep like the others.

Conclusion: The Roles and Status of the Old

To conclude, let us review the basic facts about the social position of the aged in !Kung society. Older people act as (1) stewards
of rights to water and resources of an area, (2) repositories of
knowledge, skills, and lore, (3) teachers and minders of children,
(4) spiritual specialists and healers, and (5) ritually privileged figures. None of these roles is based on the hoarding or accumulation
of power or goods, except in terms of the building up of reciprocal
obligations over a lifetime.

Young people learn these roles through direct imitation of old
people, as they spend time with them in a variety of contexts. Since
the aged are valued for their contributions, they serve as models for
the younger generation, supplementing the models that their parents provide. The young see that the elderly move into a satisfying

old age, and, in the traditional context, they see no reason not to copy them. Young people are not insulated from the enjoyable social pursuits of the old, whether these be dancing, ribald joking, or reminiscing. (This is one of the continuities of !Kung life that is quickly being disrupted, however, with changing times. Now the generations are beginning to see their destinies—and take their pleasures—in separation from each other.)

Roles of old men and women differ in !Kung society along the same lines that differentiate men and women in the society in general. Adult men are hunters and many of them are *n/um k"xausi*, or healers: aging men perpetuate these roles as long as they can and then replace them with less strenuous pursuits such as trapping, gathering, making artifacts, telling stories, and visiting. Women are gatherers, and some of them are healers; old women continue these roles and gradually vary them with more and more child care, handicrafts work, and other less physically demanding pursuits as they age. Both sexes continue to participate in the repeated, unifying trance dances, as singers, dancers, or involved spectators.

The status of the old is related to their social contribution in that the core system, acknowledging the aged and their tenure in an area, militates against conflict over resources. Moreover, the transmission of skills and lore to younger people is recognized and honored by the !Kung as an important part of the socialization of competent group members. Child care by the old frees the vigorous women and men for unhindered gathering and hunting, which have direct economic results. Spiritual discipline and healing powers, which often become highly developed in aging people, are universally respected among the !Kung, who practice very little other medicine. A class of ritually immune individuals is needed by the society to assist in transitional rites involving the young: considered as such, the old are valued for the role they play in "creating" mature men and women to carry on the work of the society.

Old Age Among the Chipewyan

HENRY S. SHARP

Before contact with Western civilization the Chipewyan were a hunting and gathering society specialized in the pursuit of the barren-ground caribou (*Rangifer tandarus*). Their numbers were small, probably less than 3,500, and they occupied an immense stretch of northern Canada in what is today the Northwest Territories. They ranged along the edge of the boreal forest from north of Great Slave Lake to points not too distant from Hudson's Bay. Their yearly cycle took many of them far onto the tundra in summer and deep into the boreal forest in winter. Wherever the barren-ground caribou went, the Chipewyan also went.

The Chipewyan were remarkable in a number of ways. Their specialization upon barren-ground caribou led them to ignore or use only secondarily such other food resources as fish, moose, and musk-ox. Their population density was roughly one per 60–100 square miles and their diet was 90 percent or more animal products. Unlike most Canadian Athapaskans, they were an aggressive people who terrorized the Inuit and constantly fought the Cree and other neighbors.

At the time of the population displacements created by the fur trade, the Chipewyan expanded their range to include the north side of the Churchill River drainage in Manitoba, Saskatchewan, and Alberta, as well as the region between Lake Athabasca and Great Slave Lake. They entered the fur trade as traders and middlemen rather than as trappers. In the new areas they became serious trappers, but in their homeland, along the treeline, trapping never replaced hunting as the primary economic activity.

The homeland of the Chipewyan is four hundred miles beyond the northern limit of agriculture and far from the major trade routes of the Northwest Territories. As a result of their isolation, the Chipewyan did not come into extensive contact with Canadian society until after the First World War, when many Euro-Canadians came north to trap. The additional predation pressure of these white trappers, coupled with the culmination of long-term changes in climate, precipitated a dramatic crash of the caribou herds in the 1940's.

The crash of the caribou herds coincided with a dramatic drop in the fur market. Within a few years the Chipewyan were unable to continue a subsistence life-style in the bush. The Chipewyan in the area where I did fieldwork settled into two villages, Stony Rapids and Black Lake, in Saskatchewan. The population increased rapidly after the measles epidemic of 1948, largely owing to improved health care, and continued to climb until birth control pills became widely used in the mid-1970's.

Population figures for Black Lake and Stony Rapids are presented in Table 1. These figures include only Treaty Indians as of December 31, 1968, updated by my field notes to March 1970. Treaty Indians constitute more than three-quarters of the population and I have no reason to expect any demographic variation between the two groups.

Chipewyan perception of a person's place in the human life cycle is based upon competence in adult economic and social activities rather than age. Competence derives from individual personality factors in women and from *inkonze* (dream power) in men. Social status is separable from chronological age. The relevant factor in determining social status is the ability to perform the tasks associated with that status; if an individual can perform the required tasks he occupies the status. The Chipewyan distinguish between seniority and old age. A person obtains seniority by virtue of genealogical position in a kinship network, which is related to the passage of time (and other factors) but only tenuously to chronological age. A person is considered elderly (hereafter I shall use "elderly" when I mean old as a negative Chipewyan value judgment) when he

TABLE I. Population of the Stony Rapids Band of
Chipewyan in 1970, by Age

Age	Number	Percent
9 and under	159	34.0%
10–19	108	23.1
20–29	61	13.0
30–39	45	9.6
40–49	35	7.5
50–59	26	5.6
60–69	25	5.4
70–79	5	1.1
80–89	2	0.4
90 and over	1	0.2
TOTAL	467	99.9%

SOURCE: Treaty List, Band 07 (Stony Rapids), Agency 672 (Carlton), Department of Indian Affairs and Northern Development, Ottawa, Ontario, pp. 3308 18.

NOTE: The Stony Rapids Band of Chipewyan includes the residents of both Black Lake and Stony Rapids.

or she can no longer function as a competent adult member of society. This dual sense of the concept of age is a behavioral rather than a linguistic distinction.

In many respects, since Chipewyan culture is so heavily based upon performance and physical capacity, the life cycles of male and female are opposite but symmetrical. Men begin their adult life with a physical strength that allows them to dominate (but not control) their spouses and a structural potential that keeps their wives subordinate. With the passage of time the man's position increases in strength. A woman remains decidedly subordinate to her husband until her children are grown. When the children of a marriage begin to function as adults, the relative positions of the husband and wife begin to reverse within the marriage (Sharp 1977). Children are bound to their parents in this system by sentiment; structural relationships with the father are of significance primarily in sorting out relationships between adult sons after they are married. The ability of the father to exercise the influence inherent in his structural position depends upon his remaining active and competent.

As a man's strength begins to fail he loses the ability to exercise this influence, leaving his position with respect to his children weaker than his wife's. At the same time, his loss of strength allows his wife to escape the physical domination he has exercised over her and indeed often allows the wife to become physically dominant over her husband. In a real sense, the position of a man within his domestic unit is one of progressive diminution of influence throughout his life while a woman's position in her domestic unit is one of increasing influence until their respective statuses are virtually reversed.

What is true within the domestic unit is generally true of the social world at large, although the variations by sex and age are not as marked within the social world. An old man is morally more valuable in the social world than is an old woman, but the old woman may have a much greater influence than an old man.

The Chipewyan are egalitarian and place a strong emphasis upon competence. Where competence is present, they are remarkably tolerant of other types of failure or deviancy. In the face of incompetence, regardless of cause, they are intolerant. Chipewyan mythology and folk literature—as well as the accounts of explorers, traders, and missionaries—are full of references to the grim treatment of the incompetent, including the abandonment of "elderly" persons during times of stress. Although such treatment has been modified in the last 20 years, largely because government agencies now care for the "elderly," incompetence is still a condition people abhor and try to avoid. In order to understand the status of "elderly" persons, then, we must first consider the status to which this is contrasted, that of competent adults.

The Life Cycle

The contemporary Chipewyan no longer have rites of passage to mark the transition of individuals or categories of persons from one status to the next beyond the three rites based upon the teachings of the Roman Catholic church—birth (christening), marriage, and funerals. All three have come to have a uniquely Chipewyan character.

The rites surrounding birth and death are of a different order than those surrounding a wedding. Birth and death are obvious and inescapable transition points between the world of the living and the world of the dead. A wedding, however, announces neither the arrival of a new person nor the departure of an old one; as the transformation of an immature person into an adult Chipewyan, it is uniquely a concern of the living. As a transition of two persons into full adulthood, a wedding is a close approximation of a rite of initiation. All unmarried Chipewyan are regarded in some sense as children, even those who postpone marriage into their forties or who never marry.

Women are considered nubile without regard to their capacity for reproduction, so that women are often nubile before they are fertile. On the other hand, the mere ability to reproduce does not make a woman ready for marriage. To be considered marriageable a woman must appear capable of functioning as an adult in economic activities, particularly traditional activities such as sewing garments, beadwork, and cooking. (The ability to care for children is assumed for all females over ten—a function of their long apprenticeship as baby-sitters.) Marriage has traditionally called for a sound assessment of the economic potential and disposition of possible spouses—an assessment chiefly made by the parents of unmarried Chipewyan rather than by the young people themselves. Though in recent years most marriages have come to be based on love, love is really the stuff of affairs (which need not terminate because of marriage). Extramarital and premarital sexual activity continue, and illegitimate births are not uncommon.

For a male Chipewyan the maturation process is not marked by any dramatic change but instead involves the mastery of the skills needed to wrest a living from the harsh Canadian subarctic. Success in economic activities, especially hunting and trapping, and the display of the implements of his livelihood (dogs, more recently a snowmobile) give evidence of the underlying magical power that, as we will see, is central to the notion of male adulthood. Once a man does marry, he becomes an adult member of the community and will remain such as long as he retains and can use his skills. When he no longer has them, or is not physically able to use them, he will be considered "elderly."

Magic

The Chipewyan believe that competence as a man is conferred by magic. This magic derives from unsought visions in which power is given by a supernatural being. The power from these dreams cannot itself be inherited or sold, but with the approval of the supernatural source, specific knowledge gained from dreams may be taught and charms invested with magic properties may be prepared and sold to men who do not have their own magic or who want to augment the power vouchsafed them.

Magical power, with one possible exception I will mention later, is the exclusive property of men. Women with supernatural power appear in myth but never in stories about real women, whether living or dead. This gives quite a different aspect to the aging process of men and women. The Chipewyan concept of magic embraces both knowledge and power. To have magical power is to have knowledge of how to do things. Magic is also secret. One may not talk about it, reveal directly that one has it, display it openly, perform it in public (magical songs may not be sung where they can be overheard), or reveal the source or dream that gives power. To do so will cause the power to vanish.

This threat of loss of power creates a problem for the individual Chipewyan male. Having magical power is useless unless the community knows a man has it, but how does he reveal the presence of something that revelation destroys? The Chipewyan answer is to judge magical power on the basis of performance: because magic brings success, success is the result of having magical power. Hence a determination of whether or not a man possesses magic, and of how much he has if he does have it, is made on the basis of his performance as a hunter, trapper, gambler, etc.

Chipewyan magic extends into areas other than the ones mentioned above, such as healing and sorcery, but ability in these areas is of a slightly different character than ability in more normal activities. Success in healing and sorcery tends to lead to political influence, whereas other forms of success assure a man the status of a competent adult. Magic for the Chipewyan is akin to our notion of "luck" in that it is a causal mechanism producing differences in performance.

The world in which the Chipewyan live is one in which they are singularly passive creatures. They live without fault for their failures or responsibility for their actions. For example, in the native view a Chipewyan hunter never misses a shot at a game animal; failure to hit the target is the result of the animal's refusing to allow the Chipewyan to kill it. The willingness of the target to be killed is a function of the magical power of the hunter, so that what for a Western hunter would be his own failure (missing a target) is for the Chipewyan a failure of his magic rather than of his person. A Chipewyan may be blamed for an error deriving from physical failure; but for a failure of magic he would not bear blame. He might be shamed or humiliated by the refusal of a creature to allow itself to be killed—unless the circumstances were so unusual that they indicated the target itself was a creature of extraordinary magical ability—but he would not be considered to be at fault for his failure.

Magical power has never been felt to prevent a man from death, at least in the Christian period, but it is felt to provide protection from the infirmities of aging. Merely to live to be old in this rugged environment is to demonstrate the possession of some magical ability, but to live a long time without losing competence is a clear indication of superior supernatural power. The older a man becomes without becoming "elderly," the stronger his magical power is believed to be, since the entire community observes his successful resistance to the aging process.

An example of the respect for a man's magical power that develops as he remains active despite growing old can be shown by something my principal woman informant, Beth, said to me in the course of a conversation about a 71-year-old neighbor in the village, George. Beth had always been fond of George's wife, but she disliked George and criticized him at every opportunity. She and I were discussing the relative magic powers of several men and she remarked of George, "Look at that old man, still walking about. He must 'know something.'" This grudging respect apparently stemmed from the fact that George had recently recovered, without hospitalization, from a case of tuberculosis.

The Difference in Aging for Men and Women

Magical power does eventually fail, however, and the Chipewyan man either dies or deteriorates physically and becomes incompetent. Unable to hunt or trap, he is forced to rely upon his relatives for subsistence. His decline can be delayed for a time by the efforts of a healthy wife and the use of young Chipewyan obtained by temporary adoption. But when a man can no longer drive his dogs and venture into the bush alone to hunt, his days as a complete adult male are ended, and he must subsist, like a woman or a dog, on meat and fish obtained by others (Sharp 1976). The Chipewyan do not value the telling of myths and tales greatly, and there are no handicrafts or other activities to which a man can turn in compensation. In the traditional bush life an elderly man, like a woman, is restricted to the few dwellings of the camp; in the village there is more room to wander at will, but the only activity with which to replace hunting is gambling, and competence at cards is a poor substitute.

The situation of an old woman in Chipewyan society is quite different. Where a man has a single paramount activity—obtaining food from the bush—a woman has three: reproduction, handicrafts, and processing food. As I mentioned earlier, women do not have magic (though female midwives may use a kind of magic in performing their specialty). Unlike hunting, women's work does not involve continuous walking, violent bursts of energy, or running, so it can still be performed by women in declining physical condition.

Women's role in reproduction is extended after menopause by the common Chipewyan practice of adopting children. Adoption among the Chipewyan does not imply the complete transfer of legal rights over a child as it does in Western society. Instead, the Chipewyan "loan" children for varying periods of time and for various purposes. Grandparents have the right to adopt a child from each of their children's marriages, and almost any woman can obtain a small child to care for without any trouble. This allows a woman to fulfill most of the duties of motherhood and be called mother, "enna," by a child independently of her actual ability to reproduce. Moreover, small children are of great service in the minor tasks of running a household (hauling water, wood, etc.) and are eagerly sought. Since many of the duties of child rearing are assumed by older children, the mother or grandmother who has or adopts several children may find her work load lessened.

The second major aspect of women's work is handicrafts, primarily sewing and beadwork, but also such other tasks as the preparation of hides for leather. This work is demanding and requires both strength and good hand-eye coordination. Even though talent varies greatly among women, a lifetime of experience gives a competent older woman a real advantage over women many years her junior. And if a woman's strength and eyesight fail with age, she can still teach her skills to younger women and supervise their work—an option that men do not have when their strength fails them.

The third aspect of women's work is processing food. Cooking is only a minor part of food processing, a task that can be entrusted to young girls under minimal supervision. Processing food means primarily cutting dry meat and splitting and deboning fish for drying. These tasks are hard, requiring considerable skill and expertise. They must generally be done outside the dwelling under uncomfortable conditions. Fortunately, the demand for food is proportional to the size of the household, and as demand increases, so does the female labor pool available to supply it. Like sewing, food preparation can be done by several women working together, and old women can supervise when they cannot perform much of the actual work themselves.

Because women's work is considered to involve the use of skills acquired through instruction and practice rather than the use of magic, women are able to remain competent adults much longer than men. Since no special powers are involved, women can cooperate in their work without any loss of face. And old women whose physical strength is waning are valued for the advice and expertise they can contribute. If being able to do it all by herself does not confer the same prestige on a young woman as hunting confers on a man, neither does needing some help destroy an old woman's self-respect and reputation as it does an old man's.

As might be predicted from the differences in the tasks of men and women, the character of old age is different for the two sexes. Many more women than men beyond a marker point of, say, 60 are "old" rather than "elderly." The "old" women are able to remain involved in the affairs of the community, and many are influential bcause of their seniority in various kin groups. Their positions individually are augmented not only by their seniority, but also by the tendency in the Chipewyan family for ties of sentiment to be stronger with females than with the more structurally significant males (Sharp, 1979).

Elderly men are not in a position to command much influence or respect. Men's affairs are centered upon the bush rather than the village or camp. For them, the increasing confinement to the village imposed by the loss of strength with advancing age is a punishment mitigated by few compensating rewards. They are ill-inclined to become involved in the issues of moral conduct or the proposed marriages that are a mainstay of village gossip. For many men the onset of old age begins in their late forties or early fifties with lung or heart disease, and they must wage a more desperate (and dangerous) struggle to be merely "old" instead of "elderly."

A good illustration of the desperation a Chipewyan man feels when his body begins to fail with advancing age is the case of my informant Beth's husband, John. Through 1971 John was able to keep most of his sons together in a hunting unit by suppressing conflict among them and by exploiting his extensive knowledge of the bush, which made them all economically successful. His magical power was well regarded, though he had given up an active curing practice some years before. In late 1971 John had a heart attack in the bush and had to be hospitalized. He recovered from the attack, but it was discovered that he had emphysema. He refused treatment for the disease and refused to stop his heavy use of tobacco. By 1975 he was so weak that he was unable to perform any work requiring heavy exertion or endurance. As his condition worsened a split developed in his hunting unit as the eldest son attempted to take control. John moved to a different hunting area in the fall of 1975 with one son, but even he was becoming increasingly autonomous.

To compensate for his growing weakness John began to spend more time alone in the bush, avoiding the village where Beth wished to remain because of his ill health. Beth considers John's attempts to continue his activities in the bush dangerous, and feels he must be watched and protected from himself as the attempted exertion will kill him. John is aware of this watching over him, but refuses to accept the need for it. To maintain his status, he must constantly risk his life—a risk he is more than willing to take to avoid being categorized as "elderly."

The Elderly Asmat of New Guinea

PETER W. VAN ARSDALE

Among the Asmat people of southwestern Irian Jaya (Indonesian
New Guinea), a mythological figure known as "the oldest man"
was said to have been responsible for establishing the traditional
ritual system by which universal balance is preserved in the Asmat
world. To some he was also known as Ndendew, the "father of the
people," because he determined where people should live, and what
cultural elements they should possess. An Asmat creation myth involves an old man known as Famiripits who carved human figu-
rines from pieces of wood, placed them in a men's longhouse, and
drummed life into them. Thus it was that among this Papuan people age was equated with knowledge, influence, and the ability to
direct the course of human development. And thus it was that in
traditional, precontact Asmat society elderly people (especially
men) whose productivity was diminishing could nonetheless enhance their prestige by increasing their ritual participation.

The Asmat, once independent and warlike, have recently become
but one pacified subgroup of Indonesian New Guinea. The rituals
dominated by old men had meaning when raiding and headhunting
determined certain of the interactions of local groups; with the imposition of Indonesian peace, however, the rituals that legitimated
the fighting lost their meaning. Deprived of their leadership in communal religion, old men have become less meaningful to society
and, perhaps, even to themselves. Although new rituals have been
introduced by missionaries and created by the burgeoning cargo
cults, former "big men" (*tesmaypits*) take no part in them, and the

prospect of reestablishing their preeminence in new roles, secular or religious, is dim.

Under the new order the Asmat have seen their complex ritual system, the product of long evolution, disintegrate within two decades. A majority of old men are now living in a "ritual void." Men who were important "big men" in 1950, deliberating for hours about which war ornaments to wear and what time to strike, are now described as "idle" by curious Western visitors. Headhunters who once gloried in recounting their battle feats and repeating the names of slain enemies to a rapt audience are now old men to whom the younger generation rarely listens.

The Role of the Tesmaypits *in Traditional Asmat Society*

Traditionally, the Asmat were a group of scattered hunting, fishing, and sago-gathering Papuan tribesmen inhabiting the coastal New Guinea region of lowland swamp and rain forest. In the early twentieth century, their bands ranged in size from perhaps 25 to 100 or more individuals each, and their total population was probably less than half the present number. Local oral history indicates that there were at least eight major Asmat subdivisions, loosely grouped by common ancestry, dialect, and geographic proximity. Asmat bands ranged over relatively well-defined areas in which their primary food, sago, grew abundantly. Women and children have always provided most of the food, but this is not the onerous task it is in many societies: during my fieldwork I calculated that the time required to obtain food was a remarkably low two days per week per person aged four and over (Van Arsdale 1978a). Indeed, work of all kinds occupies only slightly less than half of a man's waking time and slightly more than half of a woman's.

Before contact with outsiders, which occurred only to any substantial degree in the early 1950's, Asmat men not at work were busy with a complex and time-consuming pattern of ritualistic revenge warfare that involved head-hunting and cannibalism and that was intended to correct perceived spiritual imbalances and to propitiate the ancestors. Perceiving these imbalances and guiding the necessary warfare were the province of certain of the "big men" of the community, the *tesmaypits*. Hence traditional Asmat society might be described as a "selective gerontocracy"—selective in the sense that though old men organized things, not all old men were involved. For not all aged Asmat were revered; most aged males were not *tesmaypits* but simply "old men." Old men were judged "big" if they excelled in ritual, woodcarving, or "arranging things," that is if they displayed a "wealth" (*tes*) of personality attributes— a form of complex charisma—including bravery, manual dexterity, organizational ability, and/or concern for others' welfare (see Sahlins 1968).

The *tesmaypits*, particularly those who were older, controlled rights to river and land resources (especially sago groves). Because people inherited rights to resources through both parents or acquired them through marriage, the allocation of sago and river rights changed from generation to generation and required the ratification of the *tesmaypits*.

The social, spiritual, and ritual centers of Asmat society were the men's longhouses, or *yew*. Each settlement had one or more *yew* surrounded by the huts of its family members. Just as the *yew* was the principal unit of social and ritual organization in this world, so the Asmat believed that "every longhouse on earth had an associated longhouse on the 'other side,' the spirit world where the ancestors live" (Sowada 1968: 192). Births and deaths were seen as mechanisms for keeping membership relatively equal in the respective longhouses. "If a longhouse on earth became overpopulated, some members would die. If [that] on the other side became too large, some would seek out women on earth to be reborn" (Sowada 1968: *ibid.*). In most cases, it was the elder men of the *yew* who, through visions, dreams, or consultations, became aware of the imbalance between the spirit and human populations and informed all the other Asmat. They would then plan and lead rituals to propitiate the ancestors; arrange initiations, sago palm festivals, and grub festivals; and organize head-hunting raids.

Ritual recognition of the *tesmaypits* took several forms, of which the most interesting involved cannibalism. As the victorious warriors paddled back from a raid, they would sever the heads of captives as they passed junctions of important rivers. Arriving at the home village, they would then divide the flesh of the corpses according to ritual prescriptions. The brains of the dead enemy, extracted through a trephination in the right temporal bone and mixed with sago starch, were consumed by elder *tesmaypits* related to the warrior responsible for the killing (Zegwaard 1971). Less spectacular, but equally important in terms of recognizing the respect afforded the enemy, was the practice of adopting the names of enemy slain in battle. By contrast, the name of a "big man" who died peacefully was often adopted by an ambitious young man from his *yew* who hoped thus to enhance his prestige.

The ability of certain aged men "to arrange things" was not limited to the ritual context, but extended to economic and political issues such as the question of settlement relocation. Before the establishment of relatively permanent coastal villages in the mid-1950's, the Asmat changed the locations of their settlements every two to five years. In consultation with other *yew* elders, the most prestigious *tesmaypits* of a settlement pondered the possibilities before deciding where to move. The move sometimes covered no more than a few hundred meters downstream or upstream, but the ability to "arrange" it was crucial.

The Social Context of Daily Life

Through oral accounts of Asmat who were young adults during the 1930's and 1940's, as well as through a few more recent reference sources, I have reconstructed a general picture of traditional everyday life for "average" elderly men and women, not only those relatively few who were thought to be especially prestigious. What emerges is that elder *tesmaypits* were prominent, but not to the complete exclusion of other old men; that male elders dominated the public arenas but deferred to old women in their own households; and that respect for the aged was important but not all-pervasive.

Although polygyny was the ideal, traditionally only a few men were able to acquire more than one wife. Most married before the age of twenty, to women some three to five years younger. As these couples neared "old age," i.e., as their children began having children, the wives came to spend a larger proportion of their time inside the thatched family hut directing the labor of younger women, either daughters or junior wives (if the marriage was polygynous), giving them curt orders about cooking, child care, fishing, and gathering. Sexual activity probably diminished as women neared "old age," but in polygynous marriages the senior wife compensated for her husband's neglect by reprimanding the junior wives for even the smallest inadequacies in the performance of household tasks.

In the precontact era, as well as today, a woman was expected to be a subservient, efficient, docile mate. Younger women who did not measure up might be beaten—sometimes so severely that they died of their injuries. However, elderly women were much less likely to receive this kind of treatment, not so much out of deference to their age or infirmity as out of fear of the public uproar they could create. Some were so vociferous and eloquent that their husbands would not even argue with them, let alone beat them. These women reprimanded their spouses at the top of their lungs before a rapt audience of fellow villagers, young and old, who took delight in hearing an imaginative catalogue of the unfortunate husband's sexual inadequacies.

Even the most important elderly women never attained the prestige of the *tesmaypits*. But those who had established themselves as curer-sorcerers were both respected and feared. They were called *namer-o* because they derived their powers from a nonancestral spirit known by that term. Men could become *namer-o* as well, but apparently elderly women *namer-o* were considered to be both more powerful and more dangerous. In assembling firsthand oral accounts of these women, Van Amelsvoort (1964: 53–56) found that their activities centered upon disease affecting a sort of "multiple soul." The "primary" human soul is located in the abdomen, with "peripheral" souls in the head, arms, and feet. Curing and sorcery frequently focused on the stomach, and on the spirits thought to influence the soul residing there. When a sorcerer was asked to cast a spell on someone, he or she would collect leavings of the intended victim (e.g., hair, nail clippings), when possible, and certain kinds of animal feces and intestines. All such magical materials were stored in a small basket before being "shot" at the victim by an invisible bow and arrow. If victims were told what the sorcerer had done, some died within a few days (see Lex 1977 for a psycho-physiological explanation for deaths of this kind).

It should be noted that the Asmat—healer and nonhealer alike—apparently believed that whereas virtually all diseases of young and middle-aged people were caused by soul loss, object intrusion, or spirit intervention, certain ailments of the elderly were inexorable concomitants of old age. When one of these struck, people assumed that death was inevitable and imminent. (The Asmat have been known to begin the mourning ritual before breathing and heartbeat have ceased.) Old, infirm people usually were fed and minimally cared for, but occasionally those thought to be near death were left alone and untended in the corner of the family's hut.

Prolonged widowhood was a rare phenomenon because levirate marriage was common. If trends apparent in recent Asmat demographic data held in the precontact era—and there is every reason to think they did, at least with regard to widowhood and longevity (see Nag 1962: 145; Weiss 1973)—relatively few men outlived their wives. Those that did occasionally married a sister or cousin of the dead wife or were otherwise provided an opportunity to remarry within the *yew*. The only people unlikely to remarry were those debilitated by old age or injury, and they were relegated to secondary roles in household affairs. Former *tesmaypits* who became infirm were still shown deference, but they played less important parts in the decision-making process.

Old men were great storytellers. Virtually all told stories, and some who were not *tesmaypits* nonetheless were widely recognized for their ability to educate and entertain simultaneously. Each core male group (brothers and certain male first cousins) occupied a fireplace position in the longhouse. Beginning at the age of about eight, boys came to the *yew* fireplace of their father or grandfather to learn the intricacies of Asmat lore and ritual life and to hear stories about the exploits of Tewerawuts and Beworpits, the mythical and somewhat nondescript equivalents of "Jane and John Doe" in

U.S. society. Other favorite stories told of animals like Dog and birds like Cockatoo who helped the ancestors master the jungle environment and instructed humans about natural resources, especially sago.

Although elderly women did not tell stories, they played important roles in educating grandchildren. Grandmothers, whose work kept them near the huts, cared for young grandchildren while the parents were away (especially during the morning). They exercised some authority over their grandchildren, but tended to be indulgent. In turn, children treated them with warmth and confidence (Eyde 1967: 187–89). Grandparents and grandchildren were seen to stand in reciprocal relationships to one another. Hence it was not uncommon for a child to be named after a grandparent, living or dead, although the name might later be changed.

An additional hazard confronted aged Asmat before pacification: because of their physical vulnerability (real or imagined), elderly people were frequent "secondary targets" during intervillage raids. Unlike major battles, where warriors confronted each other boldly in full ornamental regalia, raids in retaliation for territorial infringements or petty injuries were conducted in secrecy. "Primary targets," such as young men or *tesmaypits*, were prestigious but risky prospects. The elderly, especially those unfortunate enough to be found working or resting alone in a sago grove, were less desirable but relatively sure targets for ambush. Even today, after pacification in the coastal Asmat region, reports still come in of aged people being killed in this fashion.

The Demographic Context

Permanent relations between the Asmat and outsiders were only established in the early 1950's, and no reliable data exist for the population in the first postcontact years. Scattered population totals for some villages have been compiled from early Dutch medical survey reports by Van Amelsvoort (1964), and they suggest that the Asmat population experienced an increase in growth rate after contact. On the basis of my own research in 1974, I concluded that the average annual growth rate of the population between 1956 and

1974 was about 1.5 percent, and that the total population in the latter year was about 42,000. Of this number, 3,167 lived in the five villages I studied near the coast. Retrospective inferences suggest that the precontact growth rate was also substantial, perhaps 1.0 percent from 1850 to 1950 (Van Arsdale 1978b).

In these settlements, where change has been more dramatic than elsewhere in Asmat, head-hunting and cannibalism have been suppressed. Individual longhouses have been abolished in favor of a single community house for the entire village, and the huts formerly scattered around each longhouse have been supplanted by straight rows of houses. Indonesian health-care programs followed those of the Dutch, and despite the introduction of new diseases from outside, my data suggest that population growth since the early 1950's has been prominently influenced by increased survival rates in cohorts spanning the ages of 5 through 29 (Van Arsdale 1978b).

Table 1 presents the age-sex structure in 1974 of the five villages I studied, based upon all individuals resident in a random sample of 72 households. Fully 41 percent of the sample is under the age of 15, and another 31 percent is under 30. Only 12.3 percent is over 45, or clearly "old." (Although age was not reckoned in years in traditional Asmat society, informants indicated that people over the age of about 45 are considered "old." Menopause signals the onset of "old age" in women.) Less than 1 percent of the sample was over 65.

More women reach "old age" than men. It is unusual for a man to live as long as 60 years, although a report substantiated by cross-checking with missionaries indicated that an old warrior by the name of Saati was approximately 90 when he died in 1970.

The Asmat population profile I describe corresponds closely to those from two other New Guinea societies first contacted in the early 1950's, the Tsembaga Maring (Rappaport 1968) and the Kepaka (Bowers 1971). Both show similarly "young" populations with only a small percentage of old people. The Tsembaga show the highest percentage (13.2) in the 45 + range, with the Asmat at 12.3 and the Kepaka at 12.0. It is interesting to note that the average

TABLE 1. Age-Sex Structure of 72 Households in
Five Asmat Villages, 1974
(N = 658)

Age cohort	Men	Women
Under 5	54	42
5–9	53	47
10–14	37	37
15–19	33	35
20–24	24	36
25–29	39	34
30–34	20	17
35–39	14	14
40–44	19	22
45–49	19	23
50–54	8	17
55 and over	5	9
TOTAL	325	333

age for the Asmat by my calculations is about 22.1 years (male, 20.9; female, 23.4). The overall male-to-female ratio is 92 : 100 in favor of females. Using methods of calculation described by Weiss (1973), I calculated Asmat life expectancy at birth as approximately 24.8 years. Those who survive to age 15 can, on the average, look forward to an additional 27 years of life, i.e., can expect just about to reach "old age." An extremely high infant mortality rate of nearly 30 percent even today prevents life expectancy from being higher. The steady population growth described earlier is partially attributable to a very high birth rate (56 per 1,000) and a crude death rate of 37 per 1,000, as calculated for 1973.

New Opportunities: A Changing Context

What, then, is happening to that 12.3 percent of the Asmat who are in the "old age" bracket? The imposition of stringent Indonesian rule has brought about fundamental changes in the traditional Asmat way of life: increased restrictions on moving settlements, the abolition of longhouses in the coastal region, the suppression of head-hunting and its ritual complex, the spread of missions, the introduction of Western medicine, the growth of population, and the advent of local development programs to exploit such resources as lumber, crocodiles, and coconut oil. With all this there has been a general disintegration of the traditional religious/magical system on which aging men used to focus more of their attention as they became less able to participate in other facets of life. In short, a "ritual void" has developed.

Since Asmat women in general had little place in ritual, the disintegration of traditional religion has had only an indirect impact upon elderly women, except in those cases where they have chosen to become involved in the new syncretic rituals, such as those pertaining to Christmas. On Christmas Day 1973, in the village of Amandesep, I observed an old woman lead small circles of women who were chanting and drumming traditional lines under the watchful eye of a catechist. This activity grew out of the notions of several Catholic missionaries, who wanted to involve women in the religious structure they hoped would replace the traditional Asmat one. It would appear that this gambit is succeeding, since a number of older women have eagerly accepted the new ritual possibilities open to them (see Clark 1973: 85). No such ritual alternatives have appealed to elderly Asmat men, however, whether *tesmaypits* or not: in several instances missionaries have urged old men to participate as leaders in church services, but none has accepted. Significantly, though, some young men have accepted such offers.

Although some traditional rituals survive (for example, elderly men in the five villages I studied still participated in *ji pok mbu*, "the bringing of the sago logs to the village for ritual storage"), the sociocultural context of ritual has disintegrated. A "ritual void" exists for aged men not merely because some rituals are no longer performed, but because the performance no longer takes place within the traditional social framework.

By contrast, women and younger men have moved to fill the "ritual void" left by the collapse of traditional Asmat lifeways. In one of the villages I studied, a cargo cult known in Indonesian as "Kepercayaan Tuhan Tanah" (Belief in the Lord of the Earth) arose in October 1966 during a period of stress brought on by the increasingly stringent demands of the Indonesian political economy. The Asmat were simultaneously faced with a diminishing supply of material goods because the Catholic mission had terminated its policy of supplying converts with tobacco, food, fishline, hooks, and clothing (Van Arsdale 1975: 157–60). As conceived by a 27-year-old man with the baptismal name of Marsellus, the cult relied upon Tuhan Tanah (described as a combination of the traditional spirit *namer-o* and God) to provide believers with a vast array of "white man's goods," which Marsellus claimed would materialize from a locked hole in the ground to which he held the key. In fact, Marsellus stole supplies from the mission warehouse to make good on his promises. Shortly thereafter, he began wearing a star-shaped pin he had stolen and the villagers began calling him "President." Although Marsellus lost his credibility when people learned that the goods had been stolen, another prophet rose to take his place. This man, named Sotor, has cleverly maneuvered longhouse factions and used his own considerable abilities as a curer to perpetuate the cult of Tuhan Tanah and expand its rituals. He has brought other young men into the cult leadership structure; promises of "white man's goods" have been transformed into promises of "unity" and "freedom." Although only 30 years old in 1974, Sotor was recognized as the most influential person in the coastal region (Van Arsdale & Gallus 1974).

Why is it that older men have not taken steps to secure places of importance for themselves in the evolving rituals of transitional Asmat society? Why is it that an elder *tesmaypits* has not used his considerable influence to become involved? Part of the answer is that the ritual context now emerging is intimately related to the rapid economic, educational, and political changes that have disrupted Asmat society. Traditional rituals developed within the framework of a diversified preagricultural economy, informal education, and small-scale political units led by elder *tesmaypits*; new rituals are evolving within the framework of a partial cash economy, formal education by both mission and government teachers, and hierarchical political leadership within the Indonesian system. The Asmat are now but one subgroup of a complex state society.

Younger men are finding opportunities within that society; older men are not. A missionary offering older men the opportunity to participate as leaders in church services does nothing to remedy the "ritual void," because this void is a product of a changed socioeconomic environment in which such men have no place. Ritual leadership among the Asmat has traditionally been the prerogative of men perceived as "big," and such "bigness" (or charismatic prestige, as we might say) is today being generated by economic, educational, and political factors that favor younger men.

Because of the strong influence household members traditionally exerted on one another in Asmat, I tested a number of hypotheses about the influence of the young on the old and vice versa in the area of educational attainments. I found that older men, and presumably older women as well, exerted a "braking influence" on educational change within the household and had more influence on young people than young people had on them. This finding is not limited to "big men," either, but is characteristic of even average old men, and the implications of it extend beyond education to economic and sociopolitical activities as well. To put it another way, those young people who are more successfully adjusting to the new ways are those who do not live in households with older people. In short, though the traditional ritual context is disintegrating, household influences remain strong (see Shanas 1975).

Despite their continuing strong influence in the household, older people have little influence outside the home. Political data indicate that most Asmat men selected for local Indonesian government offices such as *kepala desa* (subdistrict head) are under 40. Men who have demonstrated the abilities of the traditional *tesmaypits* cannot qualify for these offices in competition with those younger men who can read, write, and speak Indonesian. One example of the transformation involves Sotor, whom I have already mentioned, and his fellow villager Sakarpits. Sakarpits, who was nearly 60 in 1974, was still considered by most of the villagers to be the most important head-hunter—*tesmaypits* in the village; yet Sotor, who was only 30, had more influence. Whereas Sakarpits spent much of his time trying rather fruitlessly "to arrange things" in traditional fashion, Sotor, who had made a name for himself as the "second prophet" of the cargo cult founded by Marsellus, was active in the Catholic church and fluent in Indonesian. Similarly, when Indonesian officials had to choose a new subdistrict head in 1974, they settled on a 38-year-old man named Yacobus, despite his lackluster record in village political activities. They pointedly passed over the 60-year-old Yucemin, who was widely recognized as one of the most important *tesmaypits* in his village, and who was still a vital, active man. Yacobus was fluent in Indonesian; Yucemin was not. Moreover, Yucemin continued to speak of traditional restrictions on the cutting of prized ironwood trees, whereas Yacobus showed himself willing to negotiate with government and military officials for the cash value of timber near the village.

Rapid change has caught an entire cohort of old Asmat men and rendered their traditional way of life meaningless. That this was not the intention of those who brought about the change does not make the situation any easier for these old men, and indeed gives their dilemma a heightened poignancy.

Old Age in Gwembe District, Zambia

ELIZABETH COLSON AND THAYER SCUDDER

In Gwembe District, Zambia, becoming an elder, *mupati* ("big person"), is honorable. Growing old is distressing. Gwembe Tonga society does not idealize youth, but neither does it overlook the disadvantages associated with being old. Nobody looks forward to being called *munene* ("old man") or *mucembele* ("old woman")—the latter derived from the verb *kucembaala* ("to become old"), which when used of cattle means no longer able to work and when used of an article means worn out. Some elders have the good fortune to die before they wear out completely and are judged useless.

The impact of being old, however, differs. Relative comfort and influence during the last years of life depend largely on the elders' position in the homesteads where they live, on the resources available to those homesteads, and on the ratio between productive and dependent members of homesteads. The able-bodied assume responsibility for the care of the old more or less graciously, sometimes with loving concern, sometimes with ill-concealed resent-

This article is based on field research in Gwembe District, Zambia, in June 1949, Sept. 1956–Sept. 1957, Jan. 1960, Sept. 1962–Sept. 1963, July–Aug. 1965, Aug.–Nov. 1967, Sept. 1968, May–June 1970, May–Dec. 1972, June–Sept. 1973, and Aug.–Sept. 1976. In some years both of us have been in Gwembe, in others only one. The research has been supported by various agencies: the Rhodes-Livingston Institute (now the Institute for African Studies in the University of Zambia); the Joint Committee on Africa of the Social Science Research Council and the American Council of Learned Societies; the F.A.O.; the National Science Foundation, under Grant No. GS-3295; the John Simon Guggenheim Memorial Foundation; the Small Grants Program of the National Institute of Mental Health; the Kafue Basin Committee; the African Committee of the University of California; the Research Committee of the University of California, Berkeley; and the California Institute of Technology.

ment. This is probably true everywhere; but in Gwembe, where one can hire few services, caring for the old is an obligation inherent in the concept of kinship. To question the obligation would be to put in question one's own right to future care. Most old people therefore live with kin, upon whom they become more and more dependent.

Seven vignettes at the end of this article show how different Gwembe elders have coped with age, and how their kin have dealt with them.

The Physical Setting

Gwembe District lies in a great valley between the edge of the Zambian Plateau and the Zambezi River. It includes the entire north shore of Lake Kariba, which began to form in 1958 when Kariba Hydroelectric Dam was built on the Zambezi. The district is roughly 250 miles long and 80 miles wide. Much of the terrain is rough escarpment country, stony and covered with bush. The hot season is uncomfortably hot, although the annual mean maximum temperature is only approximately 90°F. In the cold season nights may be frosty, and at midday people shiver in the cold wind. Rains are uncertain. Famines were frequent in the past. Hunger years, when harvests fail or fall short, are still common. Many households then simply do not have enough food. Everyone grows thin; children cry; the old suffer. Transport problems in large portions of the district still make it difficult, especially during the rainy season, to import food even for those with money. It is often easier to transport people to food.

In 1949 people walked along bush paths that connected one village with another and carried their belongings on their backs or heads. By 1956 there were a few roads; it was sometimes possible to catch a lift with an official, a trader, or a missionary. By 1973 bus routes connected many villages with the railway line, and a few local shopkeepers and teachers had cars and trucks that could be hired. But transport costs were high and most traffic from village to village was still on foot or by bicycle. Village shops, almost nonexistent in 1956, became common thereafter as it became possible to import goods. By the 1970's most people lived within a mile of a shop selling salt, soap, cooking oil, blankets, cloth, and other staples. This eased supply problems of young and old alike, if they had money, but created a difference in standard of living between rich and poor.

Gwembe has no cities and only since 1965 have any small towns existed. Village life moves at an easy pace, but it requires hard work for a family to maintain itself upon the land. There is little margin of comfort. Labor-saving devices are largely absent. Women must carry water from the river, a water hole, public wells, or taps. They cook over open fires. Housewives and children must collect and carry firewood and comb the bush for food to supplement garden produce. Grain has to be stamped or ground into meal in most homesteads. Almost every household grows its own food, and this means back-breaking work during the growing and harvesting seasons (Scudder 1971).

People commonly expect to cope with sickness, death, and the care of the aged on their own. Herbalists help treat the ill. Dispensaries have become more numerous since 1956, but many people must still walk five to ten miles to reach one. Professional nurses are attached only to dispensaries or to several hospitals that are inconvenient to most villages. Nursing care is home nursing; even in the hospital, kin come along to do the bulk of the care. Few families have had servants in this strongly egalitarian society since slavery was abolished at the end of the nineteenth century. A few teachers and shopkeepers hire youngsters as household helpers; but in most families, husband and wife cultivate the fields and the wife runs the household with regular assistance only from children and other dependents. Neighbors and kin help in emergencies: villagers know that their help will be forthcoming, but there is strong pride in coping by oneself.

Caring for ill and old is the affair first of the family and then of other kin. Sooner or later the old will die at home, and be buried within the homestead in graves dug by their neighbors. It is believed that the shades of their own dead kin, taking pity upon them, will come and carry them off in a cloth like that used to carry infants. They join the dead and their own shades begin to receive offerings from the living in return for protection and to ward off anger at neglect.

The Burden of Being Old

Old people remain members of village society to the very end and expect to take such part as they can in both work and play. Old men and women join for the moment in the whirl of a village dance. Old women are summoned as midwives. Both old men and women take part in beer parties and in gatherings to settle disputes and hear local matters. The old are stalwart mourners at all funerals.

Sooner or later, however, their world contracts to the homesteads in which they live simply because their feet will not carry them beyond, or because most of those with whom they once laughed and quarreled are dead. Except for those elderly men who maintain some control within their homesteads, they become increasingly marginal. They are the first to suffer when conditions are hard. Sleeping alone without adequate covering, they shiver at night throughout the cold season. Restricted in their movements, they must endure the dust that sweeps through barren villages during the height of the dry season when others retreat to more sheltered areas. No longer essential workers in the homestead, the very old may be shifted to kin in distant regions with a better harvest, to reduce the number of bellies dependent on homestead granaries.

Inevitably the existence of very old people creates resentments. Old people themselves resent physical processes of aging within their own bodies and project their resentment on younger people who flourish while they suffer. They also resent the usurpation of their rights by juniors. Younger people, in turn, resent the drain of the old upon their sympathies, physical strength, and limited resources. Some see in the old an uncomfortable portent of things to come. We have heard middle-aged men and women comment of some very old person that they themselves have no wish to grow old like this, for this is not life (*buumi*).

Many people are reluctant to accept even the aging associated with middle-age. Women sigh over wrinkles and vanishing beauty, regretting loss of both fertility and sexual desirability. Men and women comment on how waning strength limits their ability to work. When eyesight dims, some must abandon handicrafts in which they had taken pride. Others are cut off by increasing deafness. When memory falters people embarrass themselves and annoy their companions. They repeat themselves and tire their listeners. Sexual activity is expected to decrease. In village gossip, it is legitimate to speculate on whether an old man is still potent. Sexual relations between old and young are regarded as blighting to the younger partner and are tabooed. Even continued sexual relations between an old couple are regarded as abnormal. Often they no longer sleep together, and they may even occupy separate houses.

A great many old people have trouble sleeping through the night; they rise, sit in the darkness, smoke if the coals are still alight, feel the cold and boredom, and too often brood over slights. They do not stir out for fear of being accused of sorcery, and so endure the long night. No recognition given to them in the role of wise elder seems sufficient recompense for these trials and all that is slipping away.

Some resentment felt by the old turns against other people. Not all are able to maintain the façade of good manners that usually masks the hostility generated by the flow of village life. In coping with the limitations of their own bodies, attention turns inward and the surface courtesies begin to give way. The very old may show again the greed and quick anger of childhood; then they are openly envious of the good things they see others having. As the years go by, old men and women become increasingly cantankerous and intolerant of the noise made by young children in the homestead. Raids of children upon their possessions lead to angry outbursts. The very old and the very young in a sense are competing with each other.

Gwembe grandparents and grandchildren, although expected to be friends, are unlikely to be so if the age gap is very great. Between great grandparents and great grandchildren, a barrier is assumed to exist. A woman calls her great grandchild *nkalamabeelo*, "one who sits on the thigh": she does not carry such a child on her back.

Many great grandmothers lack the strength, but the taboo probably is linked to the belief that the shades of dead kin, hovering closely behind the old, would endanger the infant. Although some women and a few men see their great grandchildren, great grandparents and great grandchildren do not belong in the same social universe. They have nothing in common except kinship, and perhaps even this is in question.

These are normal hazards of growing old. The compulsory relocation of some 34,000 Gwembe Tonga between 1957 and 1959, in connection with the formation of Lake Kariba, destroyed the familiar world of the old and thrust additional burdens upon them. Though we have no firm evidence that mortality rates increased among the elderly at this time, they tended to suffer from psychological stress more than younger people simply because decreasing energy, restricted mobility, and lessening tolerance of change made leaving a known habitat for an uncertain future more difficult to accept. No longer would they be near the graves of their dead or live in association with a familiar landscape—village sites or fields passed down to them. Ritual influence was often tied to knowledge of a particular locality, a knowledge that had little applicability in resettlement areas where members of the host population at least initially held ritual prerogatives.

For the first few years following resettlement, the elderly were at a disadvantage. They lost alluvial fields and could not expect to obtain new fields of equivalent size and value. They lost dwellings, granaries, and other household structures, and, if too old to rebuild for themselves, had to wait until younger kinsmen had housed their own wives and younger dependents. Resettlement also accelerated certain trends that widened the gap between generations. Especially important was education. Some of the compensation funds assigned to the Gwembe Treasury were used to finance a significant increase in the number of upper primary schools and the construction of the first secondary school in Gwembe District. The advantages derived from education went to the young, not to the old, whose former assets had been taken. The young gained in status at their expense. With much of their knowledge tied to an area flooded beneath 130 million acre-feet of water, old people now were hardly in a position to influence the increasingly educated youth who often looked to futures outside Gwembe.

The Magnitude of the Social Problem

In 1969 Gwembe District had a population estimated at 76,407 (some of whom were not Tonga-speakers), of whom 1.7 percent were 65 years old or older (Central Statistical Office 1975).

In our study of Gwembe District (1956–78), we have followed four villages with intensive demographic censuses at various inter vals, the latest one being taken in all villages in 1973. Those over 65 years of age were 2.4 percent of the population in 1956 and 2.1 per cent in 1973. Both the official census and our village census provide only indications of the proportion of old people. Gwembe villagers have had little interest in dating events. Few know when they were born. Birthdates we attributed to most adults are guesses, based on discovering birth order and then extrapolating from the birthdates of those few individuals whose births can be securely fixed. Ages assigned in 1956 to older men and women may be subject to a five- to ten-year error. We now know that initially we tended to under-estimate ages, but it is impossible to rework all the data to correct for this bias. Table 1 shows village population for the years 1956 and 1973, the number of men and women over the age of 65 in each year, and (within parentheses) the number over the age of 60.

These four villages may or may not be representative of the uni-

TABLE 1. Population over 65 (60) Against Total Population, 1956 and 1973

Village	1956			1973		
	Total	M+65	F+65	Total	M+65	F+65
Mazulu	128	2 (2)	0 (0)	329	5 (7)	4 (7)
Musulumba	218	3 (6)	2 (4)	270	4 (4)	4 (5)
Sinafala	238	2 (2)	5 (8)	360	0 (4)	2 (3)
Siameja	282	3 (6)	4 (4)	569	5 (8)	9 (14)
TOTAL	866	10 (16)	11 (16)	1,528	14 (23)	19 (29)

verse of Gwembe villages. They are situated in different parts of Gwembe District: Mazulu and Musulumba now are in the northeast; Sinafala in the center; and Siameja in the southwest. All four were resettled in 1958 (Colson 1971a). The Siameja census initially covered approximately one-third of the homesteads in the village, which is the largest in Gwembe District. Each of the other three was covered in its entirety. We have collected information on all residents at the time of each return visit, and have also tried to collect information on people recorded in 1956 who have since moved away. Those who live and work elsewhere, but maintain housing or return to cultivate, are counted as residents.

In 1956 this village sample contained four persons over the estimated age of 75; in 1973 there were nine. Only one person in our sample has reached the estimated age of 90 years. She was also one of two people to remain fully active after the age of 80. By the age of 82, she had given away her field and received food from other women. All others in the sample became at least partially dependent on kin by the age of 80, though most elders between 70 and 75 were active cultivators with satisfying positions in their own homesteads. After 75, old men progressively lost control over their livestock and found themselves increasingly disregarded when they tried to guide family affairs. Of the elders in our sample, seven at least became senile; six became blind and needed to be led about by a child; several became so decrepit that they found it difficult to drag themselves to the bush once or twice a day for defecation.

The age at death of elders in the 1956 census is given in Table 2.

How much of a burden the care of elders was to villagers is indicated by the fact that of 55 homesteads in 1956, 17 contained one or more semidependent seniors and 5 had seniors who were almost fully dependent on others. In 1973 only 22 of 88 homesteads had partially dependent senior members, whereas 8 contained fully dependent elders. Some homesteads cared for both partially and fully dependent elders. When the overlap is corrected for, 21 (or 40 percent) of the 1956 homesteads provided care to one or more seniors, whereas 29 (33 percent) of the 1973 homesteads did so.

The rapid increase in district population since 1949 is an indica-

TABLE 2. Age at Death of Senior People in 1956
Village Census, Irrespective of Residence
at Time of Death

Age at death	Males	Females	Total
66–70	7	7	14
71–75	3	2	5
76–80	1	1	2
81–85	1	2	3
86–90	1	1	2
91–95	0	1	1

tion that mortality rates have been falling and life expectancy increasing. Although we do not know for certain that life expectancy for elders is increasing, we suspect that it is. Leprosy and tuberculosis are now to some extent under control. So is malaria; this means fewer deaths from pneumonia. Elders today are more apt to have operations for cataracts or other disabling conditions. Bilharzia, however, has spread since 1958 as a result of the creation of Lake Kariba.

From Young Adult to Aging Elder

The old people of the 1970's grew up at a time when Gwembe District could not export enough produce to meet a large proportion of its cash needs. This was still the case in 1956. Able bodied men therefore went out to work for part of their active lives. At that time few Gwembe men or women had been to school, since there were few schools and none that took children beyond the first primary years, so men could find work only as unskilled labor. They left the village, and district, because they needed money for taxes, clothing, blankets, hoes, and a few luxuries. They also wanted to earn bridewealth to permit them to marry and set up their own households. As young men, they first sought work. After a year or so, they returned home to marry. After cultivating for a year or so, while awaiting the birth of the first child, it was off again to the towns, mines, and farms. Thereafter men alternated between home and work place until their sons were old enough to become labor migrants and their daughters (and sisters' daughters) were ready to marry and so give them claims for bridewealth and other dues against working sons-in-law. In the meantime, their wives stayed home to cultivate fields and raise children. Alternately a woman waited for her husband and chafed at having to recognize his authority when he was at home.

For a man, becoming an elder meant that he could remain at home, work toward the establishment of an independent homestead, and begin to play a continuous role in local affairs. For a woman, it meant the end of childbearing and release from the demands of young children, but it also coincided with the loss of autonomy in the presence of a now-resident husband.

The labor migration system helped to space births. It also meant that husband and wife developed a close working partnership only after the husband's permanent return in middle age, since only then would they live together year-in and year-out. Only the young wife of a polygynist elder started her married life with a permanently resident husband. In 1956, over 50 percent of the married men in our sample had two or more wives, though few had more than three. Frequently a man married several wives within a short period of years. If the women were peers, they usually came to terms and established their own working arrangements during the husband's lengthy absences.

Men, both old and young, shared the camaraderie of the common work experience; young men followed their seniors to the same work places and sometimes to the same employers. Women, both old and young, shared the routines of the village and saw their experience as a continuity. These patterns are changing. With easier travel between village and industrial centers, and greater opportunities for employment near villages, especially since Zambian independence in 1964, economic choices have altered. Some younger men today make a livelihood in the village, whereas others continue a labor migration pattern and still others settle permanently in town. Jobs are more diversified, and the search for work takes people to more places. Women, too, now accompany their husbands to town. Today women need to know about how to cope

TABLE 3. Residence of Those over 65 (60) in 1956 and 1973

Homestead of residence	1956		1973	
	M+65 (60)	F+65 (60)	M+65 (60)	F+65 (60)
Own[a] (or husband's)	7 (14)	2 (3)	15 (21)	3 (8)
Son's	1 (1)	3 (5)	0 (1)	9 (12)
Other matrikin's	2 (2)	5 (7)	0 (2)	2 (4)
Daughter's husband's	0 (0)	1 (1)	0 (0)	0 (1)
Husband's inheritor's	—	0 (0)		2 (2)
Other	—	—	—	1 (1)

[a] In these cases the elder's control appeared to be more than nominal although there comes a time in the lives of most homestead heads when control of homestead affairs passes to a son or junior matrilineal kinsman.

with town conditions as well as about how to cultivate a field or prepare a village meal; for this they often look for advice to contemporaries rather than to mothers and grandmothers.

The breakup of the previous continuity of male and female worlds gives new importance to the relationship between husband and wife. Looking to the future, this may be facilitated by changes taking place in the relative age of husband and wife. In the past, a boy or young man engaged himself to a little girl and waited for her to mature. Subsequently he courted other children who were not yet promised to a husband. In 1952, Gwembe Local Government forbade childhood betrothals and young women began to choose young men as husbands. But even in 1973 the former pattern had important consequences for elders who had matured and married before 1952. Then men had married women who were ten, fifteen, and twenty years their juniors. A woman expected her first marriage to be to a much older man; but if he died, she was inherited by one of his kinsmen who might be her contemporary or even much younger. Old men usually had much younger wives who helped to support them; old women were more likely to rely on sons.

Table 3 shows homestead residence of senior men and women in 1956 and 1973.

Old men who were still homestead heads almost invariably had wives to care for them. If they controlled fields, livestock, and cash resources, and remained relatively vigorous, their homesteads were

also apt to include married sons with their dependents and the occasional matrilineal relative. An elder with younger wives can expect to have his fields cultivated, his granaries filled, and his stock
cared for by children his wives continue to bear; and despite the
fact that their paternity may be in doubt, he continues to enjoy dignity and ease as head of a comfortable homestead even when he is
no longer an active worker. A man whose wives are also elderly, on
the other hand, can expect smaller harvests. He begins to see his authority decline and is no longer able to offer easy hospitality to age-
mates and younger men. His livestock may vanish into the pens of
more vigorous kin when he no longer can rely upon herdsboys under his own control. Matrilineal descent and inheritance do not
prevent the Gwembe Tonga man from having very real power over
his children; but as he ages, this power slackens. Daughters go off
to their husbands. Sons, as their own children approach maturity,
are likely to found their own homesteads and become less willing to
give labor to their father. If a son remains with his father, he gradually assumes control of the homestead and with it responsibility for
the care of his parents. Then only association with certain mystical powers provides the older man with a hedge against de facto
inferiority.

When a helpless old couple have no surviving children to take
care of them, eventually some decision must be made about their
maintenance. Nursing care will be undertaken only by kin, and
husband and wife come from different lineages. The solution is to
separate them and send each to a homestead headed by a kinsman.
In one instance the two homesteads were separated by only a few
yards, but this was too great a distance for the old man and woman
to traverse and they rarely saw each other thereafter.

An old man who has lost his wives is unlikely to get another. He
then becomes uncomfortably dependent for his food on the wives
of other men. In this he is like various old men who have been long-
time labor migrants and have returned after many years at work,
sometimes with a cash bonus and sometimes arriving completely
destitute. These too are cared for by kin.

An elderly widow, despite her poverty, is less handicapped than an old man without a wife. She can get along so long as she can grow her own food and cook, and can borrow a child to carry wood and water and stamp grain. Her demands on kin for labor to build a house or clear a field are sporadic and if not met at once cause her no great inconvenience. An old man needs daily services that only a housewife will provide, and other men's wives feel little obligation to cater to his whims.

Women therefore feel less dependent than do their husbands upon maintaining a marriage to underwrite security in old age. Initially married to men many years their senior, many elderly women in our sample have been widowed and inherited. If the widow is still young enough to have children and is much of an age with her inheritor, the arrangement may develop into a genuine marriage. On the other hand, if the widow is past menopause, she is likely to become only a nominal wife to her new "husband." Should she move to his homestead, she will be supported to the extent of assistance in the building of a new house when the homestead moves and permission to continue to use any fields given to her by her dead husband. Since plowing became common, a man may plow for an elderly inherited wife, but only after he has first plowed his own field and the fields of his younger wives. In return, field work and food are owed to the "husband," and occasionally the woman may make beer for him as long as she is able to do so.

Under such circumstances, aging women frequently leave inherited husbands to live with sons; less frequently they leave them to live with other kinsmen. They do not expect much tolerance from daughters' husbands and say it would be foolish to live with a daughter despite the matrilineal rules of Tonga society. Elderly women feel greater security in their relationship with sons. Even if their original husbands are still alive, they may choose to separate from them to move into a son's homestead.

An old widow without children, and without small stock and fowls to provide a cash income, usually lives in houses abandoned by younger kin and huddles over a tiny fire to warm herself in her rags, which may be well-worn and hand-me-downs. If no one sends her food or calls her to eat, she may know actual hunger as her

strength declines and her fields wear out, but she will not be allowed to starve so long as there is food available in the homestead.

The Changing Economic Position of the Elderly

Gwembe Tonga used to be subsistence agriculturalists, but since
the 1950's the economy has diversified and other occupations are
now feasible even for some of those who stay in Gwembe District.
Formerly the prized agricultural land was the fertile floodplain of
the Zambezi River and the pockets of good soil along its tributaries
that flowed out of the escarpment. The better alluvial soils supported cultivation during both the rains and the dry season. Most
of the population lived in large nucleated villages clustered around
the deltas of the tributaries. They planted maize, sorghums, cucur-
bits, legumes, sweet potatoes, and tobacco in permanent fields on
alluvial soils and bulrush millet in slash-and-burn fields away from
the rivers. Between 1949 and 1956 more and more cultivators began to open these bush gardens, since valued alluvial soils were in
short supply and the upper terraces badly needed resting (Scudder
1962: 52–61).

Alluvial soils were subject to lineage claims, which meant that
senior men and women were in a position to control allocation of
such land and themselves held a disproportionate share of the productive and easily worked alluviums. When young men began to
clear bush fields for themselves, they became less dependent upon senior kin, whose importance thereby declined. After December
1958, the formation of Lake Kariba wiped out the old holdings. It
also put a premium on the physical strength of younger men for
clearing new fields. It was now younger men who supplied fields
to senior kin, hence altering the power balance in each village—a
power balance already under attack from rapid changes occurring
throughout Central Africa that put in question the value of the experience of older men and women.

Elders, however, still held important resources after resettlement.
These included cash, livestock, and rights vested in them as repre-
sentatives of the shades of the dead. Before resettlement few people

owned cattle because the tsetse fly, carrier of bovine trypanoso-miasis, covered much of the district except for some of the high-lands and the densely settled meander zone in southwest Gwembe, where Siameja was situated. In most of Gwembe, men and women measured their wealth in terms of goats and sheep. When the ad-ministration introduced inoculation against bovine trypanoso-miasis in the late 1940's and began tsetse control measures in the 1950's, men began to invest savings in cattle and plows and to shift to plow agriculture. This again enhanced the position of men young enough to make the shift: they learned to plow and were encour-aged to clear larger fields. After resettlement, conditions for cattle continued to improve. Soon only the very poor or the old expected to hoe-plant. The system of crop management changed according-ly. Cattle and plows have become a source of current income for owners who rent them to poorer villagers. Stock sales also are a major source of income for Mazulu, Sinafala, and Siameja villages, and a lesser source for Musulumba. The wealthiest cattle-owning elders of 1973 were primarily men who had been in vigorous mid-dle age in the late 1950's. Those who were then too old or who oth-erwise were unable to invest in new ventures appeared to depend more upon income derived from claims on bridewealth and other dues. Few women bought cattle, but both men and women owned small stock. Many elders, however, saw small stock sadly dimin-ished during the resettlement period and were never able to rebuild their holdings; again it was the vigorous middle-aged men and women of the 1950's who restored their fortunes (Scudder & Col-son 1972).

Although people still have access to wild produce, big game has disappeared near populated areas and old hunting skills are rela-tively unimportant in the 1970's. The elders' knowledge of hunting, and their hunting medicines and rituals, now avail them little. Fish-ing still goes on, but again it was vigorous younger men, and their middle-aged sponsors, who were able to profit from the Lake Ka-riba fisheries during the most active period in 1959–64. A few of them have become commercial fishermen on the lake. Most purchased cattle, while some opened shops, started cash cropping, and educated their kin. These in turn became a source of remittances for their aging sponsors.

All this means increasing security for the Gwembe people as a whole, including elders. Some elders now have capital assets which return to them a regular income without large inputs of labor. They have the means with which to reward kin who give them assistance and have less need to rely on implicit threats. But probably the majority still reach old age with only a tiny store of hidden cash, perhaps a few head of livestock that they slowly draw down as the years go by, and their fields. These last they hand on to others when they can no longer cultivate them.

The Continued Influence of the Elders

In 1973 the influence of Gwembe elders, especially men, appeared to be at an all-time low. Those who were very senior at the time of resettlement suffered most since they lost both fields and whatever influence they had by virtue of their detailed knowledge of their homeland. At the same time the increased education and the movement of young people to the towns after resettlement increased the gap between them and the elders, most of whom were illiterate in both English and Tonga. Though the senior men had once gone out as labor migrants, just like young men of today, they had traveled alone, without their wives. They had gone south into Zimbabwe (Rhodesia), whereas in the 1970's young men seek work in Zambia.

For the next two generations of elders, however, we expect the situation to change. Men between the ages of 45 and 65 in 1973 used the opportunities associated with resettlement. They opened new lands, increasing the relative size of their holdings, and capitalized the fishing industry, purchasing cattle with the profits that younger relatives, who did the actual fishing, handed over to them. With plow-oxen from these and other sources, they pioneered the cash-cropping of cotton, sunflowers, and brewing sorghum that has developed since Zambian independence. Though still largely illiterate, at least in English, these men are familiar with the towns of Zambia, to which they travel for occasional business purposes. Unlike today's senior elders, they are part of a single social field with the young men, although most of their interest is focused on the rural areas (Colson & Scudder 1976). Here they control much of the cleared land, and, since little additional land is available for clearing within Gwembe District, this control carries influence over younger labor migrants if they decide to return home to settle down. Should inflation and lack of job opportunities make Zambian towns less desirable, as was the case in 1976, the influence of the elders will grow, especially if more favorable prices for agricultural produce lure young men back to the land.

As for today's senior elders, what influence they have derives from whatever wealth they have managed to retain, from the belief that they possess powerful medicines, and from the mystical power of the shades of the dead that are attached to their persons.

Most Gwembe Tonga still accept the cult of the ancestral shades (Colson 1960:122–61), despite the inroads of Christianity and skepticism. The shades of the dead are regarded as spiritual guardians of their children and grandchildren, in whose houses they receive offerings and from whom they continue to receive other recognition in the form of various dues given to those lineage-mates who are their inheritors.

Though a young man or woman may be a shade inheritor, he or she is likely to acquire additional shades as the years pass. Those who outlive their contemporaries accumulate more and more shades, most of whom are no longer known to the vast majority of the living. These shades begin to assume the malevolent character of ghosts. Shades who no longer have active roles as parents and grandparents of living descendants bring their inheritors no material benefits in the form of dues and offerings, but they do endow them with the power for harm. An inheritor who grows angry or expresses disgust at disgraceful behavior alerts the hovering shades who rush to view the offender. This makes it dangerous for old people to gossip, since they may then be accused of having directed the shades to kin and neighbors. We have heard an old woman almost tearfully protest "But I said nothing. I said nothing at all. I am always careful not to talk about people." But the fear that they will alert the shades can work to their advantage since people are reluctant to anger the old by a lack of respect.

Extreme old age is associated with ambivalent power—shades are both protectors and causers of ill. The old can either intercede with them on behalf of their kin or make them instruments of their own malevolent resentment. Old men also are believed to be actively evil in another fashion. They are believed to have invested in medicines for success and long life, and since these may require an infusion of human life force to be potent, the death of children and vigorous mature kin is attributed to the old men's ambition. Women, who are not believed to own such medicines, are less feared than old men. A man who has obtained medicine for long life will not die, even though his body is rotting away, until he rids himself of the medicine. An elder who clings to life is seen as selfish, willing to sacrifice others to his own continued existence, worthy of fear but not respect (Colson 1971b).

But elders who die in time are sincerely mourned and remembered with affection; and when their shades are summoned to the offerings, it is as cherished and cherishing kin.

A Gallery of Elders

The following biographies of old men and women show something of the variety of old people's experience. Several lived in villages not included in our census sample. Those still living are given pseudonyms.

Thomas

Thomas was born about 1893. He had been a labor migrant for many years before retiring to his village to become an elder. In 1956, he was head of a large homestead which included his remaining wife (born in 1904) and their unmarried daughter; an unmarried son and daughter by a dead wife; two married sons with their wives and infants; two married sister's sons with their wives and children; an elderly widower belonging to his lineage; and another lineage brother with his wife and children. A daughter was already married; a son had gone to live with his mother's brother in another village; and various children of an inherited wife, now dead, had also left. Thomas and his wife had enough small stock to give them a comfortable feeling of solid prosperity, and they could expect to receive both stock and cash from their daughters' bridewealth.

Thomas was a man who liked people. He had once been headman of his village but had handed on the office to another man. This seemed to leave him only more time to spend with his many visitors, whom he entertained generously. Most evenings he was visited by villagers who came to him for counsel or just to chat. His wisdom was respected and he was a witty raconteur. He pondered the meaning of events and was one of the few Gwembe people we have met with an interest in cosmology. He also was keenly interested in political matters, and took an active part in mobilizing his neighbors to oppose the administration's plans for resettlement. Finally, as a shade inheritor, he was a frequent ritual intermediary for his lineage and for the descendants of his lineage-mates.

By 1962, Thomas was living in a resettlement area he detested, bereft of the fertile soils on which he had grown tobacco and bananas. His homestead had shrunk, despite his having recruited an immigrant to the village. Thomas's older son, both sister's sons, and both lineage brothers had built separately. One married son and an unmarried son remained with him. The homestead was enlivened, however, by the presence of Thomas's divorced daughter with her young children and of two young kinswomen whose husbands were away earning bridewealth. Children from surrounding homesteads still made Thomas's area their playground, and Thomas and his wife tolerated their noise, saying "If children did not make a noise, we would begin to worry that they were ill." Both resident sons were employed locally, and though they considered themselves independent they consulted their father and gave formal recognition to him as their mentor and homestead head despite various indications that they had begun to doubt his judgment.

Thomas still had stock, including now some cattle with which his sons plowed both his fields and their own. There was already a sign of decline, however: he had had to place the cattle with his older son and a sister's son for herding because no youngsters in his own homestead were old enough for herding. Thomas's wife was still an active worker, and she was aided by the three young women. Thomas himself was beginning to slack off on field work, though he spent much time journeying the countryside and actively exploring possibilities for bond-friendships with residents of the area where he had been resettled. Fellow-villagers still spent a good deal of time in the homestead, but younger men and women were beginning to regard Thomas as a bit of a bore with his long-winded tales and his moans about the evils of their new home. His increasing forgetfulness was even more difficult for his household: he would mislay possessions and then accuse others of having taken them. Still, at nearly 70, Thomas was a force to be reckoned with, still avid for new ideas and good conversation.

By 1972 the homestead was declining, and consisted of Thomas and his wife, his divorced daughter with her children, and two married sons with their wives and children. Thomas, at 79, was going blind, was somewhat deaf, and no longer had much physical strength. His wife and the divorced daughter were the mainstays of his household and provided for his support, but his wife was beginning to grumble about the demands on her strength. Their fields had begun to wear out and no new land was available nearby. Their house was tumbling down and their sons were slow to build them another. The sons did so at the end of 1972, but the house was smaller than the one it replaced. Neither resident son gave much respect to Thomas, and neither the son who lived elsewhere in the village nor his sister's sons visited him very regularly. Both his cattle and his small stock had been appropriated by the men who had agreed to herd them, and these men resented any claims Thomas made upon the stock. Thomas himself held that he still owned three cattle. One day, when told that there was no sour milk (when he knew that his son was milking), he said sadly, "If I were young enough, I would take back my cattle and have my own pen. But I am old."

Thomas's grandsons, who ten years earlier had hung about him, openly mocked his speech and sneered at his greed for sweets, which he bought and ate in his field to avoid sharing. His growing pepperiness of temper had somewhat alienated other villagers, but his increasing isolation was also due to the fact that he did not drink beer and so was not a member of the beer parties that from 1963 on engrossed more and more time of most men and women. For other villagers he had become somewhat of a butt. He responded either by clowning or by withdrawing. There were mutters that he was becoming senile, although on a good day he could still produce flashes of his old wit and charm and dominate a gathering. For some reason, he had escaped the reputation of an active sorcerer, perhaps because he was still meticulous about paying his debts and showed his concern over the woes of his fellows. But when a grandchild died in 1973, Thomas was one of the suspects until a divination pointed the accusation in another direction.

Since 1973, Thomas has become completely blind. He is an ill old man who spends much time at hospitals or dispensaries. When he is home, his children and kin have assumed the burden of his care.

Simon

We first met Simon in 1972 when he moved to the neighborhood of one of our sample villages. He had once been a powerful active man with his own large homestead, but by 1972 he was over 80, his wives were dead, and he had left his son's homestead to join two sister's sons in a village that had remained in the general area where he had spent much of his active life. The homestead also housed his sister and her husband, as decrepit as himself. Simon's son is a progressive farmer—wealthy enough to have a car and well able to care for his father. But Simon was discontented in his homestead with its newfangled ways and finally persuaded his son to let him go to his own kin. In 1972 Simon could no longer walk—it was old age, he said, and nothing else. He spent his days sitting in the house his sister's sons had built for him. Once or twice a day he dragged himself to the bush to defecate. He ate by himself, children bringing him food from the family meal. Occasionally they stayed to listen to his memories. At other times he amused himself by playing a one-string bow and singing songs of his own composition or songs from long ago. His mind was alert, but he tired easily and he seemed to have little desire for company. He made no effort to cross the space to the house occupied by his sister and her husband, who were more or less senile. Sometimes they lay outside their house side by side in the sun, but they rarely seemed to say anything even to each other. They too were fed by active members of the homestead. All three had retired into the isolation of the very old who have little interest in anything beyond their own bodies. The people of the homestead gave them care but did not look to them for wisdom. Simon's son occasionally stopped to be sure the old man was all right and brought him food and clothing. Otherwise the days simply passed.

Sikabwele

When he died in 1974 Sikabwele was almost 90 and the eldest man in our village sample. Unlike most elders he retained control over land, wives, and other dependents, and stock—at least through 1973. And, despite his age and the common knowledge that he retained powerful medicines, he continued to be cherished, at least by some in his large homestead, until his death.

In the early 1940's Sikabwele moved across the Zambezi from Zimbabwe into Gwembe District with three wives and their children. Without sufficient tax-paying dependents to form his own village, he was required by the colonial authorities to join with kinsmen who had migrated to Zambia at a still earlier date. There he was subsequently joined by four matrilineal kinsmen, with their families, so that when we first met him in 1956 his large homestead dominated one end of the village. Sikabwele had two wives—a third had left him (but returned to the homestead after relocation to live with a son).

In the mid-1950's, Sikabwele, though at least 70, was an active cultivator, as were his two wives. They utilized over ten acres. Sikabwele was one of the first to introduce cattle into the village and to purchase a plow. With his sons and matrilineal kinsmen he had opened up large bush gardens between 1948 and 1956. At the time of resettlement he had successfully reached the goal of every adult male Tonga: he headed his own homestead; controlled land, livestock, and a large number of dependents; and was an influential man within the neighborhood. This position he was able to retain following relocation. Although his landholdings and those of his two wives were reduced to slightly under nine acres, all of his 1956 dependents, including seven married sons, rebuilt their houses within his homestead. Even his senior sister's son, who had moved out to establish his own homestead prior to 1955, rebuilt his own homestead nearby, across a narrow dirt track.

By 1973 Sikabwele, pushing 90, still dominated a large homestead. Though two married sons and three of the four matrilineal kinsmen who had joined him in the 1940's had moved out to establish their own homesteads, four sons and the remaining matrilineal kinsmen and their families still clustered around his granary and sleeping platform, where he spent his nights alone. Though his vitality was weakening, he still worked in his gardens, including his dry-season garden several miles away. Though he and his wives had begun to divide their gardens among younger kin, his cattle had increased to six in 1967. Thereafter his policy was to sell one beast every other year in order to obtain cash to meet his needs, including canned meats and sweets that he consumed alone, although his married male dependents still ate regularly with him at the noon and evening meals. Quite obviously they still cherished him: in 1973 they lovingly built him his first mud-brick house, with a concrete floor, in which he placed his spring bed and mattress along with his other possessions.

In the 1970's Sikabwele was also feared, especially by one of his elderly matrilineal kinsmen who, when drunk, raged that Sikabwele was trying to kill him with medicine. There also appeared to be a growing gap between him and his grandchildren, two of whom were in upper primary school and were subsequently to attend secondary school. The elder of these felt that his grandfather's world had little relevance to his own until the old man quite possibly saved his life. This grandson became seriously ill in 1973 after breaking a limb bone and contracting osteomyelitis, which continued to spread despite modern medical treatment. Then his grandfather treated and cured him. Thereafter he showed the profoundest respect and affection for the old man, who throughout the remaining years of his life somehow managed to avoid the indignities, the loneliness, and the indifference that so often is the lot of the very old. Even his eldest son, who had begun to detach himself from Sikabwele's homestead (by building a large and semidetached homestead of his own to which he attracted his own married sister's son), to the very end continued to eat with his father. Before Sikabwele died, he appointed this son to operate at the funeral as representative of the father's lineage, since those who should have been involved lived across the closed national border in Zimbabwe. In death, Sikabwele appeared to control his funeral just as earlier he had controlled his life.

Siabiti

In her mid-fifties in 1956, Siabiti was already blind from a disease that had afflicted her years before. She had been widowed in the 1940's and inherited by a man some twenty years her junior. She had borne one son to him before taking up residence in the homestead that her eldest son shared with another man. Prior to relocation she cultivated a riverbank garden of less than a half acre, assisted in her daily movements and tasks by a granddaughter who lived with her after the death of her own mother. After relocation, Siabiti was given a quarter-acre garden to cultivate. She shared her new home with the same granddaughter, who forfeited whatever chance she may have had for a primary-school education by caring for her grandmother.

Unlike Sikabwele, Siabiti was neglected by her sons, who seldom provided her with a blanket to protect her from the cold and the mosquitoes of the night and who only rarely catered to her other needs, such as for clothing. Yet she had a small garden to cultivate and was still able to cook for herself, so her life continued to have meaning. Her movements to her garden and to other homesteads were restricted after her granddaughter married in 1966, but one married daughter lived within shouting distance, and even in 1973 she would make her way alone across the barren space between two homesteads to pass the time of day. In the evening her distinctive and familiar voice could be heard in the midst of the gathering of women and children who nightly sat and talked around the cooking fires, several of which were within 25 yards of her house. Though obviously her life had been hard, her physical surroundings began to improve once her eldest son, a successful small-scale cotton and tobacco farmer by 1973, began to give her better care. Also, her daughter occasionally brewed beer for her so that she could sell it and use the money she earned to buy clothing.

Siagondo

Siagondo was born in 1872. She had had an adventurous youth, which had included capture and escape from Ndebele raiders. In 1956 her husbands, of which there had been several, were long dead. Her only surviving son had disappeared as a labor migrant. Her two living daughters were elderly widows whose own sons had also gone off to work and not returned. They lived as dependents in the homestead of a man who was both Siagondo's inherited husband and the husband of one of her granddaughters. Siagondo, however, had been induced to move to the homestead of a wealthy lineage kinsman who had a sense of responsibility for the old woman. At 84, she was alert and active. Two years before she had decided that she no longer would be bothered with a field, and she was cooked for by the other women of the homestead. Her kinsman supplied her with clothing and blankets—she was as well dressed as she cared to be. She ate by herself because she regarded the small children as unmannerly and did not wish to dip into the same dish with them. But she was willing to keep an eye on the babies, could chuckle over a joke, and when she was of a mind to was quite prepared to walk as much as six or seven miles to visit kin. Indeed, her memory made her the linchpin of her lineage, for its members were held together by her reminders of their common origin. Siagondo was also a mourner at most funerals in the neighborhood. After all, she had no other duties and could spend time at such occasions.

In 1962, at 90, Siagondo still lived with the same kinsman, who had had a new house built for her after the resettlement. On good days she was still a cheerful companion who was prepared to adventure on new experiences. Those who looked after her regarded her as an asset—they were sure nobody else in all of Gwembe could be as old, and they delighted in her wit. She in turn was somewhat contemptuous of the young, who were so ignorant of all she could remember. One day she said with great scorn, "Why these youngsters don't even know where Panda-ma-tenka is!" And she sang a song about the place, which had a short-lived fame between about 1880 and 1888. By mid-1963, however, she kept more and more within her house, cried about her aches, and complained of neglect and the noise of the children. People in the village began to dwell on the trials of the old when they spoke of Siagondo.

She died in 1964, having seen her great great grandchildren.

Martha

Martha was born in 1897. In 1956 she was a widow who had separated from her inherited husband and moved to the homestead of a lineage kinsman with whom her younger son had settled. Her older son was away at work and her daughters were married elsewhere. Martha was then an active woman who could hold her own in any interchange, using her bawdy tongue to great advantage. Her kinsman had given her a small field, her son had built her a house, and she had a few chickens. She was poor but self-supporting.

During the relocation her lineage kinsman and his children were permitted to join another village in the old area, but Martha was moved with her fellow villagers, including her son. During the resettlement year she was persuaded to marry an elder of her own age who undertook responsibility for building her a house and finding her a field, but the arrangement did not work. She then persuaded her son to build a house for her in the homestead of an elder with whose wives she was friendly. After all, she was still an independent woman with her own field, cleared by her son, and a few goats, beholden to nobody except her son for such services as building her house. She begged sweet potato slips and seedling tobacco plants from a kinsman with river gardens and sold the produce when the plants matured. Thus she clothed herself. This was the state of affairs in 1962, when she was 65.

In 1972 she was blind, an operation for cataracts having been a failure. She had moved to her younger son's homestead, which now also housed her older son, who had returned from work and was so disabled from a stroke that he could do little more than drag himself about. Her house was a tumbledown structure formerly occupied by her son's family. Her daughter-in-law fed her and sometimes gave her a worn dress or blanket. She still owned seven goats and occasionally sold animals to get money for clothes. A grandchild led her about while she fulminated "The people of this village are evil. They have used sorcery against me. This village is evil." She quarreled with her younger son, a day-laborer who could be brutal when drunk, and tried the patience of her daughter-in-law and grandchildren. Constantly she begged to be sent to a married daughter, thinking that somehow this would cure her troubles, but the other women of the village admonished her against the foolishness of thinking her daughter's husband would welcome her. At 75 she was a trial to herself and others.

Esther and Timothy

Timothy was born in 1896, Esther, his wife, in 1913. In 1956 they lived as members of a large compact homestead headed by another man. Timothy had already divorced one wife, who had become a leper, and their children lived with their mother or their mother's brother. His children by Esther were beginning to mature: a married son lived with them, a daughter was married elsewhere in the village, another daughter was ready to elope, and a small son was approaching adolescence. Timothy had both small stock and claims on elopement damages and bridewealth for the daughters of his two marriages. Both he and Esther were good workers and they had adequate fields. Timothy was a jolly fellow—he was not overwhelmingly ambitious, but he was well-liked—and Esther seemed content with her lot.

By 1962 they were resettled in a new area. Timothy had built with a crony who was also a lineage-mate. His older son had left the village permanently, but his younger son was old enough to help with the field work. His daughters were married and Timothy was still receiving payments from his sons-in-law. He had been able to acquire cattle and a plow, and his remaining son plowed for him. He had a small tobacco field that brought him a cash income. Timothy and Esther therefore lived in some comfort. Timothy himself spent much time at beer parties or in visiting. Esther, who was still fully active, was resentful of the signs of middle age. Her affairs with younger men led to family fights, but these were patched up and the couple went on. A young granddaughter had come to live with them to help Esther with her work.

In 1972 Timothy and Esther had their own homestead, which included their younger son, now married. They were joined by an elderly widow who needed a place to stay but added nothing to the homestead strength. Timothy still owned three cattle and some goats, but he was growing blind and did little or no work. Plowing was left to his son, who had become an alcoholic. Esther did much of the weeding and harvesting. It was she who grew and prepared the tobacco for sale, though Timothy claimed the proceeds. Esther complained more and more of their poverty, the state of her wardrobe, and the lack of a decent standard of life. Timothy and Esther quarreled frequently and bitterly. Both spent much time at beer parties. Esther at one point was determined to leave her husband. She said she was tired of his abuse and too old to have to work so hard carrying water and stamping grain. She intended, she said, to sell her groundnuts to raise money to join her older son, who lived in town. There she would not have to work hard or suffer ill treatment. An old man who commented on the matter said a man was foolish to abuse a wife when he was old since he would never be able to find another wife if she left. That time the quarrel blew over, but a good many signs indicated that Esther, now 60 years old, was impatient at having to care for her increasingly decrepit 76-year-old husband and was preparing to abandon him to his son or to such kin as would assume the burden. She had already accused him of responsibility for the death of at least one grandchild, implying that his medicines were draining life from their descendants to support his own.

Conclusion

The Gwembe Tonga are an egalitarian people who do not idealize any position in life with the possible exceptions of being the head of a vibrant independent homestead or household (for men) or the progenitrix of a large lineage (for women). Old age as such is not respected; indeed, growing old is distressing, for even the active elder tends gradually to lose control over dependents and resources, while inactive old people of both sexes are the first to suffer when crops fail and times are hard.

Although care of the elderly is as much a kinship obligation in the 1970's as it was in the 1950's, the position of the very old changes as different events affect their circumstances. On the one hand, old men and women in the 1970's have not been subject to the stress of forced relocation, as were the old in the late 1950's. On the other hand, they have less influence than the old did in 1956. They were not young enough during the resettlement years to overcome the losses associated with the flooding of their old habitat and the outmoding of their specialized knowledge. Moreover, the gap between old and young has widened since Zambian independence, influenced by the increased educational opportunities for the young and the accelerated movement of young couples to town.

Nonetheless, by 1973 rising standards of living in the village had increased the physical security of the elderly. At the same time, occupational specialization and economic opportunities had increased, and an increasing proportion of junior elders were accumulating a wider variety of resources upon which they should be able to draw in old age to give them a greater claim for respect from younger members of the community.

Respected Elder or Old Person: Aging in a Micronesian Community

JAMES D. NASON

For most if not all human beings, the passage of time is most read-ily perceived in the changes that occur as individuals age and die. It is in this process that conceptions of human life qualities, statuses, and roles are established, lived out, and transmitted to succeeding generations. Earlier researchers have demonstrated that neither the perception of time nor the qualities assigned to it are universal. Even the inevitability of death as a natural result of individual aging is not universally accepted (Lee 1959, Athos 1968, Levy-Bruhl 1966, Carroll 1956). This paper will examine the manner in which the members of a small atoll community in Micronesia classify and live through life stages, focusing particularly on how people become "old." In this community there is no single status for the senior members, but rather a number of possibilities depending on com-munity regard, other ascribed statuses, and the combination of past experience and present state of health.

The Community

Etal Island is located at 5°34'N, 153°35'E, about 257 kilometers south of Truk in the Caroline Islands. It is the smallest of the three atolls that make up the Mortlock Islands group in Truk District and has a total land area of only 189 hectares. Only Etal Island proper—the largest of the atoll's fifteen islets—has ever been in-habited, and it appears that the population has probably never ex-ceeded 500 to 600 (Nason 1975). Life on Etal before contact with the West was strikingly similar to that on most other Micronesian atolls. The community was organized into a single village with homesteads on the lagoon side of the island. These homesteads were the property of one or another of the eleven matrilineal clans in which all island residents had membership by birth or adoption. The clans were named and ranked, corporate, and dispersed among many islands, and they provided the traditional framework for social and political organization. The eleven male clan chiefs constituted an island council, with the chief of the highest-ranking clan being the paramount chief of the island. He was also the leader of one of the two territorial districts into which the island was divided, the chief of the second-ranking clan being the leader of the other. The island council, acting in concert with all adult members of the community, met regularly to consider the affairs of the island and reached decisions by consensus (Nason 1974).

Thus an islander's primary social identifications were first with the island (in a sense analogous to our notion of citizenship), then with a district, and finally with a clan and a specific lineage and homestead within that clan. The island was a politically autonomous entity, but maintained close ties with other island communities by trade and intermarriage, and was also a member of one of the two military alliances that divided the Mortlock group. Maintaining these interisland relationships was an important survival strategy for a community with limited land threatened by occasional devastating typhoons, since they expanded the functional resource base of the island.

The subsistence economy was based on a combination of land and sea resources exploited by the cooperative labor of men and women. The idea of cooperation, particularly between fellow clan members, was generalized into behavioral rules that underscored a fundamentally egalitarian ethic. Even chiefs, whose role conferred power and demanded deference, were expected to contribute economically to the society as long as they were physically able. The same principle forbade behavior that might be interpreted as haughty or arrogant, aggression (whether physical or verbal) against another member of the community; and arbitrary decision-making by chiefs or other adults. The value of cooperation was expressed in the generalized notion that one should think of the interests of the island and of one's clan before personal interests. This cooperative concept, at least in its normative sense, stems from values that are inherent in and central to family life and labor at the lineage level. In normal day-to-day life, traditionally, one is naturally expected to attend to one's family business and concerns. The difference pointed out here, however, is that a lineage head or clan chief would not ordinarily direct his group's affairs without regard to island or clan interests.

Cooperative labor was the foundation for most subsistence tasks. Men performed most of the heavy labor involved in planting gardens and in building, and they conducted mid-lagoon and deep-sea fishing. Women were expected to assist in the regular maintenance of the gardens, to contribute matting and roofing for buildings, and to be responsible for reef and in-shore gathering and net fishing. The chiefs served as managers of community labor. A paramount chief could assign a task to the entire community, a district chief to the half of the village making up the district, a clan chief to the members of the clan, a senior male head of an extended family household or lineage to the group's men, and that senior male's wife to the group's women.

Land was the most valuable commodity. According to legend, the two top-ranking clans had been the first to settle the island, and they maintained a residual title to the properties they gave as gifts to other clans as they arrived and became established. In recent times, however, clans began to grant individual members full title to land, and pieces of clan land might also be used to buy canoes, pay for services to clan members (e.g. healing), or be transferred to other clans as part of a marriage settlement or indemnity payment. Thus, although the bulk of lands were owned by clans, most adults also came to receive some property outright from their parents, despite the fact that they might not gain full title until the parents were quite old.

In traditional religion the world was an inverted bowl: the islands floated on a flat surface of water, and the heavens arched above in layers containing the fixed and immovable stars. The upper heavens were the homeland of the gods who had created the world (and since withdrawn from active interest in earthly affairs). In the lower heavens lived the deities of the sea, of war, and of such specialized activities as fishing and weaving; there, too, resided the all-important spirits of the dead. It was primarily to these ancestor spirits that people turned when faced with illness or disaster. Furthermore, these spirits were guardians of the moral order who punished members of the clans for transgressions such as disrespect to the chiefs, neglect of parents or other kinfolk, and acts of intra-island aggression. Although clan chiefs symbolically linked the living and the ancestral spirits, they used the services of spirit mediums chosen by the ancestors to invoke the advice or intercession of the spirits. There were also land and sea spirits who were almost always malicious and best avoided entirely. Spirits might cause illnesses, which could be diagnosed by knot diviners and treated by herbal specialists or practitioners of other sorts.

Life on Etal began to change from the moment of first significant contacts with Westerners in the early 1870's. Successive political suzerainties of the Spanish, German, Japanese, and American governments produced many alterations, with the most fundamental occurring after the Second World War (Nason 1970). Today the political and religious roles of the clan chiefs have been largely supplanted by an introduced Western political structure of magistrate and elected island council, and few remnants of the traditional religious system have resisted the total conversion of the population to Christianity. The clan system is only important now in the regulation of marriages. The cooperative clan-based economic system has been largely replaced by a more individualistic approach within the context of a combined market and subsistence system. These and other changes have altered many of the idealized and normative forms of social interaction, especially the nature and extent of obligations between clan mates. Nonetheless, other basic elements of the social order and the values associated with them have remained relatively untouched. A good example of such a persistent pattern is the manner in which age and aging are viewed by members of the community.

Concepts of Age and Aging

As we can see from Table 1, the people of Etal have a fairly specialized set of terms for age categories, which for convenience I have broken into four Western groupings: child, young adult, adult, and old person.

Childhood

The category "child" is used to refer to all infants and children from birth to about age 14 for girls and 16 for boys. The term applied to babies, *monukon*, meaning children from birth to one year of age, can be roughly glossed as "lying down," referring to a baby's inability to crawl or walk. The first year of life was a period of great danger and uncertainty, especially prior to the 1950's, since infant mortality was a serious problem. Even today the first birthday is marked by a celebration that acknowledges this first important

TABLE 1. Western and Etal Age Categories Compared

Western age category	Etal age category		No. of individuals	
	Male	Female	Males	Females
Child	*monukon* (0–1)	*monukon* (0–1)	10	8
	semirit at (2–16)	*semirit nengin* (2–14)	75	59
Young adult	*anuwon* (16–25)	*fopun* (14–25)	15	22
	anumwan (25–28/32)	*mesefefin* (25–28/32)	9	9
Adult	*mwan* (28/32–40/45)	*fefin* (28/32–40/45)	19	26
Old person	*chinnap* (40/45–60)	*chinnap* (40/45–60)	14	28
	atewoch (60–)		11	

SOURCE: Population data are from the author's census of Dec. 1, 1968, and include only native residents.

NOTE: The total number of males was 153, of females 152; note that what we would simply call children made up fully half of the island's population, and that old people made up about a sixth of the population.

turning point in the child's life. It is, in fact, the only birthday as such that is likely to be noted, partly because until recently, at least, few people knew or cared when they were born, and partly because calendar age is still less significant than the shifts from one age category to another as denoted by changes in status and role.

Childhood in general is a time for fun and frolic, for learning the basics of social life and etiquette, and for beginning to acquire those skills that will be necessary for adult life. Young children are greatly indulged and as a rule spend their time playing. The basic term for child, *semirit* ("not understanding"), implies that children lack the knowledge and comprehension fundamental to proper behavior. The word *fitigogo*, "childish," means behaving without respect for the established rules of social conduct. One should not fight with another member of the community, or be arrogant, selfish, uncooperative, or loud, and anyone acting in such a way would be called *fitigogo*. For a child to be *fitigogo* is tolerable; for an adult to be is not. Children are rarely physically punished because of the widespread notion that there is no point in trying to teach what may yet be unteachable. A child's parents, siblings, grandparents, and other relations care for, feed, instruct, and, in the case of grandparents in particular, spoil the child. The more specific terms *semirit at* for a boy and *semirit nengin* for a girl refer to prepuberty status, which ends when a boy is about 16 and when a girl has her first menses at about 14.

As boys and girls approach the end of childhood they must demonstrate that they are becoming useful and knowledgeable members of the community in a number of ways, ranging from showing a command of etiquette—including the proper use of kin terms and chiefly titles—to taking a more active part in the economic life of the home and community. Boys will have begun fishing, either alone or with friends, as well as helping with the gathering and processing of plant foods. Girls will have begun to assist their mothers in gathering and preparing food, in caring for younger siblings, and in other household tasks. Both older boys and girls would be expected to help care for older relatives, particularly grandparents, and may take up full-time residence with them. As an active interest in the opposite sex develops at the end of childhood, brothers and sisters must begin to avoid each other according to the formal rules of island etiquette.

Young adulthood

Young adult status has two distinct phases for both males and females. The first of these lasts until about age 25 for both sexes. During this phase, men are referred to as *anuwon*, "wild or untamed spirit," and women as *fopun*, "nubile." For a young woman this is a period of courtship leading to marriage (usually to an older man). She is expected to bear her first children and refine her skills as a food producer, weaver (in former days), and homemaker. Young men will have many love affairs, but most will not marry until they are a bit older, although there is no formal proscription against an early marriage. Young men will instead sharpen their sailing and seafaring skills and devote themselves to fishing and gardening in a serious way. Formerly, they would have become warriors. For both sexes this is considered an unsettling and unsettled phase of life, a period when love affairs and even marriages are fragile. It is a time when young people are expected to be ambitious, but are allowed to be impatient and even vain or lazy. It is also a time when they should be respectful to their seniors in the community as a mark of their own increasing maturity. Between the ages of 25 and 28–32, both men and women are expected to settle down. Men in this second phase of young adulthood are called *anumwan*, meaning "to have the spirit of an adult man." The term for women is *mesefefin*, which literally means to be "before" an adult woman. Men become *anumwan* usually when they marry with the intention of staying married; *mesefefin* is more likely to be applied to a woman when she has borne her first child in what is presumed to be a lasting marriage.

Adulthood

Though divorces may still occur, adult men and women, *mwan* and *fefin*, are expected to have enduring marriages and settled residences and home lives. They are parents and major economic producers, and specialists in areas of esoteric skills and knowledge. It is a sober period in contrast to what has gone before. During this time of life a man may turn his serious attention to any one of a number of specializations, including navigation, canoe or house building, knot divining, healing, commanding long-distance trading voyages, magic of various kinds, or, in the old days, warfare. An adult woman can similarly specialize in weaving fine hibiscus-bark clothing, in healing, and in certain realms of magic. A man may also achieve note by his success as a horticulturalist or as a fisherman. He may earn respect by the propriety of his life and the worthiness of his counsel in island meetings. Similarly, a mature woman is respected for her conduct and her skills in certain types of fishing and in maintaining a household.

The matter of propriety is of no small importance for both men and women, since it is a key measure of adult status in the fullest sense. Of course, parenting and the accumulation and management of property are also critical for adult status. Being a proper parent and a good kinsman, being generous and cooperative, working hard and keeping physically active in useful ways are all behaviors that merit respected adult standing. And the ability to accumulate more property than one had received through inheritance or to obligate others to one makes a person an influential adult in the community. The types of personal adjectives that would commonly be used to refer to a man or woman as indicators of their respected (if not influential) position in the community include, for example, "modest," "temperate," "virtuous," "humble," "industrious," "strong," "lusty," or "brave." Any person of adult age to whom none of these applies would be either not a "good" person or someone for whom others could have no serious regard. Of all of these personal characteristics, "industrious" stands out. Industry is a cardinal virtue because the small size of the community makes it essential that every adult contribute his or her share. Furthermore, laziness is by definition a default on obligations to the immediate family, the clan, the district, and ultimately to the island itself. Even one deficient adult casts a pall over the status of family and clan in a way that may have lasting effects. Finally, the essence of masculinity or feminity for adults is keyed to an active physical life. Thus, being lazy may also be thought to include being weak, cowardly, or intemperate. Laziness not only destroys the foundation of self-esteem as a competent person, but also threatens the ideals that support family, clan, and community.

Old age

There is no fixed calendar date at which time one retires from adult status and becomes an old person, *chinnap*, although formerly by the time one approached the mid-forties "old age" was not far away. Contrary to popular Western beliefs about the ease of life on tropical islands, adult life is strenuous and physically taxing and people are judged old when they can no longer do the hard physical labor required to maintain an active life in gardening, fishing, and so on. At about the same time childbearing or childgetting becomes less likely. A man or woman will begin to find it necessary to transfer strenuous duties to children, grandchildren, or other relations. This certainly does not mean an immediate end to playing important roles in the society; rather, this is a time when the nature of one's contributions changes. An old person has ceased to be a major producer of food (or of children) and has substituted lighter physical tasks and important social, political, and educational tasks. Old people are expected to take a more direct role in the instruction of young adults and children in the finer points of specific tasks or in professional specialities. Grandparents play an active role in supervising, educating, and spoiling grandchildren. But most importantly, an old person begins to turn more of his or her attention to managing property, arranging inheritances, settling conflicts, and maintaining a network of relationships with relatives and associates within and beyond his or her own community.

Being an Old Person

The process of aging itself is regarded as a natural and irreversible process that awaits everyone and leads to an unenviable period of life. There is a sense of foreboding about becoming old that can be traced to the strong desire to remain active and physically important to the community, and to the fear of becoming dependent upon others and incompetent. The motivation to remain active is clearly understandable in that it strikes at the heart of what it means to be a complete man or woman. The fact that the island's economic system is ordinarily (except in times of natural disaster) more than adequate to provide for all residents is of small comfort to one entering a stage of dependency. It is a primary duty of children to support their aging parents, but the vicissitudes of life may rob an older person of children through migration to another island or premature death. Furthermore, though every phase of life has its difficulties, becoming old carries the risk of falling prey to foolish impulses and undignified fears. Old people may be as they were as adults, i.e. generous, humble, temperate, and kind, but they may also become greedy, impatient, envious, and covetous, early signs of mental clouding that will become mental incompetence.

It is worth noting that the same term used to describe the irresponsibility of children, *fitigogo*, is applied to the incompetent or antisocial old. From the individual's perspective, mental degeneration is feared because it means loss of control over one's life and effectively wipes out whatever "credits" were amassed earlier. If an important chief becomes incompetent, for example, he does not actually lose his title but is instead quietly put to one side while his successor increasingly assumes the actual duties and powers of the office.

Though fed and cared for, confused old people are often the butts of jibes or jokes. The joking serves to indicate the ambivalence others feel about them, in part because their incompetence is a threat to their kin and the community at large. The drain on the community's economy is of much less importance than the loss to the community of whatever skills or knowledge they possessed. In addition, for kin the mental incompetence of an old person has serious consequences because it may disrupt the system by which property rights are transmitted.

Respected Elder or Old Person

Whether old age will bring increased respect and continued active participation in the community depends upon four variables: respect achieved as a mature adult; ability or desire to participate actively; specialized knowledge or skills; and control over property. The fact that one has lived longer than others does not in and of itself mean that one has become wiser or more knowledgeable and therefore more respected. A man or woman who was foolish as an adult is not expected to become wise as an elder. It is, nonetheless, expected that most old people will have counsel worth noting since they will have accumulated more knowledge about how people are related, what has happened in the past and why, and why things are the way they are now (at least to the extent that any people can address themselves to the latter). To see the significance of this, we must look at the nature of social interaction in the community.

A person growing up in a tightly knit small village like Etal inevitably learns almost everything there is to know about every other resident. There are, in effect, no secrets about how everyone is related, why certain lands are owned by certain people, and why fights have occurred over these lands. Every fault and foible, every good point and personal characteristic of fellow islanders—plus every major and minor event of the immediate past—make up a pool of knowledge that grows broader and deeper the longer one lives. In a system where precedent and a detailed knowledge of the past are vital to dispute settlement, every old person can potentially command the attention of younger members of the community by virtue of greater knowledge and experience. This is also clearly one way in which old persons can continue to serve society. Naturally, not everyone who is old will be equally knowledgeable or skillful in the use of such knowledge. There is a difference between just being old and being a respected or influential elder.

Furthermore, being a respected elder is not the same thing as being influential. Influence implies some degree of control over the actions of others. People with influence have not only wealth in land but shrewdness of mind and sharpness of practice that have led to control over property and people. An influential person, who may be an adult of any age, may also command others through his or her special knowledge and skills. In the old days, an experienced warrior had influence. These days people believed to control lethal magic can usually get what they want, as can the man whose oratory is powerful enough to move others to action. But to be influential is only tangentially related to being thought a good or bad person, since influence merely gives greater scope to either good or bad actions. A respected person, by contrast, is someone who does not cause trouble. He or she is a good relative and fellow islander and a highly regarded member of the community. Respect comes to those who have lived up to those behavioral ideals that the society has established for adult life.

An older person, however, may combine influence and respect to exert great power in decision-making. The chief is one example of a person whose role commands both respect and obedience. He has the obligation to make decisions about the lands and lives of others. If he has, in addition, lived up to the stringent standards set for proper behavior, standards that ought to apply to every adult, but most particularly to chiefs, he will be genuinely respected. But often respect and influence are not associated. In fact, if we exclude clan chiefs from our consideration, it is interesting to note that adult men on Etal, when asked to say who they most esteemed as opposed to who they thought most influential, produced two lists of names with no names shared between them. Finally, there are the old persons who are without either influence or respect in the community. This category includes older persons who have become mentally incompetent, who are unable or unwilling to take an active part in the social life of the community, who have always been regarded as insignificant, or who have lost the respect and influence they once enjoyed because they have begun to behave badly.

As I mentioned earlier, acting greedy, impatient, envious, or covetous is considered reprehensible in an old person. If such behavior becomes a pattern, it will inevitably negate whatever respect was earned in the past and will be considered an ominous herald of serious trouble for kin and community. The island's basic egalitarian ethic stresses cooperation and generosity, but the actual nature of the social system provides ample opportunities for ambitious and hard-working persons to gain more than their neighbors in a material sense. This is usually accomplished when, as an adult, an individual undertakes the acquisition of a specialist's skill or esoteric knowledge. If one becomes a successful navigator, knot diviner, healer, or canoe builder, for example, one expects to be paid for the application of the knowledge and skill. These specializations are not only significant to the life of the community but also expensive and difficult to learn. There is considerable profit to be made from the exercise or transmission of special skills and knowledge. The navigator gets a major share of the profits of a successful voyage. A canoe builder can demand not only maintenance for himself and his family during construction but also a final settlement in lands and trees. A healer or knot diviner can receive land and other properties as payment for curing a serious illness. Furthermore, knowledge is a kind of clan property, and a skilled senior navigator, for example, cannot teach his art to anyone without approval from the senior members and chief of the clan—even when the would-be apprentice is a clan member. Therefore, old people who possess these kinds of skills and knowledge are valued by their kin and the larger community, since they play essential roles and their accumulated wealth will pass to their descendants. Their loss through incompetence or death would be keenly felt, but their failure to transmit their knowledge to others would be potentially disastrous. Thus an experienced older canoe builder who was jealous of his knowledge and its secrets would be resented for his selfishness, and whatever respect was formerly his due would be lost and with it whatever renown or well-being his clan might realize from his abilities. The same would be true of other specialists.

Older people also gain or lose respect in the community by the way they administer their property. The extraordinary value of land to the island people can be seen in the way they refer to it. An adult calls his land his "food," and his village homestead his "womb." This sense of the value of land is reinforced by the se-

riousness with which land transfers and matters of inheritance are
planned and debated by senior members or the community. Land
disputes are by far the most frequent source of interpersonal conflict, and unresolved land issues may extend over several generations. To know who you are is, in large part, to know which lands
you own or have rights to and by what means they have become
yours.

As we have seen, one may gain property in payment for use of a
skill or special knowledge. There are other ways to acquire full
title: by inheritance from one's parents; by outliving the rest of the
clan; by marriage contract; as compensation for injury (e.g. adul-
tery or assault); or as a gift in recognition of services rendered
(e.g. assuming the care of an older person whose own close kin are
either unwilling or unable to do so). This last case provides an excellent example of how conflicts may arise over the way an old person controls property. It is thought foolish for an old person to dispose of all property—meaning here village or agricultural lands
held with full title, individual trees (trees may be owned even though
one does not own the land they are on), or important objects such
as canoes—because it is almost an explicit statement of intent to
withdraw from active social life in the community, an inappropri-
ate form of behavior, and leaves one even more fully dependent on
others than would otherwise be the case. The continued control of
property is one way for an old person to remain somewhat independent and to exert some control over the way he or she is treated.
An old person who has property need not fear neglect, since if kin
fail others will soon appear, hopeful of receiving the remaining
property as their due reward. Thus most old persons keep at least
some portion of what they own with full title until death. Although
it is rare for an elder to die intestate, it is rarer still for final disposition of property to occur until death appears imminent.

Table 2 illustrates the degree to which old people tend to keep
control over their property. Individuals of both sexes 45 years of
age or older controlled 60 percent of all individually owned land.
Only two men over 45 had relinquished ownership of all of their
property. For older women, however, the pattern is somewhat dif-

TABLE 2. Landowning on Etal Island by Age and Sex
(*All lands in individual ownership in 1968*)

Age	Males		Females		Total	
	Hectares	No. of owners	Hectares	No. of owners	Hectares	No. of owners
0–16	—	—	—	—	—	—
17–25	3.48	1	—	—	3.48	1
26–32	9.31	4	0.90	2	10.21	6
33–44	32.05	17	16.00	10	48.05	27
45–60	40.46	13	11.32	7	51.78	20
61+	34.63	10	5.09	5	39.72	15
TOTAL	119.92	45	33.31	24	153.23	69

ferent, because brothers are expected to care for sisters and land is typically left to sons more often than to daughters. Hence women tend to acquire less land than men and be more willing to turn it over to male kin in old age. It is also worth noting that the average age of all canoe owners was 43, and that half of all the canoes on the island were owned by men over 45. Finally, the average age of the shareholders in the island's cooperative store, a relatively recent innovation, was 41, which is an indication not only of the relative ability of older people to make investments but also of their willingness to risk a portion of their property in hopes of greater profit.

Controlling property until death is, then, one of the primary strategies for successful old age, and failure to use this strategy will make an old person lose respect and appear foolish. At the same time, attempting to hang onto all one's property is also disapproved of, since it deprives adult children of a full social position in the community as responsible property owners themselves. Either extreme can cause serious friction within a family or even a clan, and this situation is not uncommon because men in their late twenties or early thirties want lands at a time when their parents, in their late forties or early fifties, are trying to secure their own positions by maintaining control of property. The conflict this engenders may pass with time, or it may be settled satisfactorily by the intercession of chiefs or other respected persons, or it may be resolved only by the migration of children to other islands. The advent of wage labor is another source of difficulty in this area of parent-child relations. Formerly, it was customary for young people to give everything they earned to the clan chief, a parent or parent-in-law, or the two in some combination. With better education and opportunities for government employment on and off the island, young people are beginning to insist that their earnings are their own. New sources of wealth only exacerbate conflicts over property control.

Illness and Death

Death, like aging, is almost always viewed today as a natural consequence of old age and of the illnesses to which the old are particularly susceptible. A death following a long, debilitating illness is regarded as less of a loss than a death that claims an active, able person, whether young or old. Neither the older traditional religious views nor contemporary Christian beliefs in life beyond death can compensate for the sense of loss on the death of a relative or a highly regarded fellow islander. Though death is not dreaded, it is clearly not anticipated with equanimity. Any illness in an old person may presage death, so all close matrilineal relatives are obliged to rally round, providing every care and expressing concern. This is especially true when the old person believes death is close; then relatives should be willing to sacrifice anything to effect a cure or, failing that, to render all comfort possible to ease the pain of mind and body.

Dying is the last important social act that an old person performs. Prior to death he or she should both forgive and be forgiven for hard feelings over past conflicts. This is also the time when the old person will make final disposition of his or her remaining property—obviously a decision important to kin and other potential recipients, who fear that some last-minute influence might alter the expected division of property. Finally, death transforms a kinsman into an ancestor. Formerly, people believed that the spirits of old people who died angry or dissatisfied with their relatives might well decide to take revenge on them. By the same token, a new ancestor, pleased with the attention given by kin while he or she was alive, and gratified by their obvious display of grief at his or her death, would aid and protect them. Whether or not this is still widely believed, people continue to feel that the dying should pass on in an atmosphere of peace and solicitude.

An old person may also hasten the end to make public protest against real or fancied ill-treatment by relatives. Old men, more often than old women, put an end to life, usually by casting themselves adrift in a small canoe. But old people in general may be driven to suicide by grief over the loss of a loved one (a child or spouse usually), by a failed love affair, or by anger because close kin have neglected or wronged them. To prevent suicide from grief, relatives stay constantly with an old person who has suffered a loss. Should he or she commit suicide, kinfolk not only would be blamed but also would have trouble settling the estate, since suicides make no final disposition of their property. Old people who commit suicide in anger and sorrow at neglect bring even greater shame on relatives, who stand publicly accused of mistreating an old person. By threatening suicide, then, an elder can often quickly straighten out unsatisfactory relations with kin.

Changing Perspectives on Aging and Old Age

A great many changes have taken place on Etal Island and in the life of its community since the Second World War. Some of these were simply continuations of trends that had begun earlier, such as the conversion of the population to Christianity and the alteration of the political system by virtue of the intervention of foreign governments. Many of these changes directly affected the position of the elderly in the community. With the decline of the traditional religious and political systems, for example, the important roles played by clan chiefs—usually older men—faded to the point of extinction. Gone, too, were many of the specialist roles and activities that formerly earned respected status for adult and senior men and women, e.g., navigation, long-distance trading, spirit mediumship and knot divining, magic, and warfare. The influence of wage labor in a Western market economy on changing relationships between young adults and older parents has already been noted. The trend toward mandatory Western-style education has also played its role in this and other changes in island life that have altered the position in which older people find themselves.

Now people are more likely to respect someone for Western education than for careful observance of island mores. Similarly, the control of cash has now become as important as the control of land. Perhaps most important, though, is the fact that improvements in diet owing to larger incomes and imported foodstuffs appear to be acting in concert with improved health care to elevate life expectancy. Between 1948 and 1958, for example, only 11 percent of the island population died at or beyond the age of 70, whereas 34 percent died between the ages of 45 and 69. But in the following decade only 20 percent of deaths occurred between 45 and 69 years of age, whereas 60 percent occurred at or beyond age 70. Thus in the future the island can expect, barring devastating natural disasters, to have a population with a growing number of older persons who will require sustenance and care. Moreover, the implications of this demographic shift go well beyond the obvious economic prospects. Up to now it has been common practice for older islanders to maintain residences separate from those of their children for as long as possible. This has been feasible because grandchildren have moved in to help out as required, but it may clearly become impossible as more young people go off-island for employment and education. Moreover, village boundaries may have to be enlarged to accommodate expanded housing for more old people living longer; and the decline of clan organization, which traditionally took responsibility for the care of older clan members, raises the question of who will look after the burgeoning population of old people. Finally, the purely economic consequences cannot be overlooked in any case where the number of individuals who are dependents is increased, particularly in a setting where the potential subsistence resource base is as limited as it is here (see Nason 1975).

The increase in life expectancy and in the general level of health for adults will surely raise the chronological age at which one becomes an old person. Similarly, the increasing respect for the educated young combined with the possibilities for economic independence through wage labor may well mean marriage and the assumption of adult status at earlier ages than was formerly the case. It is difficult to anticipate the effects of this trend on relationships within the community, but as parents live longer and hang onto their assets longer, while children become adults sooner, conflicts between generations over land are likely to become more frequent and more bitter.

Becoming an old person in the community on Etal Island is a process that may take several forms, ranging from existence as an unremarkable old person to life as an important and respected member of the community. It may also bring about loss of whatever respect or influence a person once had. Indeed, the position of an old person is inherently precarious because of changes in mind and body. The elderly on Etal would appear, on the face of it, to have problems common to elders everywhere. What makes Etal different, perhaps, is the degree to which kin have been expected to render support when needed, and the power of the old to exercise some control in ensuring that support.

Recent economic and political changes, however, are challenging the traditional strategies of this generation of old people at the very time when modern medicine may have lengthened their life spans. For the short term, I predict a period of increased tension between old people and their adult children as the island economy modernizes. However, the next cohort of elders, those who are now middle-aged, will have an opportunity to equip themselves more effectively for old age in modern Micronesia.

Growing in Respect: Aging Among the Kirghiz of Afghanistan

M. NAZIF SHAHRANI

The Kirghiz of Afghanistan, a small community of about 2,000 Turkic-speaking people, live in the high-altitude valleys of the extreme north and northeast of the Wakhan Corridor, an area also referred to as the Pamirs of Afghanistan. They alone have successfully retained their traditional nomadic way of life, for their fellow Kirghiz who live in the neighboring Soviet Union and People's Republic of China have experienced radical change during the past several decades.

The Afghan Pamirs consist of two high valleys running roughly southwest to northeast between the major ranges of the Hindu Kush to the south and the Alchur Range to the north. Once part of the Silk Road, the main highway of trade and communication between China and Western Asia, the Wakhan Corridor, and the Afghan Pamirs are today one of the most remote frontier areas of the Republic of Afghanistan, sandwiched between the Soviet Union to the north, Pakistan to the south, and China to the east. The minimum elevation in the valleys of the Afghan Pamirs is approximately 13,500 feet, and the climate is accordingly severe, with great extremes of temperatures, long, harsh winters, and a brief growing season of less than three months in the spring and summer. Access

This paper was written while I was a postdoctoral Research Fellow at the Center for Middle Eastern Studies, Harvard University. Financial support for the research on which this paper is based was provided by the Foreign Area Fellowship Program of the Joint Committee of the Social Sciences Research Council and the American Council of Learned Societies. I also received a Grants-in-Aid Fellowship from the Wenner-Gren Foundation for Anthropological Research. I want to express my gratitude to all three institutions for their generous support.

to the area where the Kirghiz live involves more than ten days' travel on horseback after the end of motorable roads.

Traditionally, the Kirghiz drove their herds of sheep, goats, yak, and camels to graze in the high valleys of the Afghan Pamirs during the summer months, returning to warmer, low-altitude valleys farther north in the winter. Although sometimes a few households could be expected to remain behind in the high pastures through the winter (seeking temporary sanctuary from officials or rival Kirghiz groups), permanent year-round occupation of the Afghan Pamirs began only in the 1930's, when the Soviets gained firm control over Turkic Central Asia and closed their frontier with Afghanistan. Some 250 Kirghiz households had taken refuge in the mountain pastures of the Afghan Pamirs following the Russian Revolution and for more than a decade had been allowed to graze their herds in Soviet territory in return for fees. However, after the establishment and maintenance of closed border policies by the Soviet Union, these Kirghiz became totally confined to the high valleys of the Afghan Pamirs. In addition to losing their winter pastures to the Soviet Union, these Kirghiz subsequently lost their access to market goods and revenue earned through service to caravan traders traveling through their territory when, in 1949, China followed the Soviet Union's lead and closed the frontier between Chinese Turkistan and Afghanistan.

During 1972–74, when I conducted my research, the Kirghiz of the Afghan Pamirs numbered some 1,825 people living in 333 family/household units (called *oey*). When we compare this figure with the 1921 population estimate of 2,000 given by Mowlana Burhanuddin Kushkaki (1923 : 286–87), we see that over the past half century the Kirghiz have maintained a demographic balance despite the cold, hypoxia, and exposure of their high-altitude habitat. This balance has been achieved with difficulty, however: approximately 30 percent of all children born die during their first year, and another 16.7 percent die before puberty. Moreover, female mortality is high during the reproductive years owing to complications involved in pregnancy and childbirth (Shahrani 1979 : 118–29). Many births are premature—probably induced by hypoxia (McClung

TABLE 1. The Composition of the Kirghiz Population by Age and Sex

Age group	Total	Male	Female	Sex Ratio Male	Sex Ratio Female	Percent of total
0–9	476	234	242	49.2%	50.8%	26.2%
10–19	399	223	176	55.9	44.1	22.0
20–29	289	149	140	51.6	48.4	15.9
30–39	233	130	103	55.8	44.2	12.9
40–49	172	87	85	50.6	49.4	9.4
50–59	108	52	56	48.1	51.9	5.5
60+	148	71	77	48.0	52.0	8.1
TOTAL	1,825	946	879	51.8%	48.2%	100.0%

1969:50)—and premature infants as well as many others are frequent victims of respiratory complications, particularly during the nine-month winters. The Kirghiz diet is poor (particularly during the winter months), consisting chiefly of dried milk products, tea, and bread, and the complete absence of fruits and vegetables contributes to poor health and the high mortality rate. The unsanitary conditions common to the pastoral nomadic life and the lack of any kind of health-care facilities add to the difficulties.

Table 1 shows the composition of the Kirghiz population by age and sex. It is worth noting that in the youngest age group there are slightly more females than males, but that in the subsequent four age groups, which cover the reproductive years, males outnumber females. This suggests the importance of pregnancy and childbirth as a cause of death for women. It is also worth noting that over 65 percent of the Kirghiz population are in their economically productive years (ages 10 to 59), and that only about 8 percent are 60 and over. These figures contrast with the available population statistics from urban and rural Afghanistan, which indicate that less than 50 percent of the population is between 14 and 65, or in the productive years (see Dupree 1970, 1971; CINAM 1973).

Like other Turkic-speaking peoples, the Kirghiz view the process of growing old as one of achieving greater wisdom, respect, and privilege, and so they hope to grow old. The aura of reverence for the old among the Kirghiz finds support in the most basic organizing principles of their society—in their kinship system and in their religion. Kirghiz kinship terms, particularly terms of address, are assigned not only on the basis of sex and generation, and on the basis of categories of lineal and collateral relations (i.e. agnatic, uterine, and affinal), but also on the basis of chronological order of birth. All unrelated individuals in the community fall into three terminologically distinct age categories analogous to those of a person's immediate agnatic relatives. These categories are (1) *chung* (elders), members of ascending generations and senior members of the sibling generation; (2) *teng tush* (age-mates), some members of the sibling generation and some members of the immediate ascending and descending generations; and (3) *yash* (youth), all those who are younger in a person's own, adjacent, and other descending generations. Therefore, male and female *chung* and *yash* are always addressed with appropriate age-specific agnatic kinship terms of address, which are otherwise applied specifically to members of one's own *oey* unit (family and household). Personal names, rather than kinship terms of address, are applied to members of one's *teng tush*, as is common within the Kirghiz *oey*.

Household Economy and the Economics of Growing Old

Membership in an *oey* (the word means both "yurt," the portable felt tent in which the Kirghiz live, and those who live in a yurt— i.e. family/household) is central to the Kirghiz social order, for the high-altitude pastoral way of life the Afghan Kirghiz have adopted requires the cooperation of at least four to six people for the proper management of the herds and the carrying out of daily routines. An adult male and an adult female can set up a herding household, but they will face a constant struggle until they have several male children of working age (about age seven or eight) to help them. We can thus understand why the Kirghiz show a great desire to have a large number of children, particularly boys. Yet children are regarded not only as a source of labor but also as a form of security in old age and even as a means of salvation after death.

About 80 percent of Kirghiz *oey* consist of elementary families (e.g. nuclear families, nuclear families with additional relations, and incomplete families, such as a widow[er] with children). The remaining 20 percent are patrilineal extended and composite (polygynous) families. Authority in the Kirghiz *oey* is in the hands of senior members, with the *oey bashi* (head of household) generally being the most senior male. (In the absence of any adult male the senior female will become head.)* The *oey bashi* exercises complete authority over the household, and represents it in its social relations with the community. In principle, the household head alone owns the family's yurt and its contents, the herd, and any other tangible goods the family may have claim to, and he may dispose of them without the consent of other members. The household head also arranges his children's marriages. An important consideration here is the marriage's potential impact on the future well-being and security of the senior household members: a Kirghiz mother, in particular, wants her daughters to remain close enough to continue to help her, especially when she begins to slow down with age. Hence young women are often given in marriage to members of the same lineage, and preferably to those who camp nearby. By the same token, when a bride is needed for a young male household member, preference is given to a close female relative, since it is culturally assured that she will provide help, care, and respect to her in-laws. As a result, the Kirghiz display very high frequencies of bilateral first-cousin (parallel and cross cousin) marriages and lineage endogamy (Shahrani 1979:158–61). (An added advantage in close kin marriage is the relatively lower cost of wedding festivities and the modest exchange of bridewealth and dowry goods.)

In a household with more than one son, monopoly over the eldest son's labor sometimes ends when he is provided with a wife, a yurt, and animals from the family herds in a form of anticipatory inheritance. Sons are married in the order of their birth, and after the wedding they set up independent households either in the paternal camp or nearby. A very close interdependence between the eldest married son's household and the natal household continues as long as the parents live, but all sons are expected to make and re-

*I found that in 54 households (about 16 percent) senior women either were heads or exercised great authority.

ceive periodic visits to and from their parents and to help them in any way possible as they grow old. As each son marries in turn and sets up his own household, he relinquishes the responsibility of looking after the paternal household to his younger, unmarried siblings, who share the household labor. However, if one parent dies prematurely after the marriage of an eldest son, the newly formed household may be reunited with the paternal *oey* so that the son can look after the widowed parent and his younger unmarried siblings. The youngest son, or an only son, never leaves his natal household. He and his wife and children remain as an integral part of the parental household. On the death of the father, this son inherits the yurt, the family herd, and the camping grounds. Political influence and prestige, however, fall to the eldest son. Kirghiz parents who have only daughters can assure their welfare in old age by an arrangement known as *kuch keyow*, whereby they bring in a son-in-law who will provide them with services for at least seven years and who may be adopted into the household permanently.

Growing up in the *oey* is not substantially different for girls from what it is for boys: girls learn domestic skills and learn to perform certain tasks that fall to women in Kirghiz society, and after about the age of eight they regularly help the adult women. Most girls have to manage an independent household after their marriage, since unless a girl is an only child, or unless she marries a youngest son, she and her new husband will set up their own *oey*. When a daughter-in-law does live with her husband's parents, she is generally expected to work under the authority of the mother-in-law and is given little or no say in the household decisions.

As the first crucial change of status for a Kirghiz woman, marriage is publicly symbolized by wearing a white shawl instead of a red one.* But it is a woman's reproductive success that brings about the ultimate change in her position within the *oey* and Kirghiz so-

---

* The color of female clothing is related to age in many particulars: unmarried girls wear only bright red; young married women exchange their red shawls for white ones but continue to wear bright red until about the age of 35; women of about 35–50 wear more subdued colors, such as various shades of green and blue; and elderly women generally wear only solid colors of gray or blue.

ciety at large, for giving birth to children who survive is the only way a young wife gains permanent membership in her conjugal unit and affinal group. Should her husband die after she has borne children, she may marry a younger brother (junior levirate) or close agnate, or she may remain unmarried and manage the household of her husband's heirs.* Bearing children and rearing them to adulthood is, therefore, the main avenue to higher status, prestige, respect, and security for Kirghiz women. Women without children are unlikely to enjoy emotional or economic comfort in their old age. A childless woman will probably be divorced; or, if her husband should die prematurely, she may join a polygynous household as a junior wife. A polygynous household may result if the first wife bears no children or only girls, or if her children die young. Indeed, most of the 24 existing households with two wives came about at least partly through the encouragement or consent of the first wife in order to ensure children for the household. In one household with three wives, the senior wife had had two children die and had miscarried several times, so she and her husband arranged his marriage to the second wife, who turned out to be barren. A third marriage, contracted for the husband some five years later, produced a child that did not survive and then, happily, a healthy son. All three women share and enjoy the child-rearing tasks.

Plural marriage for the purpose of producing children is a viable alternative only for the rich; for the many poor families who have either no or relatively few children, adoption is the rule. Adoption of both young boys and young girls, particularly orphans of close agnatic kinsmen, is quite common among the Kirghiz. Childless families may sometimes request one or two children for adoption from close relatives who have large families, and relatives sometimes spontaneously offer children to a childless couple. Married couples without children (natural or adopted) have little chance of

* The Kirghiz Islamic laws of inheritance make very limited provisions for the wife of a deceased man. A childless widow can inherit only a quarter of the household property, the remainder going to close male relatives of the deceased. A widow with children receives only one eighth of the property, the children getting the rest. This leaves widows largely dependent for their economic support on male relatives.

success as herders and consequently little chance of reaching a successful old age for reasons that have to do in large part with Kirghiz herding arrangements.

The majority of Kirghiz herds are owned by about twenty households, which allocate their livestock among poor herders under both long- and short-term arrangements. A major determinant for the allocation of animals, especially under the long-term contract known as *amanat*, is the size of the available labor force in a herding unit. For example, a newly married young couple could arrange for 100 sheep and goats and ten or fifteen yak under the *amanat* system, which would give them a living but would not enable them to accumulate capital of their own. However, should they rear several children to maturity, access to a larger herd of, say, 500 sheep and goats and a large number of yak through *amanat* is assured. Such a family also has the option of hiring out one or more of their sons as shepherds, who earn five to ten sheep a year for their services and may thus start their own small herd. By contrast, as childless couples grow older and weaker and become unable to look after herds year-round, they might be able to get only a small number of animals during the spring and summer under the short-term arrangement known as *saghun*, "milk animals," which would not assure them of adequate year-round subsistence.

There are simply no elderly childless couples among the Kirghiz who are economically and emotionally secure. Among the 333 Kirghiz *oey*, only 27 contained just two members (married couples). Of these 27, only two consisted of elderly couples. One, a 78-year-old man and his 60-year-old wife, had produced nine children, all of whom died before the age of nine. They owned only six yak of their own. The other couple, a 60-year-old man and his 55-year-old wife, had had an only son who died at the age of eight. They did not own any animals of their own, but they had access to about 40 sheep and two milking yak under the *amanat* system. They complained bitterly that they did not have adequate labor and that they were at the mercy of their kinsmen, with whom they moved camp. The death of one of the partners will oblige the survivor to join the household of a kinsman, which is always done with a degree of reluctance. My observations lead me to believe that the chances of childless couples reaching old age are very low. Those who survive to grow old will likely suffer from lack of care and attention when they need it most. Successful parents, by contrast, have the assured help and continued services of their growing children, and later they have the guaranteed support and care of at least one of their offspring and his or her spouse and children.

Respect for the Aged

Kirghiz social structure not only provides economic security for the aging but also guarantees a measure of emotional and spiritual security—and above all respect—during the later years. The senior members of the *oey* are never completely retired; they retain their managerial and decision-making privileges over the *oey* and remain active and productive for as long as their physical condition permits, and for as long as they wish. Soon after a man's sons are able to take charge of his herds he begins to transfer herding responsibility to them. Similarly, a woman slowly decreases her participation in daily domestic chores at her own pace as she grows older.

The knowledge and skills of household elders represent a tremendous resource for the young. Old people play a major role in the socialization and care of their grandchildren, and thus are rarely isolated or idle during their later years. Those who reach old age and are fortunate enough to have the support of children and grandchildren spend a great deal of time performing acts of piety such as praying, fasting, reciting the Quran (Koran), aiding the poor and needy, and even making the pilgrimage to Mecca (more than twenty older men and women have performed this religious duty during the past decade alone). Elders are extended a great deal of respect, in accordance with Kirghiz expectations of kinship behavior and social etiquette. When an older person approaches a camp, those who are younger will come out to greet him at some distance from the yurt, help him dismount, tether the horse, and invite him into the yurt. Once inside the house, he is seated in the most comfortable place at the farthest point from the entrance (a place of honor) and served the best available food appropriate to the time of day and season. Similar courtesies are extended to elders leaving the camp. In public gatherings the elders occupy the places of honor, are served first, and are given the choicest portions of food. Younger people are expected to be quiet and attentive in the presence of their elders at all times.

Age is also an important prerequisite to certain political ranks and determines access to economic resources and information. Yet the Kirghiz are aware of the difficulties an exclusive focus on chronological age can entail, as this proverb makes clear:

> Aqel-leg bala wonbeshda bash,
> Aqelsez bala otezga kersa yash
>
> [An intelligent boy at fifteen is a leader,
> An unintelligent boy at thirty is a child].

Age is important, but it is not sufficient in itself to assure anyone a political office. Those who aspire to political rank and social recognition have to demonstrate first their success in learning to perform the role of household head. Thus the rank of Be (camp leader) is generally occupied by the head of the most successful herding unit in a camp or cluster of camps. By the same token, the office of Aqsaqal (lineage elder, which literally translates as "white-bearded") is assumed by the most successful household head within each lineage. The Aqsaqal of the most successful and powerful lineage in turn claims the position of Khan, the head of the whole of Kirghiz society.

All political ranks in Kirghiz society are, in principle, nonhereditary and nonelective. They are assumed by the most likely candidates and legitimated through public consent at each level of society. They are solely the prerogative of senior males, which means that men below the age of 40 and women are usually excluded. Candidates for leadership are expected to have acquired and demonstrated certain personal qualities necessary for the posts, among which are skill in public persuasion and oratory, sound judgment, impartiality, and honesty (in sum, those qualities associated with being a good Muslim). Success as a herder and father is important, too. It takes many years for a man to demonstrate his worthiness for office, and the higher the office the more time it takes.

Let us take as examples three men in leadership roles at different political levels. The first is a Be, a camp leader of about 50 who heads a household made up of his two wives (aged 58 and 26), two sons (24 and 20), two daughters (5 and 2), and one adopted daughter (14). He claims to own 40 yak and two horses and to have access to some 300 sheep and goats from the Kirghiz Khan under the *amanat* system. He claims private ownership of pasturage and has corporate rights over a summer camping site with a number of his kinsmen who camp with him year-round. Two years ago he purchased a plot of agricultural land, and he now harvests about 300 pounds of grain annually. He camps with five households of agnatic kin and is recognized as the Be of this camp and another neighboring one of five agnatically related households. He is older than most, but not all, of the other household heads and is clearly the most successful herder among them. He is able to offer help to the households in his camps when they are in need, and he entertains all visitors. He is known as Ghani Be by everyone. Ghani Be is a relatively articulate, knowledgeable, dignified, and respected man who can read the Quran and Kirghiz material written in Arabic script. His influence is generally limited to his own camps and to some near neighbors. His role as a Be is acknowledged both by the Aqsaqal of Alapa lineage, of which he is a member, and by the Kirghiz Khan.

Our second example is a 70-year-old man named Hait, who is commonly referred to as Hait Be. He is an Aqsaqal, but the Be form is used with his name because he has been the leader of his camp for a long time. Hait Be is the head of one of the two largest Kirghiz households, which consists of fourteen members spanning four generations. He owns approximately 50 sheep and goats, 20 yak, and two horses, and he has access to about 200 sheep and goats from the Khan and another rich herd-owner under the *amanat* system. He owns seasonal camping and pasturage grounds in four areas, and he claims to have brought under the plow the only cultivated land at Langar, on the way to the Little Pamir at an altitude of over

12,000 feet. His household cultivates the land and harvests about 1,500 pounds of grain a year. Hait Be was born to a former slave family (a Chinese father and Kanjuti mother) owned by a prominent member of the Alapa lineage. His family was freed and fully enfranchised as members of the Alapa, the third-largest Kirghiz descent group, with a membership of some 26 households and 140 people. Hait Be is now the undisputed Aqsaqal of the Alapa lineage. Some years earlier he had much larger herds, but he lost the greater part of them through natural disasters and personal misfortune. Highly respected, and regarded as a very persuasive orator and a fair arbitrator, Hait Be accompanied the Kirghiz Khan in 1959 when he traveled to Kabul for the first time to pay homage to the Afghan monarch.

Our third example is the Kirghiz Khan himself, Rahman Qul. He is 62 years old and has married three times, producing eleven children (nine boys and two girls), who range in age from two to 42. His first wife, the mother of his four oldest sons, died fifteen years ago, but his second and third wives (aged 45 and 30, respectively) are alive and live with him. Five of his sons are married, and four of the five reside with him in the same camps year-round. The second-oldest son and his wife live with the Khan's sister, who adopted him during his youth. Two of the Khan's youngest sons (each by a different mother) have been given to their respective maternal grandparents, with whom they live.

The Khan was brought up in an influential household. His father was a literate and highly religious man who was the Aqsaqal of the Qochqar, the largest Kirghiz descent group. (At present, the Qochqar number 35 oey and about 220 people.) He had made the pilgrimage to Mecca, but he was never Khan. He also instructed his four sons in the basic skills of reading and writing. Rahman Qul was the second son, and he married and maintained his own household before his father died in the early 1940's. (His older brother died shortly after his father.)

Rahman Qul began herding with only a few hundred animals, but he was able to build up his herd in a short time. Then Soviet raiding parties undid his efforts in the late 1930's and early 1940's, even taking him prisoner during one raid, with the result that he spent nine months in jail in the Soviet Union. In 1946, following a Soviet raid on his camp, he led most of the Kirghiz in a retreat into the Pamirs of neighboring Sinkiang Province in China, where they spent three years. After the establishment of Communist China in 1949, however, Rahman Qul and his followers were obliged to fight their way back into the Afghan Pamirs. His bravery, good judgment, and military prowess during these exploits earned him the high opinion of his people. Upon his return to Afghanistan he rebuilt his own herd and introduced many innovations to help improve pasturage conditions in general and to regulate the use of the limited available resources in the high valleys. These innovations included irrigating new areas, creating new ponds and lakes, and cultivating fodder for winter use in well-fertilized areas such as winter camping grounds. Rahman Qul is also credited with introducing the system of herd management known as *amanat*, and his tremendous ingenuity over the past 30 years has resulted in a severalfold increase in the Kirghiz livestock population. His personal flock now numbers over 16,000 sheep and goats and about 700 yak, most of which are distributed among more than 135 households under the *amanat* herding arrangement. Many more families benefit from his herds under the short-term traditional herding arrangements known as *sayhun*, "milk animals."

The Khan is without doubt the richest and politically most powerful person in the Pamirs. He has a good command of Persian as well as several Turkic languages, and he can also read and write. He has been to Mecca twice and to Kabul many times since his first visit over twenty years ago. Rahman Qul established good relations with the highest government officials during the monarchy and again during Daoud's republican regime (1973–78), and he was received both by the monarch and later by the president several times.*

The Be, the Aqsaqal, and the Khan all are involved in dispute set-

* The Khan led most of the Kirghiz out of the Afghan Pamirs to northern Pakistan following the Soviet-backed April 1978 coup in Afghanistan. Reports indicate that the Kirghiz decision to leave their territory may have been prompted by Soviet provocation and direct hostilities toward them following the coup.

tlement, generally through mediation and *nasehat* (persuasion), whether individually or in council with other heads of households. The resolutions they arrive at are generally redressive and conciliatory, and are rarely based on punishment. In addition, Be and Aqsaqal represent the interests of their respective groups against other such entities, and the Khan acts as an intermediary between the Kirghiz and the outside world, including the national government of Afghanistan.

Some Specialized Roles of Older Men and Women

The dominant position of the elderly among the Kirghiz results from their effective control of economic resources and political power, which is intimately linked to the great knowledge they have acquired through long lives. In general, old men have an extensive knowledge of Kirghiz oral history, local ecology, and curing rituals, just as old women have special knowledge of certain arts and crafts and are considered especially versed in the problems attendant on births, both human and animal. Let us turn now to some of the roles this specialized knowledge allows older men and women to fill.

One important role for older men is that of *bakhshi*, or ritual curer/shaman. The services of a *bakhshi* are sought to diagnose and cure illnesses thought to be brought about by malevolent *jin*. A prospective *bakhshi* has to develop a relationship with a benevolent *jin* and accumulate ritual knowledge over the years through association with an accomplished practitioner. A person may have a chance encounter with a benevolent *jin*, or an aging practitioner may choose to pass his personal *jin* on to a would-be *bakhshi*, but men under 30 are thought to be unable to "see" a *jin* or establish a friendly relationship with one. All four of the *bakhshi* over 40 are heads of households of from four to nine people, and all are relatively successful herders. They are remunerated for their services, and their special ability is appreciated and admired by most people. Recently, however, some opposition has been aired by the religious purists, including the Khan, who regard such practices as non-Islamic.

Another important role filled by older men is that of *mullah*, or religious teacher. All *mullah* enjoy respect among the Kirghiz, but old *mullah*, who are thought to have great experience and knowledge, are regarded with the greatest respect. In many public gatherings I noticed the Khan defer to an old *mullah* by offering him the place of honor and the first bite of food. The *mullah* teach the young Kirghiz the basics of religion and reading and writing. In addition, their services are sought for all life crises—births, illnesses, marriages, deaths, and funerals—and they assist political leaders at all levels in resolving disputes and conflicts between individuals and groups.

Most elderly Kirghiz men are steeped in their local history and ecology. Several are known for their veterinary abilities and are called in to perform minor surgery upon the animals. And two of the best silversmith-jewelers, known as *usta* among the Kirghiz, are men of over 70 who are going blind. The best *erchi*, or traditional Kirghiz epic-singers, are also older men. The person with the most remarkable repertoire of *er* (epic songs) is a 75-year-old man named Fazil. I recorded a section of an *er* entitled *Olja Bi o Keshim Jan* (after the names of the principal male and female characters in the story), which took more than an hour and a half to recite. Fazil says that he is the only person in the Afghan Pamirs who knows this section of the epic in its entirety, and that he first learned it when he was eighteen. In addition to many standard epics, he recites a number of *er* he has composed himself in memory of some of his deceased relatives and famous ancestors. The *erchi* traditionally played important roles as entertainers during the long winter nights, at weddings, and at funerary feasts; their importance has been undercut in recent years, however, by the advent of transistor radios.

There are no female *bakhshi* or *mullah* among the Kirghiz. There are, however, many older women with remarkable skills in weaving, embroidery, tailoring, felt crafts, and so on, whose competence and ability to transmit these skills to the younger women of the household provide them with security and authority. A few older women who have proven themselves successful mothers are widely sought out for their special knowledge concerning fertility, pregnancy, delivery, birth complications, nursing, and the diagnosis and curing of those conditions and illnesses not attributed to *jin*.

One of the better-known women who enjoys a good reputation is a 60-year-old widow with a number of children and grandchildren. She proved to be an excellent informant on Kirghiz categories of illnesses, symptoms, and cures. Unlike the *bakhshi*, this woman suggested remedies for illnesses ranging from the common cold to tuberculosis that consisted of a wide variety of concoctions and dietary restrictions. The concoctions are mostly made of local herbs and extracts of organs of certain birds and animals. She is frequently consulted on problems of both human and animal health.

Old Age and Death: The Kirghiz View

The Kirghiz view growing old as a process whereby one gains knowledge and wisdom by virtue of experience. They are fully aware of the physical deterioration associated with aging, but they do not acknowledge mental deterioration (beyond an occasional lament over a lapse of memory). Words such as senility have no equivalents in the Kirghiz vocabulary, nor is old age described in negative terms such as "declining years." In fact, those who live long enjoy fairly active lives; people completely confined to the home as a result of old age are virtually unknown. Loss of sight, either partial or complete, is common among the older Kirghiz, but blindness does not terminate active participation in family and camp affairs since young grandchildren act as guides.

The aged in Kirghiz society become more religious, and as a result they seem to experience little or no anxiety about death and dying. (It is worth noting that several men in their late fifties told me they were older—closer to 63, the age at which the Prophet Mohammed died.) Kirghiz funerary and memorial rites have significant implications in this respect, for they ensure salvation for the dead. During funeral rituals the Kirghiz generally give away some of the personal belongings of the deceased as *esqat* (alms or penance for omissions of religious obligations) to gain merit and salvation for the deceased. For those who die old and leave a wealthy household, the amount of goods and livestock given out can be substantial. The survivors of an aged, important person will give commemorative feasts on the third, seventh, and fortieth days after death. Also, the anniversary of the death of a person of consequence was traditionally celebrated by a *mehreka*, which consisted of many days of feasting and playing *olagh tartish* ("goat snatching," a game played on horseback) and the building of a sizable domed structure of sun-dried mud bricks to enclose the tomb of the deceased. Although this practice has been discontinued in recent years, many domed tombs still stand as evidence of earlier *mehreka* held in the Pamirs.

In concluding, I want to emphasize that growing old in Kirghiz society is viewed essentially as a process of growing wise, of gaining in respect and authority. The primacy of seniority among the Kirghiz finds its best expression in the basic socioeconomic and reproductive unit—the *oey*. The small numbers of people who survive the rigors of pastoral nomadic life in a harsh, high-altitude environment to reach old age enjoy their later years in the safety and security of their *oey*. Old age is cherished as a triumph and rarely, if ever, considered a problem.

Growing Old in Rural Taiwan

STEVAN HARRELL

No visitor to the green countryside of northern Taiwan can fail to notice the older residents of the red-brick villages. Gray-haired grandmothers and great grandmothers, dressed in the usual baggy black pants, white cotton shirt, and plastic zoris, move slowly from house to house to hear the latest gossip, or sit on porches or in front rooms dispensing advice, exchanging rumors, or perhaps caring for children whose mothers are doing heavier work. Old men, most often crew-cut, congregate in stores, in each other's houses, or squatting on the ground outside, and talk politics or reminisce. They look well-fed and usually in good shape, and are adequately clothed by their own meager and rather monotonous standards. The more fortunate among them rarely need to do any hard physical work, and those few who do often perform it with a strength and endurance that excites the admiration of the visiting foreigner. Here is a society where old people are respected, treated with politeness and deference, and well cared for. Yet many feel sad and useless. This is especially true for the men, who have experienced a decline in power—if not in respect—from middle to old age. For the women, never very powerful outside the family, the transition is sometimes easier, and old age is usually more pleasant.

Taiwan is of course only one small part of Chinese society. The Chinese who settled Taiwan from the seventeenth century through the nineteenth represent only two of the many regional subcultures of the great mainland empire: the Hokkien of Zhangzhou and Quanzhou prefectures in southern Fujian province, with whom we are mainly concerned here, and the Hakka of southwestern Fujian and northeastern Guangdong. Though they have preserved the linguistic and cultural forms of their mainland Chinese ancestry, the villagers of Taiwan today have behind them a history of two occupations—one by the Japanese from 1895 to 1945, which brought in its train modern education along with agricultural and some industrial development, and another by the Chinese Nationalists, since 1947, which has brought a new system of universal education along with economic changes that may eventually break down the social structure of Taiwan's still quite traditional villages. Moreover, in modern Taiwan the rural villages do not present a cross section, either economically or educationally, of the island's population. In general the rural people are poorer, less educated, and less aware of Western cultural influences than Taiwan's growing urban middle classes. So we must be careful not to equate rural Taiwan with Taiwan as a whole, much less with China as a whole, in its solutions to the problems of aging. Yet neither should we err in the opposite direction, since rural Taiwanese culture today is a vigorous variant of Chinese culture, and may well have much to tell us about the way old people are thought of and behave in other parts of China, at other times in history, and among other social classes.

The Category "Old"

It is difficult to know exactly how to define the Hokkien term *lau*, "old." Certainly people in their 80's and 90's belong in that category; indeed they are objects of real veneration. Anyone over 70 or even 65 is probably considered old, though many at this age are still active both in earning money and in political and community affairs. The transition between middle age and old age appears to come somewhere in the mid-60's for most people, and consists of a series of related changes. Men begin to retire for reasons other than wealth or sickness, and women begin to leave the management of the household, not just the routine chores, to their daughters-in-law. Parents of brothers who have set up separate households show their age by their inability to control the previously joint family. Women let their hair grow gray instead of dying it black, and begin to be addressed as *Ha-pou* ("great-aunt") rather than *obasan*, the Japanese term used for middle-aged women. Men take a smaller and smaller part in the management of family affairs, especially if their sons' sons are approaching maturity. Not all these changes happen to every person at once, but they are all signals of approaching oldness.

By these standards, old people do not constitute a large part of the population of today's Taiwan countryside. In Ploughshare, the village where I spent ten months in 1972–73, only 26 women and 18 men in a population of approximately 700 were over 60 in 1973, only six women and four men were over 70, and only four women were over 80. Of these 44 old people, five—all over 70—were physically or mentally disabled: one female nonagenarian was totally senile, though of sound body, and another was deaf; an 84 year-old woman was blind; and one man and one woman in their 70's had chronic illnesses. The rest were healthy enough to be reasonably active, some of them remarkably so. The 82-year-old lady who was my next-door neighbor used to run up and down the street chasing away the ducks that threatened to befoul her new concrete porch, and the oldest man in the village, a 77-year-old farmer, was widely admired for his ability to contribute to community work projects.

Interestingly, the proportion of old people seems fairly typical for Chinese rural communities. Sidney Gamble, in his 1928 survey of Ding Xian (Ting Hsien), a county on the North China Plain, found 8.5 percent of the population to be over 60 and 3.0 percent over 70 (Gamble 1954:58). Fei Xiaotong (Fei Hsiao-tung) (1939. 22) reported that people over 60 constituted 6.3 percent of the village of Kaixiangong (K'ai-hsien-kung) in 1936, and those over 70 were 1.4 percent, exactly the proportions I found in my survey of Ploughshare. This is true despite the fact that health care services were incomparably better in Taiwan in 1972 than in any part of China in the 1920's and 1930's. Apparently a decrease in infant mortality has balanced an increase in longevity, leaving the actual proportion of old people about the same. But since children constitute a greater percentage of the modern population, old people make up a greater proportion of *adults* in the community now than ever before.

The Chinese View of Old Age

We will examine the position of old people in Chinese society in terms of two factors: cultural ideas about how old people should behave and be treated, and how they actually behave and are treated. We will find that the way people treat the aged is a compromise between the dictates of cultural values and practical exigencies.

Chinese culture places a high value on old age. Veneration of the old is bound up in the Confucian system of social ethics, which underlies most of late traditional Chinese elite social philosophy and which, in modified form, has permeated all classes of society even into modern times. In Confucian ethics, society is seen as an organically interrelated system in which people are expected to play certain roles relative to each other, the end being social harmony to the benefit of all. Traditionally, the relationships considered most vital to the harmonious workings of a society were between ruler and subject, parent and child, husband and wife, elder brother and younger brother, and friend and friend. Most moralists and almost all the common people considered that between parent and child the most important. The parent should act toward the child with (M) *zi*,* "nurturance," and the child should return this with (M) *xiao* "filial piety" or "absolute obedience." Indeed, *xiao* may be called the cardinal virtue of traditional Chinese social ethics. It is an obligation children owe their parents not only as a contribution to a harmonious social system, but as a meager and partial return for the gift of life, a debt that can never be repaid in full.

To be *xiao* means many things, but at a minimum it entails absolutely obeying one's parents, showing them respect at all times and especially in front of others, caring for them in their old age, generating grandsons to carry on the patriline, and performing the rites

---

* Mandarin Chinese terms, romanized according to the Pinyin system, are preceded by (M) on their first usage; Hokkien terms, romanized according to the Bodman system, are indicated by (H).

of ancestor worship for them after they die. The obligation of *xiao* is absolute and for most people outweighs all other bonds of kinship and citizenship. It applies equally to fathers and to mothers, and in the case of a married woman is transferred to her husband's parents, though important ritual obligations to her own parents remain. Even sons who are acting independently would be considered unfilial for doing anything that publicly contravened the wishes of their parents. Since almost all old people are parents either naturally or by adoption, *xiao* is in many ways the most important cultural value contributing to high regard for the aged.

Because the gift of life can never be repaid, the obligation of *xiao* continues after the parents' death in the form of ancestor worship. This entails, among other requirements, carrying out elaborate funeral rites, securing a favorable burial site according to the principles of geomancy, placing an ancestral tablet on the home altar, and providing sustenance through daily incense offerings and through food and mock-money sacrifices on holidays and deathday anniversaries. Neglecting the rites of ancestor worship is said to bring severe supernatural retribution upon the descendants' families (Ahern 1973). In short, skipping an offering or leaving out a tablet constitutes a fundamental breach of basic social relationships, tantamount to forgetting to feed an aged and helpless parent. Even those who doubt that ancestors actually come to eat the food offered them on holidays, or that illness can be caused by ancestors angry at being neglected, still regard ancestor worship as a legitimate extension of the fundamental obligation of *xiao*.

Moreover, the high valuation of the aged in China extends far beyond respect for one's own parents. Chinese culture traditionally has had many symbolic ways of emphasizing the high status of old people. To begin with, the very word "old"—(M) *lao*, (H) *lau*—is a mark of respect. A government official or a head of household was always referred to by inferiors as (M) *lao-yeh*, "old master," in the same way that teachers even today are called (M) *lao-shi*, "old teacher," even if they are young high school graduates standing in front of a classroom for the first time. To address a middle-aged or older man as (M) *lao xiansheng* or (H) *lau sien-si:*, "old Sir," is positively flattering, in contrast to the merely polite (M) *xiansheng* or (H) *sien-si:*, "Sir." In Hokkien usage even parents are most politely referred to as *lau-be* or *lau-bu*, literally "old father" or "old mother."

In addition to linguistic customs there are many other cultural forms that express veneration for age as such. For example, in contrast to Western practice, birthday celebrations are held only when there is something noteworthy to celebrate, that is on the 60th, 70th, 80th, 88th,* and 100th birthdays. These are days of great honor for the person feted, and banquets often involve a hundred or more guests for a ten- to twelve-course meal. Relatives, friends, and politicians present gifts of scrolls bearing phrases praising longevity, and pigs may even be sacrificed to the Heavenly Emperor, a ritual performed only on the most important occasions. In lineage communities in other parts of China, the formal ritual leadership of local lineages devolved upon the eldest member of the most senior generation of the group, and banquets associated with ancestral rites were often restricted to males of 61 years and older (Baker 1968 : 65, 68). Such formal gestures of respect are accompanied by an attitude of general politeness to old people in everyday situations. Very young people especially are expected to speak politely, to defer in conversation, and not to disagree in any but the most circumspect terms with those older than themselves. Naturally, there is a difference between the respect owed to one's parents and that owed to other older people, especially non-kin. The first is an expression of *xiao* and an absolute obligation, the second a mere courtesy though one taken very seriously.

This pervasive respect for old age confers many advantages on old people. First, they are ensured as physically comfortable an existence as possible, for it would be shameful as well as a breach of *xiao* to neglect their needs for food, clothing, or medical care. Second, whatever people may actually think of their own and others' parents, they never ridicule or insult old people for being old-fash-

---

* Since the Hokkien word for "nine," *kau*, is homophonous with *kau*, "dog," any birthday containing a "nine" (i.e. 89 through 99) is considered unlucky and avoided.

ioned or losing their mental acuity. Third, the family-centered nature of care for the aged means that old people are always active participants in family and community affairs, and have daily contact with younger adults and children both inside and outside the family. A common Taiwanese stereotype of Americans is that they consign their parents to old folks' homes, an act that seems to the villagers not so much cruel as nonsensical. In short, the obligations of *xiao*, combined with the many symbolic and conventional aspects of deference to old people, ensure that the basic needs of the aged are taken care of without question, and that old people receive attention and respect from more junior members of the family and community.

But the problem of old people has another aspect. In Taiwanese society, even traditionally, old people had very little actual power in most families. Men who retired from active farming or other work soon lost touch with the family economy, and younger men in their middle years rose to positions of prominence in the family, especially after brothers divided their households and patrimony. In the community the younger generation, thanks to their greater vigor and activity, took over most local political offices. With modernization, the old have become increasingly marginal; not only are they making little contribution to the economy, but they may even be totally ignorant of the new commercial and industrial contexts in which their juniors work to bring the community the increased prosperity of today. In this situation, juniors must see to it not only that their elders are respected and cared for, but that they do not interfere too much in the economic and political activities of their children's families and the community.

We shall next examine the ways in which the old people, though respected and deferred to, are eased out of power and the kinds of reactions they have to being "kicked upstairs." We must consider the two sexes separately, for growing old is quite different for Taiwanese men and women. Paradoxically enough, women, who are unquestionably treated as inferiors and even oppressed from childhood through middle age, are usually happier and less lonely in their final years than their once-powerful husbands and brothers.

Becoming an Old Man

Let us, then, first outline the process of Chinese family organization from the standpoint of its male members. Ideally, in each generation a conjugal family of husband, wife, and children will grow
first to a stem family, consisting of parents, a married son with wife
and children, and unmarried sons and daughters; and then to a
joint family, where parents live together with two or more married
sons and their wives. Not every family will attain this ideal in each
generation, and of course those families in which the parents die
before or soon after their sons marry are irrelevant to a discussion
of aging. Other families will reach the stem stage but never become
joint, either because they have only one son or because only one
son remains at home after his marriage. But we can take the typical
experience of the division of the joint family as a prototype of what
happens when fathers are displaced by their sons.

The joint family is above all a solidary economic corporation for
property management and the control of production and consumption; as such, its most powerful figure is the one who redistributes
the earnings of the various members (Cohen 1976). This is most
often the senior male, the father of the married sons. As head and
redistributor, the father in the prime of life exercises firm control
over the entire family economy. At the same time, the father may
represent the family in formal and informal village political affairs,
and have contacts with other local family heads and with important political and business figures outside the village community.
The power of the father is eventually undermined, however, primarily by the breakup of the joint family structure. The sons, though
they are members of the joint family, are also members of smaller
and more intimate conjugal units consisting of themselves, their
wives, and their children; ultimately these nuclear family units will
separate, each forming a household of its own. They will divide
their property and their budgets, and will construct separate cooking stoves and no longer share food with each other. They may, for
all this, remain in the same house, or some or all of them may build
new houses or additional rooms if the old quarters are too crowded.

There are several aspects of the structure of the joint family that lead to its eventual division. For one, daughters-in-law usually are more than eager to emerge from the strict and often unpleasant control of their mother-in-law. Also, since joint family income is distributed more or less *per capita* but patrimony is divided *per stirpes* (equally among the sons), it is likely that smaller conjugal units within the extended family will be eager to divide in order to get a larger share of the family income (Cohen 1976:196). Further, grown sons themselves establish political and social contacts, making them less dependent on their father's representation; thus once the sons have decided to leave the joint family, their father is generally powerless to stop them. When an old man's sons have divided, his position in the family is destroyed, and usually with it his position in the community.

To be sure, the old man will be cared for in one way or another, and in most cases will continue living where he always has. Three kinds of solutions are common. First, a share of the inheritance may be put aside for the retired parents as (M) *laoben* (old-age capital). This money may be given over to whichever son's household the old people decide to eat with and used to provide for their needs. Alternatively, if both the parents are alive and reasonably able to fend for themselves, they may simply take their *laoben* and run their own household with it. Finally, there may be no provision for *laoben* in the division of the property, but the aged parents may simply rotate between the households of their sons on a monthly or semiannual basis, or may live in their own quarters but eat with the different sons in turn. These rotating solutions are particularly common where sons, after dividing, continue to live in the same building.

At the same time, the old man will be offered the deference and respect—formally at least—that accrue to the aged in rural Taiwan. People will be polite to him, take him into conversations, compliment him. If he reaches an important birthday, his sons may spare no expense to throw a tremendous bash and arrange to have him showered with commemorative scrolls from far and wide. Never mind that their motive may be to increase their own political contacts and to create and reinforce webs of mutual obligation with their own important friends and associates. If the old man is still physically active and mentally acute, he may receive a certain amount of genuine esteem from younger members of the community. For example, the oldest man in Ploughshare, a 77-year-old farmer, missed no opportunity to be in the middle of things by helping at public occasions. One thing he liked to do was put up the stage for operas; another was lead a funeral procession to the grave, scattering the requisite mock-money to appease the ghosts along the path. I once heard a young man say to several other young men, "Look at old Ti:—he's almost eighty and he can still do more work than we can." He could not, of course, but they admired him nevertheless.

On the other hand, an old man who can no longer do physical work is most pitiable. I remember clearly a scene in a Taiwanese farming community where I did a summer of fieldwork. At the time of the rice harvest, my assistant and I were approaching a farmhouse when we saw a stooped-over, gray-haired man emerge and walk slowly along the field-path with a sickle in his hand. We thought it a little strange, but said nothing and entered the house to ask questions about ancestor worship. We were told that only grandfather knew the names of the remote ancestors, and that he had just gone to help with the harvest. We had to wait only a minute before grandfather returned with his sickle. Clearly, the harvesters had informed grandfather that he should not trouble his venerated self with such taxing work, and he had recognized that he was impeding their work and reluctantly departed. Because grandfather turned out to be quite deaf and perhaps a little senile, it is not strange that he was not allowed to help. But the interesting thing is that he tried, knowing full well that his bent-over body would be of little use in cutting rice. He went, I think, because that is what able-bodied farmers do: they work in the fields. He was sent back not only because he was physically frail, but because he had reached the point where his opinions in this context no longer mattered.

One might think that old men, removed from positions of authority, could take consolation in the support and respect they receive from others, but this seems to be only partly true. Respected they may be, but they are rarely loved by their juniors. This lack of affection, paradoxically, stems from the nature of the ordinary peasant interpretation of the father-son relationship and its embodiment of the virtue of *xiao*. To have a filial son is so important that one cannot afford to be gentle or understanding with him. To make children respect you, you must make them fear you (Wolf 1970: 44). Having filial sons to provide necessities in old age is too important to leave to chance; any leniency, it is thought, may give children the erroneous impression that their parents are soft and tempt them to fudge on their filial obligations. A mother's remonstrances to her sons are nonetheless typically tempered with affection and tenderness, but a father's seldom are. By the time sons reach their teens, they typically talk to their fathers only when necessary, and rarely converse freely with them. The harshness and distance in this relationship are particularly marked in the farming family, where the father will eventually yield his control of the family estate to his sons. The father may resent his sons for their potential usurpation of what he regards as his rightful place, and the sons for their part may resent their father for keeping them from exerting their own authority as heads of individual families. Stern detachment may work for the father as long as he heads the family; the chances are his sons will behave in a filial manner. They may even provide for him generously when he becomes too old to make decisions for the family. But they will not love him, and when he does become old, frail, and powerless, they will probably avoid him.

An old man, of course, comes in contact with other younger persons besides his sons, but his relations with these others are even more severely limited. His daughters are of little concern to him once they pass early childhood, and most marry out long before their father becomes really old. When a married woman visits her parents' home, she often speaks fondly of seeing her mother and brothers, but seldom mentions her father at all. And a daughter-in-law traditionally offers her father-in-law very little—good care and some deference, but certainly no companionship.

To whom, then, do old men turn for companionship, or just to pass the time? Primarily to their own age-mates: to friends, sometimes wives, and occasionally sisters. Cronies are perhaps the greatest source of companionship for old men in rural Taiwan; many groups of old men can be seen sitting by the hour in front of the ancestral tablets, or squatting outside in good weather, exchanging thoughts and reminiscences. Occasionally, as well, old men can simply join in the general men's conversations that take place on front porches or in butcher shops, but they will be listened to less attentively than the younger men.

Old men sometimes also find relationships with their wives and sisters quite satisfying. A man and his wife may not have got along at all well when they were young and the man's mother was part of the picture. And indeed there was no particular expectation that they would get along. As long as the man and the working members of his family supported his wife, as long as she did the requisite chores, as long as the babies kept coming, little else mattered—not sexual satisfaction, not friendship, certainly nothing resembling the Western concept of romantic love. But old couples with basically compatible personalities often grow close as they grow old. Their lives change—the family divides, the man's jealous mother is no longer there to guard her son from the intruding daughter-in-law— and their common interests bring them together emotionally. Old couples sitting together talking are a familiar sight in Ploughshare, and in some cases the close relationship begins to develop while they are still heads of a joint family containing their undivided sons.

Brother-sister companionship is rare, simply because most women marry out of the village and seldom see their brothers afterward. But separated brothers and sisters often speak fondly of one another, and the closeness of feeling between elderly brothers and sisters who did reside in the same village was always quite striking to me. There were two such pairs in Ploughshare, and the members of each seemed to be nearly inseparable. One widower in particular was nearly always to be found at his sister's house, which he had built free of charge, and often went with her to gather firewood or pick tea on her mountain land. It seems that men often have fonder childhood memories of their sisters than of their brothers, since their sisters were never their rivals for the family estate. So sisters, like wives, make good old-age companions if one gets along with them and they are nearby. But not all old men are so fortunate as to have compatible wives or nearby sisters; for most, companionship is found primarily in their aged male friends.

Becoming an Old Woman

The aging experience of Taiwanese women is very different. Basically, as a woman grows older her lot improves. As a young daughter-in-law, recently married into her husband's family, she is the lowest of the low. Her mother-in-law resents her claims on her son's affections and assigns her the dirty household tasks that she herself had been assigned by her own mother-in-law a generation earlier. Even if her husband likes her, it is not good form to pay too much attention to her; and of course he may not even like her.

As she matures, however, she undergoes several changes in her social position that directly affect her status and comforts as an old woman. First, she becomes mother of a son, either by birth or by adoption. This is significant both because she gains a modicum of respect from her husband's family, and because she now has a lever, a potentially powerful adult male whom she will eventually attempt to control. Second, she gradually becomes accepted by those informal conversation groups and gossip networks that Margery Wolf calls the "women's community" (1972: 37–41). Third, when her son marries she herself gains a daughter-in-law to whom she can in turn assign the heavier work around the house and at the laundry ditch.

But most important in understanding a woman's position in old age is the growth and maturity of her son. As many writers have pointed out (Wolf 1970: 43; Yang 1945: 128), a mother, unlike a father, disciplines her children with a mixture of fear and affection. Hopefully the boy will learn to respect and defer to his mother, and she is not above threatening him in the crassest terms and beating him soundly on occasion. But she does not feel so constrained to be cold and distant with him as his father does, and this makes a difference when she grows old. Whereas a father's authority over his sons weakens severely when the household divides, the mother's hold on them, based partly on affection, declines much less. Many middle-aged men seem genuinely fond of their aged mothers, and often sit and talk with them during leisure hours. A woman understandably grieves when her sons set up separate households; after all, she no longer has daughters-in-law to boss around. But she retains their support and affection, and that makes her loss of authority a lot more bearable.

The arrangements for material support of an old woman in Taiwan are similar to those for an old man. If able-bodied, she may be left with *laoben* to fend for herself, especially if she is difficult to get along with. Together with her husband, or alone if she has been widowed, she may be rotated from son to son, eating with each for a specified interval. If mother and son live in the same building or within walking distance, this works well enough; it works less well where an aged mother is forced to walk many miles every few months to stay a short while with a son in another village or in the city of Taipei. If an old lady remains in the same house with one of her sons, she will almost always insist on taking the oldest, most run-down rooms for her own. Most seem to care very little for material comforts; they wish only that the headaches or the back pain would go away or that they could see as well as they used to. Perhaps because Chinese women never had much power in the first place, the deprivations of old age seem less hard on them than on old men.

Keeping busy may also lighten the burden of being an old woman. If she can no longer perform heavy domestic tasks, such as doing the family laundry or hauling water, she can still be a help around the house. She can mend, if her eyes are good; she can sweep and tidy up; she is usually delighted to care for the grandchildren while her daughter-in-law sweats at the spring or the well; and she can cook an occasional meal if she feels like it. In short, unless she is actually disabled an old woman can feel useful, and this probably contributes to the relative ease with which women experience growing old.

A few old women are not merely useful but genuinely powerful in a way that younger women rarely are. These few are the famous matchmakers, the go-betweens for both traditional arranged marriages and modern "love marriages," both of which still involve complex ceremonial exchanges between the bride's and groom's families (Wolf 1972:112–13). The old woman with bound feet who dresses down the most powerful man in the community in Margery Wolf's *The House of Lim* (1968:139) is not exactly a typical female octogenarian, but she is far from unique.

Alternatively, old women can both occupy themselves and gain a certain respect by becoming the nodes of village gossip networks. The 82-year-old great-grandmother who lived next to me in Taiwan had this talent. She would stand in her doorway and invite passers-by to "come sit and chat—I'll bring a bench out for you." Before long, six, eight, or a dozen people would be congregated in front of her house, talking of whatever was current. This woman was in no way powerful—she came from a poor family and had never taken a very active part in community affairs. But she had carved a satisfactory niche for herself, keeping abreast of happenings and having company most of the time; and everybody—old and young, male and female—liked and respected her for what she did.

Finally, old women are freer than almost anybody but small children and village idiots. An old woman can speak her mind without fear of censure on just about any topic; she can go topless in the summer heat; she can sleep all day and stay awake all night. People may get annoyed, but they will not reprimand her. It is as if, having raised her sons to maturity, having given over the household management to her daughters-in-law, having fulfilled her responsibilities, and having given up her authority, she is free at last. And if she is well and able, she will try to enjoy that freedom.

But we should not exaggerate the joys of old age in Taiwan, even for women. My 82-year-old neighbor, a most pleasant old woman and not one to burden other people with her troubles, often seemed sad nevertheless. "I'm old," she would say, "old, sick, and about to die." She frequently spoke of her ailments, though seemingly without complaining: her eyes were no good anymore (this was one reason she gathered followers on the porch rather than watching television inside); she had headaches and dizzy spells; her teeth (a remarkable collection of rather useless-looking enamel and gold dentures) were so bad she could not eat meat or fresh fruit. She had sons and grandsons, she had great-grandchildren, and it seemed a distinct possibility that she would see her great-great-grandchildren before she died. But her old body hurt, and there was little that could be done about that. In this she was certainly not alone; most old people in Ploughshare seemed to suffer from some kind of chronic aches and pains.

Whatever her real or imagined medical complaints, my neighbor, who could still run after ducks and ride straddling the back of her grandson's motorcycle, was essentially of sound body and keen mind. Those who are physically or mentally disabled in old age are another story. A 70-year-old woman who lived down the street had suffered a debilitating illness the year before we arrived in the village. All day long she sat in a wicker chair in her son's front room staring out at the street. Occasionally someone would stop and talk to her, but she barely had the spirit to respond. Sometimes, when the weather was nice, her son would carry her in her chair out into the sunshine; but he and his family were too busy with their knitting business to pay much attention to her. Otherwise, she just sat, as did her neighbor, a formerly active man who had been similarly stricken. The senile, of course, as in all other societies, are the saddest of all. My landlady's 91-year-old adoptive mother was a case in point. On the one hand, this totally wacky crone was a source of amusement to all and sundry. Stories about her made the rounds of the village: once she woke up at 4 A.M. and claimed somebody had stolen all her raggedy hand towels; another time she came home a bit confused and accused her great-grandson of turning their house around while she was out. Everybody laughed, but there was a darker side to her senility that perhaps indicates more than anyone realizes the vulnerability and insecurity of the aged. Two or three times when the old woman was staying in our house, her adopted daughter, our landlady, went to the city and left her children to care for their grandmother. Each time, though they fed her and attended to her needs, the old woman accused her daughter of abandoning her or at least of locking the refrigerator so that she would have nothing to eat. In a way, it was as if this senile old woman was powerless to repress the kind of basic fears of old people that the clear-minded would never dare to mention: fears of desertion, starvation, or neglect in the absolute dependency of old age. Perhaps Chinese parents do indeed see filial obedience as being based on fear; and perhaps old people feel apprehension that once they become feeble and powerless there will be nothing left to make their sons and grandsons continue supporting them.

Probably to their credit, villagers neither tried to humor the old woman during these scenes nor even allowed her to get away with creating them. When she accused her daughter of locking the refrigerator or insisted that her towels had been stolen, everyone including her own great-grandchildren and our octogenarian neighbor—argued with the ancient one, and argued quite vehemently. They seemed to be practicing some sort of "reality therapy," trying somehow to show her that nobody, least of all her daughter, was out to get her. At the same time, since she was so unaware of her actual surroundings anyway, people made no pretense of being deferential or respectful. When she complained several nights in a row about how impossible it was to sleep in a bedroom she was temporarily sharing with two of her grandchildren, her daughter simply moved her to the corner of the kitchen. A day or two later, when I asked the younger woman how the old one was doing, she motioned mischievously to me to come peek; I followed her into the kitchen where we both snickered at the ridiculous heap snoring away on the cot in the corner.

The Chinese Way: How Well Does It Work?

We can evaluate the Taiwanese solution to the problems of dealing with old people from two perspectives. First, we can look at the way the society meets the needs of the aged by providing material comforts, companionship, security, and a feeling of usefulness. Here I think the record is mixed. Old people's material needs are cared for, no doubt; and most have companionship of some sort, from younger people as well as their own age-mates. Old women fare somewhat better in regard to companionship, since unlike old men they tend to have the affection of their sons. Security is not a problem; old people are so rarely left to fend for themselves that few if any have any fears on this score. Finally, as regards usefulness, we should say that old people are generally given an opportunity to help out wherever they can, that skills or strength rarely go to waste. Women, whose skills depend less on physical strength, obviously fare better in this regard and suffer less from their declining usefulness.

From the second perspective, that of the younger generation, we see that the Taiwanese have effectively solved the problem of removing old people from positions of authority when their ability declines. The young give their elders all the care, deference, and symbolic honor required by *xiao* even as they are edging them out of power. For even in a society based on filial piety, the young must in the course of things make their way to the top.

Old Age in a South Indian Village

PAUL G. HIEBERT

Growing old in India takes place under the pervasive influence of the Hindu religion. Probably as much as any religion, Hinduism provides its followers with explicit and detailed plans for living, in which aging is charted as a series of progressively higher stages of human activity. To be sure, not all Indians scrupulously observe religious precepts. But whether aging Indians follow or depart from the course laid out by Hinduism, their lives tend to exhibit complex variations in the interplay between Hindu cultural rules and what we may term human life-strategies.

In this paper we shall consider examples of this interplay in Konduru, a south Indian village of some 3,000 people where I did fieldwork in 1963–65 and again in 1974–75. Konduru is situated on the northern edge of the Nallamalai hills, about 120 miles south of Hyderabad in the state of Andhra Pradesh (see Hiebert 1971). Our primary focus will be on the roughly three-quarters of Konduru's population that is Hindu. The Hindus are divided into 24 castes, 21 of which are considered "clean" and the others "untouchable." Though the untouchable castes are few, their members constitute one-third of the population of Konduru. Among the clean castes, the highest are the "twice-born" Brahmans, Kshatriyas, and Vaishyas (Priests, Rulers, and Merchants, respectively).* Ranking below these are the "once-born" Shudra castes, comprising various categories of farmers and workers who are allowed to associate with

---

* Indians are born into their castes, which are named for certain traditional occupations or roles. Caste names in this paper are capitalized (e.g. Goldsmith); they do not necessarily indicate a person's occupation.

and serve the upper castes. The untouchables are regarded as polluted from birth by their ritual status and by the work they custom-
arily do, and they are kept at the margins of the village and of
society.

As in other peasant societies with high birthrates and subsistence
economies, the aged make up a relatively small segment of the population of Konduru and its district. Nearly half the population are
under 20 years old, and only about 23 percent are 40 or above. If
we take 50 as marking the onset of old age, when Indians believe a
man should have sons able to assume responsibility for the household, then there are about 200 "old" men in Konduru and a few
more elderly women (Andhra Pradesh 1966:108).

Ideally, old age in Konduru brings with it security and esteem in
village and family life. Within the intricate and far-reaching functions of the caste and network systems of the village, the old men
play many of the leading roles. The caste headmen, for example,
are generally the oldest men of the senior lineages of the caste. Together with caste and village elders they serve in *panchayats*, the informal councils that operate at many levels to settle local problems.
They are a traditional, highly effective alternative to the modern Indian legal system. Few disputes in Konduru that might be expected
to reach the law courts ever get that far; most are settled by means
of *panchayats* (Hiebert 1971:101–30).

In family life the elderly are similarly important. They often
dominate the joint (or extended) family, in which old parents live
with their married sons and unmarried children in a common
household, and which Konduru villagers regard as the ideal domestic arrangement. The patriarch should have built up a trade, occupation, or estate and turned it over to his sons, thereby freeing
himself and his wife from material worries. He should have acquired a reputation in the community, enabling him to represent his
household at caste festivals and rites such as marriages and funerals, and to serve in *panchayats* and other caste and village councils.
The patriarch's sexual drive and need for offspring should have
been satisfied, allowing him to give up conjugal relations with his
wife and spend his time in relaxation and reflection, served and

honored by his descendants, while his wife oversees the management of the household.

Considerable planning can go into the attempt to assure this kind of security in old age. Normally, for example, a son and daughter-in-law will care for the aging parents, but if a couple has only daughters they usually try to arrange at least one *illitum*, or adoptive marriage, in which a son-in-law becomes their son and heir. These matches are not always easy to make, for there is some stigma attached to the adopted son-in-law (villagers say that his wife wears the pants). Nevertheless, adoptive marriages constitute 5 percent of a sample I took of 207 marriages in Konduru. Childless couples generally seek to adopt a child, often from the husband's brother. Alternatively, the husband may take a second wife in hopes of having offspring. Should these strategies fail to produce children, some couples turn for support to more distant kin such as a patrilateral nephew; but to appeal to relatives in this way brings a measure of shame.

Partly as an outcome of these efforts the social goal of the joint family is often realized in Konduru; in any event almost no old people live by themselves. In a sample of 79 households drawn from five clean castes, I found a total of 71 persons over age 50, and only one—a widower—lived alone. Of the 71 old people, 27 were men, and 14 of them lived in true joint families. (Untouchables, because of their precarious social and economic existence, show a smaller proportion of true joint families.) Of the 13 men who were not heads of true joint families, eight lived in partial joint families—two widowers and six who had seen one or more of their sons permanently leave the household. The remaining five comprised two who lived with their barren wives and two who lived with mistresses, plus the aforementioned solitary widower.

Of the 44 old women found in the sample, 20 lived with their husbands and additional family, and only four lived with their husbands alone. The remaining 20 were widows, none of whom lived alone; six were in joint families, and the other 14 had a son and perhaps other relations in the household.

Although old Konduru villagers are seldom forced to live alone,

social and economic circumstances are often barriers to their comfort and security. Poverty and illiteracy restrict many of the old to
toiling for day-to-day survival. The 1961 census of the Konduru region showed that 80 percent of the men and 40 percent of the
women aged 60 and over were still working, mostly in subsistence
agriculture. Some have no sons to support them and some work to
avoid boredom, but a great many belong to families too poor to get
along without their incomes. The census found that over 85 percent
of the old men and 99 percent of the women were illiterate. Illness
and mental incompetence among the aged present a pathetic picture, and serve as familiar themes in village proverbs and folklore,
as for example in the *Panchatantra*:

> Slow, tottering steps the strength exhaust;
>   The eye unsteady blinks;
> From driveling mouth the teeth are lost;
>   The handsome figure shrinks;
> The limbs are wrinkled; relatives
>   and wife contemptuous pass;
> The son no further honor gives
>   to doddering age. Alas! (Ryder 1953:295–96.)

A major source of insecurity for aged parents is the inherent tendency of the extended family to fragment as the sons and their families mature. If the patriarch dies, the family usually divides within
a few months; and if it does so while he is still alive, the breakup
represents only the final stage in his loss of authority. Earlier, there
may be tension among the women of the household, sometimes
tentatively resolved by establishing separate cooking hearths.
Grown brothers frequently quarrel over present or future administration of the family estate that is their patrimony. The conflict
may smolder a long time before the father's authority is openly
challenged, but if he becomes mentally incompetent the sons may
divide sooner. With the breakup of the joint family the care of the
parents and unmarried siblings devolves on the eldest son, who receives an extra share of the inheritance. In general it is easier for an
old couple to maintain a joint family than for either of them alone

to do so. As we shall see later, it is also easier for a widower than a widow to keep sons and their families together.

This sketch of aging in the context of Indian family structure must now be considered in relation to the powerful, all-embracing nature of Hinduism. Village elders sometimes explain the instability of the extended family in religious terms; Hindus, they say, should turn their thoughts from worldly matters toward God in old age. But the Hindu religion exercises a still broader influence. As a Konduru villager reaches old age, Hinduism can have a variety of impacts on his life, depending, as we shall see, on what strategy he employs and in which social or religious arena he functions.*

Hinduism describes in vast detail an organically ordered universe in which everything—god and demon, person and caste, animal and object—has its place within a hierarchy. The stages of human life are but small steps in this scheme, with old age occupying a special status as the time of a person's highest spiritual development in preparation for death. Further, Hinduism supplies a map for living; it defines human goals, outlines alternatives, and lays down principles and rules that govern each stage of life. The religious injunctions for men, whom we shall examine first, are much more explicit than those for women, but men still have at their disposal a wide range of religious options over the course.

Old Age and Men's Lives: Strategies for Aging

Having lived as a householder according to the rules, the twice-born, with firm resolve and his senses in subjection, should abandon all his belongings and enter the forest, leaving his wife to the care of his sons.

He should continually study the Vedas, and be self-controlled, friendly to all, spiritually composed, ever a liberal giver and never a receiver, and compassionate toward all beings.

Having thus passed the third stage of his life in the forest, he should renounce all attachments to worldly objects and become an ascetic during the fourth part of his life.

He should always wander alone, without any companion, in order to

---

* The theoretical model used here and the terms "strategy" and "arena" in this context are derived from Bailey 1969.

achieve spiritual perfection—clearly seeing that such attainment is possible only in the case of the solitary man who neither forsakes nor is forsaken.
(*The Laws of Manu*, chap. 6, verses 1, 8, 33, 42 [Jhā 1922:198–206].)

Hinduism prescribes its most highly elaborated life plans for the elite of society, men of the twice-born castes. They are educated to read and interpret the scriptures, like the *Laws of Manu*, and to follow them as a guide to life. Most Konduru villagers, being illiterate, get their Hinduism instead from the extensive oral literature. Those who depend on this literature, who include high-caste women and lower-castes of both sexes, are encouraged to emulate the religious ideals of the elite but are held to a less rigorous standard.

One of the most important religious concepts in the Hindu scriptures is that of the four stages in a man's life. By the time a man has reached maturity, roughly 45 to 55 years of age, he should have completed the first two stages, student and householder. As a student he should have acquired knowledge. As a householder he should have satisfied his drives for sex, status, and material property in the areas of marriage, society, and business, respectively. After these two stages he is ready to leave worldly affairs and to pursue wisdom and *moksha*, or liberation from the endless cycles of rebirths. Ideally he should move on to the third and fourth stages: he should become first an ascetic, withdrawing from sexual relations with his wife and retiring into meditation, and then a mendicant, renouncing society itself in his search for ultimate spiritual truths.

The concept of the four stages plays an important part in the old-age strategies of Konduru villagers. But tension between the demands of everyday living and the ideal of total withdrawal from society produces diverse results in their life histories.

The strategy of reinterpreting the rules

For Lakshayya, a member of the Goldsmith caste, the question of becoming a mendicant (*sannyasin*) was unavoidable. He was a Panchala, that is, a member of a cluster of artisan castes that once were ranked low but now adhere to the customs of the Brahmans and claim high status. Like his father and grandfather, he was an *achari*, a scholar of Vedanta. He was a devout man with grown sons who could take over his work and care for his wife. Should he leave the warmth and security of his home for the rigors of the forest and begging bowl like his friend Ranga Rao in neighboring Padra? Rao had renounced the world, left his high government position, and gone to live in an abandoned temple in the forest. There he lived, revered by villagers in awe of his sacrifice, and provisioned by a growing band of disciples.

But Lakshayya chose the path of abstract meditation at home, cared for by his wife and sons. He described his thoughts in two small books, *The Essence of Vedic Philosophy* and *The Path of Ratiocinative Meditation.* * In these he justifies his actions by interpreting literally certain scriptural passages that most sages have taken figuratively, and by spiritualizing other passages that the sages have taken literally. Orthodox gurus have traditionally accepted literally the injunction of mendicancy and taken as metaphorical the writings upholding the role of the householder. In his books Lakshayya, seizing on ambiguity in the texts, argues that marriage and family are a prerequisite for compliance with the other religious precepts.

Lakshayya does not reject mendicancy, he spiritualizes it. He warns that the *sannyasin* wandering alone in the forest may still be caught up in desires—if nothing else, the desire for *moksha* itself. On the other hand, he maintains that *mental* mendicancy and detachment can be practiced in the midst of any situation in life. In his old age Lakshayya tried to live up to this ideal. He lived as a householder but aspired to a higher plane of spiritual contemplation.

As things turned out, Lakshayya's strategy of reinterpreting the rules and choosing his own course of action achieved a moderate

---

* A thousand copies of each were printed and distributed to his disciples, all of whom live in Konduru and the surrounding villages. Narayanamma, an old childless widow, bore the publication costs of the second book, claiming that of all the seven kinds of good works as described in the Hindu scriptures—digging a tank, building a Brahman village, constructing a temple, planting a garden, having a son, finding a treasure, and writing or dedicating a book—the last was the greatest.

success. He gained a reputation in the village as a *jnāna*, or sage, and attracted a number of disciples, among whom was another Panchala, one Narayya of the Ironsmith caste. Narayya also gained a reputation as a *jnāna*, in part because he competed successfully with other disciples within Lakshayya's circle, in part because the villagers accepted as legitimate Lakshayya's reinterpretation of the rules.

The strategy of manipulating the rules

Rules lend themselves not only to reinterpretation but also to exploitation. In pursuing a strategy, a person may deliberately seek goals other than those toward which the scriptural texts are aimed. Because people are operating in a number of different contexts at any given time in their lives, it is possible to play a double game. Thus Patabi, of the Merchant caste, a middle-aged man whose high-caste status prevented him from divorcing his intolerably domineering wife, used the scriptural texts to justify his action and announced that he would become a mendicant, take up meditation, and seek *moksha*. Donning an ocher robe and tying his hair on top of his head, he left the village to tour the important religious shrines of India. Five years later, having heard that his wife had given up hope of his return and gone to live with her parents in a distant village, Patabi returned to Konduru. There he reopened his shop, cut his hair, and took a low-caste Shudra mistress.

The villagers were critical of Patabi's motives in becoming a mendicant—as in fact they are of the motives of most wandering mendicants who periodically pass through the village. But Patabi did not care. He had taken advantage of a religiously sanctioned course of action in order to achieve the goal of escaping from a burdensome marriage.

The strategy of operating by alternative rules

Lakshayya, Narayya, and Patabi all followed the injunctions of Manu, even though they did so according to their own interpretations or to serve their own ends. The Brahmans Krishna Chari and

Balayya chose another religious path. They are among those Hindus who hold that liberation is gained not through meditation and wisdom (*jnāna marga*) but through selfless love and devotion to God (*bhakti marga*). Krishna Chari is the local temple priest and a Shri Vaishnava, or member of a sect whose chief tenet is that the worshiper must abandon everything and take refuge in the god Rama. Balayya is a Smārtha, a family priest who reverences all the principal deities. Both men claim that religious life in the village is declining, and that it would decline further if they withdrew into mendicancy. Therefore, they say, they must remain in the village to minister to their fellowmen, seeking liberation through service rather than renunciation.

Although Krishna Chari and Balayya do not reject the path of mendicancy, they point out that it is open only to twice-born males, who make up less than 5 percent of Konduru's population. To be sure, an occasional Shudra or even an untouchable renounces the world, but the villagers are not sure of the validity of such action. On the other hand, *bhakti* creates a religious field open to men and women from all levels of society who have the time to spend an hour or two before breakfast in purification rites, to attend temple festivals, religious fairs, and devotional song services, and to participate in wedding and funeral rituals.

Many more, too ignorant to understand abstract devotional rites or too burdened by the daily responsibilities of life, choose to follow the pathway of duty (*dharma marga*). For instance, there is Pentayya, of the Barber caste, who brings a weekly offering to the local Rama temple, cracks a coconut as an offering to the icon, and takes away the blessing of having been in its presence. When illness strikes the family he makes a special offering to the god; and if it is particularly serious, he vows to go on a pilgrimage to the shrines at Tirupati to offer his hair to the Lord Venkateshwara if the patient is cured. Above all he performs the rites and duties (*dharma*) to which he and his caste of Barbers were born, and thereby helps to maintain the social order so that the more spiritually advanced may attain *moksha*. For himself, he hopes for a heaven after death and a higher status in his rebirth.

The strategy of nonparticipation

Not all Konduru villagers seek religious goals in old age. Balayya, of the Farmer caste, is content to remain in the sociopolitical arenas of his earlier life. Balayya continues to help in the fields, although his sons now do most of the work. He has time to spend on other matters, occupying himself chiefly by visiting friends and participating in village politics. On behalf of the local Congress Party he has made several trips to the city of Hyderabad. Though he does not object to his wife's faithful observance of family and temple worship, and on occasion joins in a Hindu festival himself, in general he takes little interest in religious matters.

Venkatnarayana, of the Merchant caste, is another case in point. As the village's most prosperous wholesaler and moneylender, he is too caught up in his business successes to give much attention to religion. He pays his dues to the gods by making sizable donations to the annual religious fair, and by sponsoring the itinerant Brahman priest who serves as guru to the Merchant caste in that region. When this priest is in the vicinity, he stays at Venkatnarayana's house, and the neighboring Merchants gather on the porch to hear him read and expound their caste scriptures. But Venkatnarayana spends his days counting or lending money, calculating interest, and measuring rice that he lends out as seed. Those of his younger brothers and his married sons who live with him complain behind his back that he is holding on to power too long, but short of breaking away and losing his financial support, there is nothing they can do.

The no-strategy bind

Papayya, an untouchable, has only one option open to him: to live he must work. He has a married son, but between the two of them they can barely earn enough to feed a growing family. During the agricultural season, from June to December, Papayya is out in the fields plowing, drawing water with oxen, guarding the ripening crops from thieves and wild pigs, and threshing the grain. From January through May there is little demand for day labor other than some construction or well-digging, so Papayya has some time to visit friends, attend family weddings, and watch the village religious fair. As an untouchable he remains an outsider at all the major village festivities, which center around the Rama temple. Although some untouchables have hereditary rights to beat the large leather drums that lead the religious processions, they, like Papayya, are forbidden to enter the temple itself (despite state laws to the contrary).

Old Age and Women in Village Life

Whether she be a child, or a young woman, or an aged woman, she should not do any act by herself, even in the house.

In childhood she should remain under the control of her father, in youth under that of her husband, on the husband's death under that of her son; the woman should never have recourse to independence.

Till her death, she should remain patient, self-controlled, and chaste— seeking that most excellent merit that accrues to women having a single husband.

She who does not fail in her duty to her husband, having her thought, speech, and body well controlled, reaches her husband's regions and is called "Good" by all gentlemen.

(*The Laws of Manu*, chap. 5, verses 146–47, 157, 164 [Jhā 1922:171– 83].)

Women should live under the control of the successive men in their lives, the Hindu scriptures have it, and ostensibly this is by far the most common pattern in Konduru. The wives of Krishna Chari, Farmer Balayya, Lakshayya, and Lakshayya's disciple Narayya take care of their households and serve their husbands. They spend little time outside their homes except perhaps to visit a friend, make a brief trip to the shops, go to the temple, or attend a wedding. Yet despite their subordinate position, women live much of their lives in areas where they exercise a great deal of leadership. The mother of a large extended household controls not only servants, daughters, and daughters-in-law, but also a sizable family budget. Many women set aside part of their dowry or family income in the form of money and jewelry, or carry on a small trade on the side as a hedge against family misfortunes. Many are the village stories of women who have drawn on their reserves to keep the family alive when their husbands became ill or lost their jobs.

Women, particularly those from the lower castes and from poorer homes, also participate in work groups. For example, Old Rathnamma has organized a team of women that she contracts out to do field work such as transplanting and harvesting crops. For her services she receives a small share of the team's wages. Balamma and Venkamma, the two wives of a member of the Washerman caste who has the hereditary right to wash the clothes for more than 40 families, assist their husband. (He took a second wife because he needed more help.) In recent years daughters-in-law have joined the family work force, and Balamma and Venkamma spend more of their time taking care of the home and watching the children. Krupamma's husband is a potter, and she helps him prepare the clay. But aluminum ware is cutting heavily into their sales, and they are beginning to have to look elsewhere for work to supplement their income.

The daughter

Despite the male dominance over a woman's life sanctioned by Hinduism, social realities, as Vatuk points out (1975:149–51), tie the woman more closely to other women who are central for her at each stage: her mother, mother-in-law, and daughter-in-law. Childhood years, spent under the control of the mother, are often warm and free. Though girls are given responsibilities by age six or seven, mainly helping their mothers in the kitchen and caring for their younger siblings, parents are aware of the difficulties their daughters will face after marriage and frequently pamper them. After marriage, women retain lifelong ties to the family of their childhood, receiving hospitality, presents, and support if their own marriage founders.

The mother

A woman's success lies in marriage and motherhood. She is exhorted by the family and temple priests, by passing bards and dra-

matists, and by her parents and elders to be like Sita, the loyal wife
and humble follower of Rama. Most women do indeed marry. In
the 1961 census, over 99 percent of those 60 and over in the Konduru region listed themselves as married or widowed, and less than
1 percent as separated, divorced, or never married. (The last figure
may be artificially low; low-caste families that permit divorce remarry their women to other men but are unwilling to admit it has
taken place.)

Formerly courtesanship was a legitimate alternative to marriage.
Girls born into the Courtesan (Bogum) caste were selected for their
beauty and trained in the skills of music, dance, and lovemaking.
When they came of age they were married to the local temple deity.
The patrons who paid the wedding costs had first claim on the girls'
favors, but the Courtesans served worshipers from all the upper
castes. They were not considered prostitutes, and ranked high
among the Shudras because of their service to the gods. Occasionally parents from a clean caste would pledge their daughter to the
temple deity in gratitude for a favorable response to their prayers;
and such girls, too, were trained to be Courtesans. Their offspring,
like those of the other Courtesans, were considered Bogums and
could marry Bogum men and establish regular families.

Old Courtesans not only trained and supervised their temple
charges, but also participated in important religious rituals. They
were considered particularly favored since as brides of a god they
could never become widows. The custom of dedicating girls to the
gods has died out, and Lakshmamma, now in her sixties, is the last
of the Courtesan temple women in Konduru. She lives with her son
and leads all the processions in which the icon of the god Rama is
taken from the temple through the streets of Konduru and to the
nearby fields.

The first years of married life, when a bride is new to the domain
of her mother-in-law, are often difficult ones (Vatuk 1975:149). A
young woman must move into a new home, perhaps in a strange
village, and learn the duties of a wife from her mother-in-law. For
important festivals she may go home for a visit, escorted by her
husband. There she is given clothing and a warm reception, but in

time her husband or his relative comes to take her back. As her responsibilities in her husband's home grow, such visits become less and less frequent. A wife gains respect when she bears a child, particularly a son. Barrenness is cause enough for a husband to demand a divorce or take another wife.

The mother-in-law

A woman reaches her best years when she herself becomes a mother-in-law and manages an extended household. Now she is cared for by her husband and sons, and respected and served by her daughters-in-law and grandchildren. Now it is she who delegates housework to the daughters-in-law and goes out to shop or to sell vegetables or other products in the market. Under less pressure to spend as much time as possible pleasing her husband, an old woman has more leisure than before to visit in the courtyard with other old women, or to play with her grandchildren while their mother works. And even when the mother is free, grandmother has first rights to the children's attention.

Not all women achieve these rewards of old age. We have already noted that many old women have to work hard for their subsistence; they may work on their own account or contribute their income to the family, and their tasks can range from simple food-gathering to organizing work teams. Many lose their husbands. Whereas less than 30 percent of men 70 and above are widowers, almost 95 percent of women of the same age are widows. The difference reflects in part the fact that men often marry women much younger than themselves, and also that higher-caste widows do not remarry no matter how young they are—even in cases where the man dies before the marriage is consummated. Widows of the low castes and widowers of all castes generally remarry up to age 50. Beyond that age all people are expected to turn their thoughts from sensual desires toward God.

Lacking patriarchal authority in a male-dominated society, a widow cannot easily keep an extended household together. Lakshayya's widow managed to do so for a few years following her husband's death; but when Narayya died his three sons separated and his widow lived with the eldest. Muggayya's mother was widowed when her two sons were small. With the assistance of relatives she ran the small family farm, and her sons remained together with her until about five years after their marriages. But when they became more prosperous, they quarreled and separated. Now the aged mother lives with Muggayya, her younger son, because her relationship with the older son is tense.

Disengagement

For a woman, as for a man, old age is ideally a time for withdrawal from the mundane duties of life and for relaxation and reflection on the life beyond. When a bride moves in, her mother-in-law should begin to transfer household responsibilities to her; and well before the onset of physical and mental degeneration, the matriarch should turn over to her daughter-in-law the keys that symbolize authority in the home. It is considered the duty of the younger woman to serve her mother-in-law. She should comb and braid the old woman's hair, massage her legs when she goes to bed, and care for her when she is weak or sick. The daughter-in-law should assume responsibility for the cooking and cleaning in the home, and later for handling the finances and managing the household. She should save enough to tide the family over in times of difficulty. Above all she should respect her mother-in-law.

In practice an old woman will generally delay giving over authority to her daughter-in-law as long as she feels physically and mentally capable of handling affairs. She is glad to let the younger woman do the menial tasks but reluctant to relinquish the management of the house. The result is frequently a growing tension between the two that may not end when the older woman finally has to give up control because of disability or illness.

The normal reaction of an old woman to this kind of tension may be to complain of neglect to her neighbors or to blame her son for his wife's behavior. A tragic exception may have occurred when Shantamma grew feeble and her daughter-in-law wrested control of the household from her. A few months later Shantamma was found drowned in the well where she had gone to draw water. Villagers were uncertain whether she committed suicide in bitterness at the family's rejection of her or accidentally slipped and drowned. A judgment was necessary, for if she died by accident she would be cremated with full religious rites as a Brahman, whereas if by suicide she would be considered polluted and buried like a lower-caste. After hurried consultations among leading members of the family, she was cremated the same night near the well with a minimum of ceremony. But villagers continued to gossip about the bad feelings in the household that had preceded her death.

Religion becomes increasingly important in the lives of older women as they disengage themselves from family responsibility. Some women spend considerable time each morning propitiating the gods in their homes, and occasionally they take offerings to the temple. It is not uncommon to find women in the circle of disciples attending a Hindu saint or a guru. Since women are allowed to follow the guru of their choosing regardless of their husbands' caste or religious affiliation, many women follow a guru to find freedom from constraints imposed on them at home.

A dying woman, like a dying man, can nearly always be confident that she will not be left alone. She spends her last days at home cared for by the family, and when the end seems near relatives and friends gather to say farewell. They continue to express their love in the preparation of her body, the funeral rites, and the annual rites for the ancestors. The father may have the leading role in society and in religion, but it is the mother who has the closest relationship with her sons and daughters. In the end it is the mother who is revered most in the home and remembered most lovingly.

Coast Salish Elders

PAMELA T. AMOSS

The Coast Salish Indians of western Washington State and British Columbia still live on the wooded coasts and valleys of their forebears, but the human world they live in is very different. Despite massive social, economic, and cultural changes, contemporary Coast Salish elders still enjoy rank comparable to that of the old people in precontact society. The prestige of modern elders, like that accorded their ancestors, is based on a recognition of their contribution to the group. Only the nature of their contribution has changed.

In premodern times, the old were valued for their special skills in food procurement and processing, for their knowledge of building and canoe-making, and for their ability to produce items of practical or prestige value. They were repositories of knowledge and ritual expertise. They also made important contributions to group solidarity by holding together the extended family households. Modern old people procure little food and earn little or no money to buy any. Their knowledge of techniques and skills is of little economic importance. Although concern for the old still holds the scattered family groups together, under modern economic conditions the production and consumption unit is the nuclear household, not the extended one. Yet old men and women maintain prestige and high social rank through their control of scarce information about the old ritual practices and through the spiritual power people believe they possess. Far from losing ground as Coast

Sections of this paper were adapted for a paper entitled "Cultural Centrality and Prestige for the Elders: The Coast Salish Case," to appear in Christine Fry, ed., *Dimensions: Aging, Culture, and Health* (New York: J. F. Bergin, 1981).

Salish society has changed, they have actually improved their position in the last twenty years.

The Coast Salish challenge the conventional wisdom that rapid social change is detrimental to the old. Drawing heavily on Simmons (1959), Cowgill and Holmes argue from the experience of modernization that rapid social change will inevitably damage the old (1972:9). If this is not so among today's Coast Salish elders, part of the explanation may lie in the confusion between modernization and social change (on this confusion see Achenbaum & Stearns 1978). Modernization is a term applied to a special case of change, the recent history of the Western world. It is not yet clear that the rest of the world must follow the Western example in all particulars. We need more information on what actually happens when non-Western peoples "modernize," that is, become more industrialized, urbanized, bureaucratized, and integrated into the world economic system. In particular, we need more information about the impact of all this on the elderly. If, as Cowgill and Holmes claim, modernization is hard on the old, is this simply because the old cannot handle change, or because changes make it impossible for the old to contribute in traditional ways and block them from learning new ones?

Clearly the issue is not social change per se, but whether social change allows old people opportunities to reestablish themselves in useful roles. Press and McKool (1972) identify four factors that predict high rank for old people: contribution, control, advice, and "residual" prestige (prestige that lingers because one or more of the other components was important earlier in the person's life). When change destroys old people's ability to manage one or all of these components, they lose rank. Change, however, need not interfere with all of the components; and even when it does, old people may find opportunities to develop new arrangements where they control, contribute, or advise.

Obviously, if the old lose a monopoly over vital resources, their position will be threatened. The classic example of this kind of economic revolution is the introduction of steel axes to the Australian Yir Yiront, which broke the power of the senior males, formerly the exclusive owners of all stone axes (Sharp 1952:84). Similarly, where the old dominate through ritual rather than economics, the discrediting of beliefs will result in their having to find a place in the new ideology or go the way of the old Asmat men discussed by Van Arsdale in this volume. Although social and cultural change introduced during the period of early contact with whites was destructive to the position of Salish elderly on both these scores, more recent change has provided the present cohort of elders with an opportunity to improve their social position. They now find themselves in a period when people want to affirm their Indian identity and need the old to legitimize their claim to an exclusive cultural tradition. In fact, such a tradition has persisted through all the vicissitudes of recent Indian history. Much of the old world view still finds expression in the religious beliefs and practices of modern Coast Salish. But for the purposes of solidifying the group and drawing its boundaries, what really matters is that people should believe they possess a genuine tradition. So although many of the active old people are developing new solutions out of old ideas, both they and their younger relatives emphasize orthodoxy, not innovation. The contemporary aged are taking advantage of the current enthusiasm for the old ways both to perpetuate what is most central in the old values and to improve their own position in the social group.

To understand how old people are profiting from contemporary concerns with ethnicity, it is essential to see the cultural tradition and historical process out of which the present situation has developed.

The Precontact Position of the Aged

Our picture of the position of old people during precontact times is tentative, being based on the scanty reports of early observers and the memories of old people's impressions of aboriginal life recalled from childhood or heard from their grandparents. Nevertheless, the evidence suggests that old people were honored and deferred to because they made real economic contributions to group survival and because they were repositories of vital information of both a practical and a ritual nature.

How was "old" defined in precontact times? Apparently not

chronologically, because the Coast Salish, like most preliterate peoples, did not keep close track of age. It was defined rather by a combination of generational position and physical functioning. The importance of generational position can be deduced from kinship terminologies that illuminate both the kinds of relations prescribed between classes of relatives and also the native concept of the ideal human life span (Geertz 1966:20). Although information is limited, we do know that in at least one Coast Salish group, the Klahuse of mainland British Columbia, adults were named teknonymously, suggesting that generational position defined the most important roles (Barnett 1955:132). A person moved through a sequence of statuses from youth to old age. A new family cycle began again with the birth of a great-grandchild. The terms for great-grandchild and great-grandparent were the same, suggesting that they were in some sense equivalent: one ended when the other began (Collins 1974:88; Hess 1976:105; Smith 1940:174; Elmendorf 1960:347; Spier 1925:74). Following this line of reasoning a person would have become "old" on the birth of his or her first grandchild.

People were considered old when they could no longer perform the full range of adult tasks appropriate to their sex and station. When men could no longer hike miles to kill game and pack it home again, and when women found it hard to bend and stoop to pick berries or dig roots, they would begin to shift the major part of these jobs to younger relatives and turn to the tasks reserved for older people. The heavy physical demands of men's work suggest that men may have become functionally "old" sooner than women, but menopause was a complicating factor. A woman was "old" for certain purposes when she could no longer bear children, even if her food producing and processing abilities were still in their prime. Old age did not bring leisure to either sex, but only a shift from the physically more demanding tasks to those where skill, patience, or experience were more important than strength and speed.

The chronological age at which people were classified as "old" seems to have been younger than that at which modern Coast Salish become elders. As Simmons has pointed out, most preindustrial societies raise people to the rank of elders earlier than industrial societies (1959:6). I would estimate that most precontact Coast Salish became "old" according to the combination of criteria suggested above in the last half of the fifth decade of life.

Old age not only brought new responsibilities, it conferred freedom from certain restrictions. Among the Upper Skagit—and probably elsewhere, too—old age, when one's reproductive responsibilities were discharged, was the time for love affairs (Collins 1974:232). People found the prospect of an alliance between beautiful youth and experienced old age romantic. Unlike contemporary Western culture, which accepts such a relationship between an older man and a younger woman but stigmatizes the reverse, Coast Salish people found the old of either sex suitable lovers for the young.

Many of the taboos that applied to people in their youth and maturity were waived for the elderly. Women past child-bearing age could no longer pollute hunters or their gear, nor would they contaminate the berry patches or offend the salmon. Old men no longer had to observe the discipline of sexual abstinence and fasting that were incumbent on active hunters and fishermen. Certain foods forbidden to the young were reserved for the old. With the raising of these restrictions new avenues of spiritual power opened up to both men and women. The old were often caretakers for people in dangerous liminal states—successful spirit questers, girls at menarche, women in childbirth, warriors returned from battle, mourners, and the recently dead. A grandmother was an ideal attendant for a girl at her first menstruation, because she was not only wise, experienced, and concerned about her granddaughter but also impervious to the girl's sacred contagion (Elmendorf 1960:439).

Old people were always treated with respect and deference. Young people were taught to be courteous to their grandparents and to other people of that generation. All elders were addressed with kinship terms appropriate to the age difference. This pattern reflected a cultural theme of subordination of younger to elder, but it also represented a fear that slighting old people might be dangerous: anyone who had lived a long time must have had good supernatural helpers still ready to avenge any insult to their human partner. It was assumed that a person's spiritual power increased throughout life. Although children and adolescents were enjoined to quest for spirit visions, mature people might also look for additional help or receive new gifts from the guardians they had encountered first in their youth. Only the advent of life-threatening illness was taken as a sign that a person's spirit helpers had left for good. Religious specialists—whether shamans, mediums, or people who knew magical spells—were almost always old. Shamans often received their visions in preadolescent quests but usually did not practice until they were at least middle-aged, because powers acquired early in life needed time to season and develop full potency. Old people took prominent roles in the winter-season ceremonials, when people whose vision-quest encounters had given them a song and dance performed publicly in a gathering of fellow villagers and visitors from nearby communities.

In a preliterate society, old people are almost always the repositories of important cultural traditions. They not only transmit traditional information and beliefs, they also contribute their own insights to a living and growing corpus. The Coast Salish elders, too, were the keepers and creators of traditional lore in the form of genealogies, family histories, and myths. Although every old person probably knew all the myths told in his local group, not everyone was an equally skilled raconteur. Nor did everyone have the right to tell stories that belonged to other families. Those who had a gift for telling the stories well, and the right to tell them, would recite them during the long northern winter evenings in the big communal houses.

Part entertainment, part moral code, part religious dogma, the myths were one of the major devices old people used to instruct the young. Mature adults bore children and fed them, but it was the grandparent generation that raised them. The archetype of the pitiful figure in Coast Salish mythology is the child without grandparents to instruct him: deprived of legitimate access to knowledge, his only recourse was to eavesdrop on the instructions given more fortunate children by their grandparents. For grandparents taught the children how to prepare for the all-important spirit quest, how to conduct themselves in polite society, how to give speeches at potlatches or funerals, and even how to perform many practical tasks of everyday life. Among some groups, it was the grandparent who gave the child his or her first formal name. Consequently, a successful person was said to be one who had "listened to his grandparents' words" (Barnett 1955:144).

Leadership in all areas except warfare was in the hands of old people (Haeberlin & Gunther 1930:59). Although there were no hereditary political offices, members of wealthy and influential families dominated village politics and were responsible for maintaining intervillage alliances through networks of marriage and potlatch alliances. Political leaders were supposed to be wise, gentle, courteous, forbearing, and old. They never traded insults with ill-bred people, but maintained a dignified silence in the face of criticism. Undoubtedly the experience gained through many years of observing and interacting with fellow villagers and the widespread network of friends and affines in other villages made it possible for such people to achieve their ends through persuasion and influence. The war leader, by contrast, was usually a younger man who demonstrated the efficacy of his fierce spirit-helpers by his violent disposition. People deferred to him, but he had almost no influence in any activity other than offensive raiding.

Although all political and economic leadership was in the hands of the old, it was restricted to elders with large, wealthy families. Poor old people, like poor young ones, had little real power. In a society where a person's place depended on kinship ties, an old person without grandchildren was in as pitiable a state as a child without grandparents. But even poor old people were treated with an outward show of respect. And one of the most generous acts a wealthy person could perform was to give something to a poor elder at a potlatch, because it was assumed that the gift could never be repaid. Young people of good families were taught to be helpful to all older people. One informant related that when he was a boy his father used to send him to carry water for an impoverished old woman who lived alone near them (Barnett 1955:142). Whenever he helped her, she made cryptic references to how she would thank him by sending him supernatural help when she died.

Despite the real power and influence of many elders and the overt respect shown to all old people, there are indications that people did not all rejoice at getting old. Twana youth were taught never to call anyone "old" in his or her hearing (Elmendorf 1960:431). No doubt people mourned the loss of full competence in adult roles, despite the special privileges they would enjoy as elders. Furthermore, old age and death are inextricably linked, and Coast Salish ideology offered little consolation for the prospect of death— life after death being only a poor shadow of life in this world (Collins 1974:232). Even the guardian spirits who sustained a person through every earthly crisis left as death approached (*ibid.*). In addition to this general burden weighing on every older person, elders who became mentally incompetent, though supported by their families and tolerated by the community, were neither honored nor cherished. Despite this darker side to aging, it seems clear that most healthy old people in precontact times participated fully in community life, and that the more fortunate dominated it.

Change in the Position of the Old After Contact

Solid historical information on what conditions were like for old people during the period shortly after the first contact with whites, is very limited. We do not even know how the disastrous epidemics affected the percentage of the elderly in the population. We can estimate, based on other sedentary hunting and gathering groups, that before contact old people amounted to only about 3 percent of the population. Although the earliest period of white contact, the maritime fur trade, probably had little noticeable effect on the position of the old, it has been suggested that the new source of wealth may already have begun to undermine native institutions because it allowed younger men to acquire wealth outside the traditional kin and village networks. In the first half of the nineteenth century, when the Hudson's Bay Company established fur-trading posts in Coast Salish territory at Fort Nisqually in southern Puget Sound and along the Frazer River to the north, signs of strain were apparent. Hudson's Bay observers at Fort Nisqually reported a young man who claimed a vision empowering him to enrich all his followers. Although innovations were often legitimized by visions, this entrepreneur was unusual because he was a young man seeking religious leadership. We do not know whether he would have been accepted, because both he and his visions were discredited when he was caught robbing graves to supply his miraculous wealth (Bagley 1916:157–60).

After the treaties signed in the 1850's removed the final obstacle to white settlement, the economic and political base of Indian society changed radically in a relatively short time. The economic foundations of Indian life were almost completely changed. Indians began to work for wages—digging clams, logging, or the like—so that a person no longer depended for subsistence on close ties with his elders and his sibling group. With the shift from hunting and gathering to wage labor, old people's knowledge was no longer relevant. And since most jobs available to Indians required full physical strength, there was no opportunity for old people to update their skills. At the same time that new opportunities were opening up in the labor market, Indians were being moved from their traditional village sites and concentrated on reservations. With the breakup of old multifamily households, elders found themselves relatively isolated and deprived of their position as senior advisers in the large households.

Challenges to the native ideology robbed elders of their dominant place in the religious life of the people. Old rituals were either suppressed by missionaries and Indian agents or abandoned as useless by a progressively demoralized people. Deprived of supernatural legitimation for their roles as trainers of the young, old people lost the influence they had traditionally had over their grandchildren.

The conditions eroding the position of Indian elders during the last half of the nineteenth century did not apply everywhere with equal force. Although Indians living in southern Puget Sound or around the major centers of white settlement were subjected to intense pressure to accommodate themselves to new patterns, farther north—along the inner shores of Vancouver Island and along the headwaters of rivers draining into Puget Sound—where they were left more to themselves, the older patterns persisted longer. Shamans, most of whom were old, became in many places the targets of suspicion and hostility among their own people, who attributed the high infant death rate from introduced diseases to their malevolence. Old people of no particular distinction, however, whose family networks remained intact still probably enjoyed the support and affection of their children and grandchildren even if they no longer were able to make economic or ritual contributions to family well-being. And in many families, grandparents continued to raise the young. But, in general, elders who managed to preserve their positions did so on the strength of their individual abilities to adjust to new circumstances.

During this period, religious leadership apparently passed into the hands of young men. In the 1880's the Indian Shaker Church was founded, which became the most successful of several revitalization efforts among Puget Sound Salish Indians. The leader, John Slocum, was only 40 years old when he was said to have died and returned to life, urging Indians to reject the old shamanistic religion and to give up drinking, smoking, and gambling. Slocum was still too young to be considered an elder. He was working as a logger— a young man's job—and his eldest daughter was just going through her first puberty seclusion. Slocum's father offers an interesting contrast to his innovative son. When John fell ill a second time, the old man insisted on calling a shaman over the objections of John's wife, Mary. It was at this point that Mary began the involuntary trembling, called the "shake," which is still the sign of the Holy Spirit's presence to Shakers. Strengthened by her inspiration, Mary sent the shaman packing and cured John herself. Predictably, the most outstanding early Shaker converts were also young people (Amoss, in press). Shaker ritualism rejected the symbols of aboriginal supernatural forces and the practices of the old faith. Ritual forms were borrowed instead from both Protestant and Catholic Christianity. Although the most important concepts from the old world view survived under new symbols, this overt rejection of the old ways further eroded the influence of the elderly.

During the period of early white contact, and later when the Indians were being completely subjugated to an alien political and economic system as well as bombarded by the messages of a proselytizing religious system, the old people found themselves at a disadvantage. Although cultural themes emphasizing the importance of respecting the elders persisted, the old were unable to compete successfully for new sources of power and were reduced to whatever individual strategies they could devise to assure themselves a secure place in Indian society. The early history of Coast Salish acculturation thus supports the assumption that rapid social change displaces the old. But the situation in the 1970's presents a striking contrast: contemporary elders have somehow managed to secure an esteemed place in society. This change cannot be explained by claiming that Indian society is now stable, because economic, political, and cultural change is impinging on Indian people to a degree unprecedented since the initial period of white settlement in the last half of the nineteenth century. Rather, Indians now see value in affirming their unique position within American society, an enterprise to which old people not only contribute but to which they are essential.

Contemporary Coast Salish Elders

In general, contemporary people become elders later than their ancestors did. Generational position, appearance, physical vigor, chronological age, and personal choice all combine to dictate when a person will begin to act like and be treated as an elder. Elders usually have adult grandchildren, but younger people may become elders when their last senior relative dies and they must assume positions of family leadership. The old system of kinship terminology has fallen into disuse and with it, presumably, the view that an individual is an actor in a cycle that continually renews itself every fourth generation. Only the way Indian names are treated suggests that the concept of the individual as an ephemeral manifestation of immortal social position persists. Names, now as in the past, pass in the family line. There are many names, so that two people rarely have the same one. Names are used only on formal occasions, and a person can only use a name he has been given after he has hosted a gathering to announce it publicly. In native usage, a person does not "have" an Indian name; he "carries" it and is responsible for making it grow in honor and significance. Patterns of bestowing names have changed; some modern elders are giving names not to their grandchildren but to their great grandchildren.

Although Indians are benefiting from the same factors that have raised life expectancy for other Americans, the effects have come to them more slowly. Even though older people are living longer now, the high birth rate and improved survival rate among the very young have kept the percentage of Coast Salish old people low. Only 5 percent are over 65 years old; of these, 53 percent are women (D. Smouse, personal communication).*

Although some contemporary old people make economic contributions to the family, elders contribute most significantly in the religious sphere. Modern Coast Salish people participate in a number of institutionalized religions. Some are Roman Catholic, some Protestant, some Pentecostal, and a few Mormon. A sizable number belong to the Indian Shaker Church. Many participate in the revived aboriginal-style winter dancing rituals. Furthermore, a number are active in several of these religious systems at once, because most Coast Salish people feel that their access to spiritual consolation or supernatural help should not be limited to any one channel. Nevertheless, the most dedicated and fervent participation is reserved for the winter ceremonialism, the Shaker Church, and the Pentecostal Church, all of which encourage the expression of individual inspiration in altered states of consciousness. Of these, the two systems that are most unequivocally Indian and that discourage non-Indian participation—the Shaker Church and the

* This information comes from the Annual Report (April 1977) of the Labor Force submitted to the Western Washington Agency of the BIA by the tribes of Western Washington. Since only tribal groups recognized by the BIA report, a number of Indians are not represented and the figures vary in accuracy depending on the reporting procedures of the tribes. Mr. D. Smouse, Programs Officer, Western Washington Indian Agency, kindly supplied the figures.

aboriginal-style winter dancing—offer the greatest scope for older people.

Both Shakerism and spirit dancing exalt knowledge of the old ways, something only older people possess. (Not all old people, however, have such knowledge.) Furthermore, although inspiration can come to any believer, one grows in spiritual power by learning how to cooperate with the spirit, whether the Holy Spirit in the Shaker Church or a person's individual guardian spirit in the aboriginal tradition. Since power increases with experience, older people are stronger than younger people. And finally, long life itself is thought to be proof of strong power.

Although elders are important in the Shaker Church, their role is perhaps most central in the aboriginal-style spirit dancing rituals (Kew 1970; Amoss 1978). These ceremonies are held in the winter, when the individual spirit guardians of the participants return and inspire them to perform their spirit songs and dances. At big gatherings held every winter weekend on reservations in British Columbia and Washington State, people come to dance and to help others dance by singing and drumming for them. Families who want to give names to their children or memorialize their dead act as hosts. Before the dancing begins, the host families make their announcements and pass out presents to thank the guests for witnessing the event. Elders are essential to all this, and also to the rituals that precede and follow the large public gatherings, for the following reasons.

First, because of particular historical circumstances, elders are the only ones who know how things should be done. In most communities during the 1940's and 1950's, the formative years of today's young and middle-aged people, the old-style rituals were moribund and rarely performed. Thus the elders who remember the times when they were still being practiced are in particular demand as advisers.

Second, old people, even though generally poor, contribute directly to the ritual occasions by giving goods and money and by participating. They not only know how speeches should be made, they make them. They not only remember how the deceased's photo should be displayed at a memorial, they may carry it around during the ceremony themselves. They are the ones who know all the other important people and remember their Indian names, which must be used on formal occasions. When family regalia should be displayed —inherited masks, or rattles, or the like—it is the oldest people in the family who know what to do. Not only do old people bestow family names, they remember the genealogies that should be announced when a name is given.

Third, elders control the initiation process that is the only route to full participation in the winter dancing ceremonial system. Though any Coast Salish may attend, only properly initiated spirit dancers actually dance at winter gatherings. Dancers may be of any age, but the majority are in their late teens or early twenties and have been initiated, if not at the behest of their family elders, at least with their consent. In theory, a man or woman is initiated as a dancer because he or she is troubled by a possessing spirit. The initiation process establishes a cooperative relationship between the two. In fact, a person so troubled is not always initiated, because the initiators may not want to take on the responsibility, or because the person's family may be unwilling to give permission or unable to meet the expenses involved. And not everyone who is initiated has first been troubled by a possessing spirit: every year, some young people are initiated at the request of their elders to control their rebelliousness, depression, or self-destructive behavior (Amoss 1978; Jilek 1974). People believe that old dancers, who specialize in initiations, can induce spirit possession and the accompanying song and dance in a person who has had no previous spiritual encounter. Although the initiators will not act without family approval, they may refuse a candidate they consider too difficult. "Bringing in" a dancer is dangerous because mismanagement can cause serious illness or even death. Again, experience is at a premium. A few initiators are only middle-aged, but the most prominent are old—with the gray hair that symbolizes accumulated power and experience.

Old people also have a virtual monopoly over the other ritual roles that control the welfare of others. Shamans, who have the power to inflict fatal illness and to cure it, are all old. Mediums, who can see ghosts and who officiate after funerals, when food is burned to placate the ghosts, are also old men or women. And it is the elders who use the family-owned ritual privileges invoked on public occasions for the good of the whole community. Although inherited or shamanistic powers have no place in Shaker ritual, older Shakers are often believed to have special gifts for curing or for diagnosing the cause of spiritual or physical trouble. Some older Shakers also combine their Shaker gifts with help from their Indian powers.

Three examples will illustrate how particular old people manage their participation in ritual life.* The first, Raphael Jack, is a dominant figure; the second, Bobby Due, is limited by factors beyond his control; and the third, Roseanne, concentrates her efforts only on her own family.

Now in his late seventies, Raphael Jack has been a religious functionary all his life, but he has shifted his primary affiliation from the Shaker Church to the Pentecostal Church to the Spirit Dancing arena. A practicing shaman, he also owns an important inherited ceremonial privilege, which he uses for the public good when he performs, and is a medium to whom people turn when troubled by ghosts. He withdrew from the Pentecostal Church, where he had become a very successful preacher, and returned to the "Indian Way" during the early years of the winter dancing revival in Washington State. He contributed to that revival and has devoted himself to fostering it.

He has the spiritual strength to initiate new spirit dancers and has brought in many of the young and middle-aged dancers. Jack has a large family and claims a distinguished ancestry, so his leadership in the ceremonial system rests on inherited right as well as on personal power. Known throughout the larger ceremonial circuit, he is often called from considerable distances to heal the sick. Although most people still trust his spiritual strength, a recent pro-

---

* To protect their privacy, I have used pseudonyms for these people and the others I describe later.

tracted illness led some to wonder if his spiritual partners were withdrawing from him. "Raphael is the last one around here," they say, "we don't know what we'll do when he's gone."

Bobby Due is not in good health. He suffers from arthritis made worse by obesity. Despite his troubles, he looks strong and vigorous. It comes as a surprise to learn he is in his nineties. When there are visitors, he is usually cheerful and alert. He doesn't talk about feeling depressed, but when he is alone he sleeps all day. His own relatives seldom come to see him. Until recently he lived with a family who were paid by public assistance to look after him. They were careful to feed him and see to his needs, but they seldom took him to big gatherings, and he was alone for hours at a time with nothing to do and no one to talk to. Several years ago when he could still walk around, Bobby used to go to spirit dances regularly, whenever he could get a ride. He was always recognized publicly, given presents, and thanked for attending. He seldom sang his spirit song, but everyone knew he had one. In his youth Bobby was a passionate Shaker, a missionary, and a healer. He loves to tell how he and fellow Shakers "brought the Shake" to his home country and of the many people they converted. Some years ago, Bobby drifted away from Shakerism into spirit dancing, and he believes that he has cut himself off from the Holy Spirit, the power inspiring Shaker healers. He and Raphael Jack are alike in that neither believes he can combine shamanistic spirits with the Holy Spirit; this reflects an older, more exclusive interpretation of the Shaker faith, one not shared by many young and middle-aged Shakers. Although Bobby Due's ability to enhance his position by participation in the ritual circuit is drastically limited because he cannot attend most gatherings, the old values are still useful to him because the people he lives with are very careful to avoid antagonizing his spirit-helper by neglecting him.

Now in her late sixties, Roseanne is another example of a person who is "religiously musical." Raised a Roman Catholic, she resisted involvement in traditional Indian religion even when her brother was initiated as a dancer to cure the deep depression he suffered after Roseanne's first son died as a baby. In her middle years she became a devout Pentecostal Christian, and she still believes herself to be "saved," although she has not participated in Pentecostal worship for some time, having instead been active as an Indian dancer and, most recently, having joined the Shaker Church. She now divides her time between winter ceremonials and Shaker services. A strong-willed woman, she has found in religion a way to come to terms with her disappointments and to find the recognition she needs. She has drawn the rest of her conjugal family into all her conversion experiences. With her they were first Pentecostal Christians, then dedicated spirit dancers, and now Shakers. In all three systems she has often been the focus of extraordinary ritual activity. While a Pentecostal Christian, she received a gift of tongues "from Africa," which was interpreted as a calling to the African missions. She claims she was strongly tempted to go to Africa but refused because her children were still young. As a spirit dancer she was often visited with new songs that required the services of shamans or other specialists to express properly. Nor is she a lukewarm Shaker; when the Holy Spirit comes to her, she sees visions and is moved to cure and help. Her strategy for social recognition has been to rely on the authority of her religious experiences rather than to claim traditional learning, though she knows more aboriginal lore than many of her contemporaries and still speaks her mother tongue fluently. Unlike Raphael Jack, who scrupulously maintains his reputation for generosity, Roseanne neglects her obligations to make gifts on ceremonial occasions. For this reason, she does not have the influence in the wider ceremonial circuit that other people with her religious talent do. Her major concern has been to use her spiritual power to influence her own family.

Several years ago, when she had a serious break with her oldest daughter, Roseanne began to suffer chest and back pains. Concerned, one of her sons consulted Bobby Due, who is "part Indian doctor." He said that she had been deeply hurt by her child's behavior and that her Indian spirit had been disturbed. Now, because of her sorrow, she was troubled by a new song that should be publicly performed at a gathering hosted by her family. The ritual of bringing out the new song rallied community support for Roseanne and solidified disapproval of her unfilial daughter. In this case, the ritual restated the value of children respecting their elders by emphasizing the supernatural dangers attendant on a breach of the norm. Roseanne emerged from the experience decked with new supernatural honors, and her daughter bowed to the heavy social pressure and was reconciled with her mother.

Roseanne's experience illustrates how the pattern of old people dominating in religious ritual is consciously emphasized. Every public occasion where the elders appear—managing, controlling, advising, and participating—is punctuated by speeches that reiterate the necessity of respecting them and heeding their advice. Far from excluding the young from these arenas, the elders are at pains to make sure that the young participate in supportive roles. Although only 28 percent of the people in the two communities for which we have actual figures are initiated spirit dancers, there are at least as many more who participate in other capacities (Kew 1970:127; Amoss 1978:138). Young people who are not spirit dancers can drum and sing to help the dancers, tend the fires that burn in the big houses, help in the parking lot, wait on tables when guests are fed, and take gifts from the hosts to the witnesses who are being honored during the formal proceedings. Middle-aged people also participate, but more often as speakers, dining-room managers, ushers who seat the guests, etc. All age groups are fully engaged, but it is the old who are running things.

The power old people achieve through the ceremonial system comes at a price, however. Just as elders use the ideology to constrain the young, so the young and middle-aged can use it to evade some measure of control. Once part of the dancing fraternity, a person can use the demands of his guardian spirit as an explanation for withdrawing from the family or avoiding certain responsibilities, and other people cannot object or even ask questions about it. Apparently, from the viewpoint of the elders, the disadvantages are minor compared with the advantages.

It is also important to note that the old people who dominate the ritual arena do not form any sort of solidaristic group. Indeed, ritual specialists often actively compete with one another and are not above gossiping about the inadequacies of their age mates. Shamans occasionally cooperate on a case, but ordinarily a successful ritual leader like Raphael Jack seeks help only from his own kindred, and perhaps some of his affines. The only issues on which the old will all agree is the importance of respect for the elderly.

And finally, though ritual participation is the most common route to prestige for old people, not all old Coast Salish are able or willing to participate in old-style religious activity. There are other strategies they may employ to contribute, control, and advise. There is, however, variation in the prestige of individual old people depending on the plan they follow and how successful they are.

Ellen Tommy and John Halarise are elders who refuse to participate in the winter ceremonials. Ellen still commands respect for her general knowledge of the old ways. John, however, has chosen to remain aloof from most communal activities and makes no effort to be considered knowledgeable on the old religion.

Ellen Tommy is unusual in her refusal to be involved in the Indian ceremonials. A widow in her mid-seventies, she knows more than she will admit about the ceremonial system, although she never participated willingly. As a young married woman she was required to drum and sing for her husband, who controlled a very powerful set of divining poles that exorcised evil influences or found lost things. He was often called to "run his poles," and she went with him, but she never felt at home with his supernatural helpers. After she left her husband, she turned to Pentecostal Christianity, which provided her a home, an explanation, and a sense of purpose in life. She believes in the powers of Indian doctors and spirit dancers—although she thinks some of the contemporary dancers are fakes—but she believes the power comes from evil sources. Ellen's surviving child and her grandchildren are staunch Pentecostal Christians who, although not so devout as she, follow her lead in rejecting the winter dancing. Ellen lives in her daughter's big, busy household, where her influence has the maximum effect on the family. Although subjected to considerable pressure from her age-mates, she stands firm. She is not, however, hostile to all the old rituals and has tried to reintroduce old customs to contemporary funerals.

When her brother died a few years ago, Ellen laid out all his belongings after the funeral meal and invited friends to take them away. She did not, as has recently been the custom, have them burned. As she explained, in the old days "only the Canadian Indians burned things; we gave things away, we didn't burn them." The reason was the same: if the close kin kept the deceased's belongings, his ghost would be drawn back and might cause them harm. Ellen Tommy's rejection of the usual custom in favor of an earlier local pattern was accepted and may even provide a model for others who do not want to burn the deceased's possessions. Her knowledge of the old customs, her respect for the old values, and her command of the old language allow her to extend her influence beyond her family, even though she will not participate in the ritual system that provides the surest route to prestige for most of the other successful elders.

John Halarise is an example of an old man who has declined both the responsibilities and the rewards of being an active elder. Now 80, John is the son of a prominent tribal leader. John feels incapable of following his father's path. "I can't speak in public," he says, "it's just not in me." So when other old people stand up to thank their hosts and exhort the young, John sits quietly. He has, however, definite opinions on how the old ways have been corrupted by contemporary interpretations. "In the old days," he says, "them Indian dancers they really *had* something. Now they're just jumping around. They ain't got nothing." Although his religious beliefs do not prevent him from attending or even participating, he does not see any real value in the current rituals and holds himself aloof. Unlike Ellen Tommy, who advocates an alternative to participating in spirit dancing and who is always looking for Christian interpretations of old customs, John is simply not interested. He remembers how, as a young man in the heyday of the Washington timber industry, he worked in the woods, and he loves to recount his logging exploits. When he retired from logging, he tended his own farm and is proud that he never needed to accept any public assistance. Married twice, he lives with his much younger wife and their foster child on the land his father left him. He is content with what he has and in remembering what he did. The need for recognition, which motivates some of his contemporaries, does not affect him. Since he does not participate, his influence is slight in his home community and he is virtually unknown beyond it. Yet even people like John Halarise, who choose not to participate at all, benefit from the halo effect radiating from the most successful participants.

Conclusion

The case of the Coast Salish elders who are taking advantage of their unique position to reaffirm the ideological bases of Indian identity shows that rapid social change of itself is not necessarily a threat to the elderly. It may even come as a boon to them. It is the direction of social change that is important for old people, and how it will affect their ability to control, contribute, and advise.

Modern Coast Salish old people have access to all three prestige-generating components through the revival of Indian religious ceremonies. In this area they have near-exclusive command of the advice component, because they are the ones who claim and who are believed to have preserved the old traditions from the past. Insofar as Indian religious expression has become diagnostic of real Indianness, the old people who hold the keys to it are the focus of Indian identity. Many are actively promoting the revival and encouraging the participation of their younger relatives, even to the point of sometimes having them initiated without their prior consent. Far from being the helpless victims of change, this case shows that given the right conditions, elders can not only profit from it, but may even become active agents of change themselves.

References Cited

Eisdorfer: Foreword

Beattie, Walter. 1978. "Aging: A Framework of Characteristics and Considerations for Cooperative Efforts Between the Developing and Developed Regions of the World." Background paper prepared for the expert group meeting on aging, United Nations, N.Y., 3–5 April.

Cowgill, Donald, and Lowell D. Holmes. 1972. *Aging and Modernization*. New York.

Hauser, P. M. 1976. "Aging and Worldwide Population Change," in Robert H. Binstock and Ethel Shanas, eds., *Handbook of Aging and the Social Sciences*. New York.

Kay, David W. K. 1977. "The Epidemiology and Identification of Brain Deficit in the Elderly," in Carl Eisdorfer and Robert O. Friedel, eds., *Cognitive and Emotional Disturbance in the Elderly*. Chicago.

Kramer, Morton, Carl A. Taube, and Richard W. Redick. 1973. "Patterns of Use of Psychiatric Facilities by the Aged: Past, Present and Future," in Carl Eisdorfer and M. Powell Lawton, eds., *The Psychology of Adult Development and Aging*. Washington, D.C.

Maddox, G. L. 1978. "Will Senior Power Become a Reality?," in Lissy F. Jarvik, 3d., *Aging Into the 21st Century*. New York.

McKain, Walter C. 1972. "The Aging in the USSR," in Cowgill & Holmes, *Aging and Modernization*.

Mumford, Lewis. 1968. *The Urban Prospect*. New York.

Myers, George C. 1977. "Future Age Projections and Society." Paper presented at the World Conference on Aging organized by L'Institute de la Vie, Vichy, France.

Tobin, Joseph Jay. 1978. "The American Idealization of Old Age in Japan." Paper presented at the 11th International Congress of Gerontology, Tokyo, Japan.

Amoss and Harrell: Introduction

Ahern, Emily. 1973. *The Cult of the Dead in a Chinese Village*. Stanford, Calif.

Amoss, Pamela. 1978. *Coast Salish Spirit Dancing*. Seattle, Wash.

Arensberg, C. M., and S. T. Kimball. 1940. *Family and Community in Ireland*. Cambridge, Mass.

Butler, Robert. 1975. *Why Survive: Being Old in America*. New York.

Cohen, Myron L., 1970. "The Developmental Process in the Chinese Domestic Group," in Maurice Freedman, ed., *Family and Kinship in Chinese Society*. Stanford, Calif.

Cowgill, Donald, and Lowell D. Holmes. 1972. *Aging and Modernization*. New York.

Foner, Anne, and David I. Kertzer. 1978. "Transitions over the Life Course—Lessons from Age-Set Societies," *American Journal of Sociology*, 83: 1081–1104.

Fortes, Meyer. 1949. *The Web of Kinship Among the Tallensi*. London.

Guemple, D. Lee. 1969. "Human Resource Management: The Dilemma of the Aging Eskimo," *Sociological Symposium*, 2 (Spring 1969): 59–74.

Hughes, Charles. 1960. *An Eskimo Village in the Modern World*. Ithaca, N.Y.

Levine, Robert A. 1978. "Adulthood and Aging in Cross-Cultural Perspective," *Items*, 31/32 (4/1) (March 1978): 1–5.

Levi-Strauss, Claude. 1970. *The Raw and the Cooked*. New York.

Neugarten, Bernice, and C. Hagestad. 1976. "Age and the Life Cycle," in Robert H. Binstock and Ethel Shanas, eds., *Handbook of Aging and the Social Sciences*. New York.

Opler, Morris E. 1936. "An Interpretation of Ambivalence of Two American Indian Tribes," in W. Lessa and E. Vogt, eds., *Reader in Comparative Religion* (3d ed.). New York.

Ortner, Sherry B. 1974. "Is Female to Male as Nature Is to Culture?," in Michelle Zimbalist Rosaldo and Louise Lamphere, eds., *Woman, Culture, and Society*. Stanford, Calif.

Simmons, Leo. 1945. *The Role of the Aged in Primitive Society*. London.

Spencer, Paul. 1965. *The Samburu: A Study of Gerontocracy in a Nomadic Tribe*. Berkeley, Calif.

Van Stone, James. 1974. *Athapaskan Adaptations*. Chicago.

Vatuk, Sylvia. 1976. "Raya Population of Raypur: Age Pyramids." Paper presented in the Departmental Colloquium of the Department of Anthropology, University of Washington.

Wolf, Margery. 1972. *Women and the Family in Rural Taiwan*. Stanford, Calif.

Weiss: Evolutionary Perspectives on Human Aging

Acsadi, G., and J. Nemeskeri. 1970. *History of Human Lifespan and Mortality.* Budapest.

Armitage, P., and R. Doll. 1961. "Stochastic Models for Carcinogenesis," *Proc. IVth Berkeley Symposium on Mathematical Statistics and Probability*, 4:19–38.

Black, F. L. 1966. "Measles Endemicity in Insular Populations: Critical Community Size and Its Evolutionary Impact," *J. Theor. Biol.*, 11: 207–11.

———. 1975. "Infectious Diseases in Primitive Societies," *Science*, 187: 515–18.

Black, F. L., J. Boodall, A. Evans, H. Liebhaber, and G. Henle. 1970. "Prevalence of Antibody Against Viruses in the Tiriyo, an Isolated Amazon Tribe," *Am. J. Epidemiol,*, 91:430.

Burnet, F. M. 1974. *Intrinsic Mutagenesis.* New York.

———. 1976. *Immunology, Aging, and Cancer.* San Francisco.

Burnet, F. M., and D. O. White. 1972. *Natural History of Infectious Disease.* Cambridge, Eng.

Coale, A. J. 1957. "How the Age Distribution of a Human Population Is Determined," *Cold Spring Harbor Symposium on Quantitative Biology*, 22:83–90.

———. 1972. *The Growth and Structure of Human Populations.* Princeton, N.J.

Cohen, M. N. 1977. *The Food Crisis in Prehistory.* New Haven, Conn.

Comfort, A. 1979. *Aging: The Biology of Senescence* (3d ed.). New York.

Cook, P. J., R. Doll, and S. A. Fellingham. 1969. "A Mathematical Model for the Age Distribution of Cancer in Man," *Int. J. Cancer*, 4:93.

Cutler, R. G. 1972. "Transcription of Reiterated DNA Sequence Classes Throughout the Lifespan of the Mouse," *Adv. Geront. Res.*, 4:219–321.

———. 1973. "Redundancy of Information Content in the Genome of Mammalian Species as a Protective Mechanism Determining Aging Rate," *Mech. of Aging and Develop.*, 2:381–408.

———. 1975. "Evolution of Human Longevity and the Genetic Complexity Governing Aging Rate," *Proc. Nat. Acad. Sci.*, 72:4664–68.

———. 1976a. "Nature of Aging and Life Maintenance Processes," *Interdiscipl. Topics Geront.*, 9:83–133.

———. 1976b. "Evolution of Longevity in Primates," *J. Hum. Evol.*, 5:169–202.

———. 1979. "Evolutionary Biology of Senescence," in J. A. Behnke, C. E. Finch, and G. B. Moment, eds., *A New Look at Biological Aging*, pp. 311–60.

Doll, R. 1971. "The Age Distribution of Cancer: Implications for Models of Carcinogenesis," *Proc. Roy. Stat. Soc.*, Part 2:133–66.

Emlen, J. M. 1970. "Age Specificity and Ecological Theory," *Ecology*, 51:588–601.

Hamilton, W. D. 1966. "The Moulding of Senescence by Natural Selection," *J. Theor. Biol.*, 12:12–45.

Hayflick, L. 1975. "Current Theories of Biological Aging," *Fed. Proc.*, 34:9–13.

———. 1976. "The Cell Biology of Human Aging," *New Engl. J. Med.*, 295:1302–8.

Hershey, D. 1974. *Lifespan and Factors Affecting It*. Springfield, Ill.

Howell, N. 1976. "Toward a Uniformitarian Theory of Human Paleodemography," in R. Ward and K. Weiss, eds., *The Demographic Evolution of Human Populations*. London.

Keyfitz, N. 1968. *An Introduction to the Mathematics of Population*. New York.

Keyfitz, N., and W. Flieger. 1968. *World Population: An Analysis of Vital Data*. Chicago.

Kohn, R. 1971. *Principles of Mammalian Aging*. Englewood Cliffs, N.J.

Livingstone, F. B. 1958. "Anthropological Implications of Sickle Cell Gene Distributions," *Am. Anthropol.*, 60:13–22.

Mann, A. E. 1975. *Paleodemographic Aspects of the South African Australopithecines*. Philadelphia.

Medawar, P. B. 1952. *An Unsolved Problem in Biology*. New York.

Pollack, Otto. 1980. "Shadow of Death over Aging" (editorial), *Science*, 207:1419.

Preston, S. H. 1976. *Mortality Patterns in National Populations*. New York.

Preston, S. H., N. Keyfitz, and R. Schoen. 1972. *Causes of Death: Life Tables for National Populations*. New York.

Preston, S. H., and V. E. Nelson, 1974. "Structure and Change in Causes of Death: An International Summary," *Pop. Studies*, 28:19–51.

Rosenberg, B., G. Kemeny, L. Smith, I. Skurnick, and M. Bandurski. 1973. "The Kinetics and Thermodynamics of Death in Multicellular Organisms," *Mech. of Aging and Develop.*, 2:275–93.

Russel, J. C. 1958. "Late Ancient and Medieval Populations," *Trans. Am. Phil. Soc.*, 48, No. 3.

Sacher, G. A. 1975. "Maturation and Longevity in Relation to Cranial Capacity in Hominid Evolution," in R. Tuttle, ed., *Antecedents of Man and After. Vol. I: Primates: Functional Morphology and Evolution*. The Hague.

———. 1976. "Evaluation of the Entropy and Information Terms Governing Mammalian Longevity," *Interdiscipl. Topics Geront.*, 9:69–82.

———. 1977. "Life Table Modification and Life Prolongation," in C. Finch and L. Hayflick, eds., *Handbook of the Biology of Aging*. New York.

Service, E. 1975. *Primitive Social Organization* (2d ed.). New York.

Shock, N. 1960. "Some of the Facts of Aging," in N. Shock, ed., *Aging: Some Social and Biological Aspects*. Washington, D.C.

———. 1961. "Physiological Aspects of Aging in Man," *Ann. Rev. Physiol.*, 23:97–122.

Strehler, B. L. 1977. *Time, Cells, and Aging* (2d ed.). New York.

Swedlund, A., and G. Armelagos. 1975. *Demographic Anthropology*. Dubuque, Iowa.

Ubelaker, D. 1974. "Reconstruction of Demographic Profiles from Ossuary Skeletal Samples: A Case Study from the Tidewater Potomac," *Smithsonian Contributions to Anthropology*, No. 18.

Ward, R. H., K. M. Weiss, and R. Chakraborty. 1980. *Age Patterns of Cancer. I. Models for Parameterizing Risk with Age*. (In preparation.)

Weiss, K. 1973. *Model Life Tables for Anthropological Populations*. Society for American Archaeology, Memoir No. 27.

Weiss, K. M., R. Chakraborty, and R. H. Ward. 1980. *Age Patterns of Cancer. II. Application of Risk Model to Worldwide Data*. (In preparation.)

Williams, G. C. 1957. "Pleiotropy, Natural Selection, and the Evolution of Senescence," *Evolution*, 11:398–411.

Hrdy: "Nepotists" and "Altruists"

Alexander, R. D. 1974. "The Evolution of Social Behavior," *Annual Review of Ecology and Systematics*, 5:325.

Angst, W. 1975. "Basic Data and Concepts on the Social Organization of *Macaca fascicularis*," in I. Rosenblum, ed., *Primate Behavior*. New York.

Bernstein, Irwin S. 1968. "The Lutong of Kuala Selangor," *Behaviour*, 32:1–15.

———. 1969. "Spontaneous Reorganization of a Pigtail Monkey Group," in C. R. Carpenter, ed., *Proceedings of the Second International Congress of Primatology, vol. 1: Behavior*. Basel.

Blaffer Hrdy, Sarah. 1977. *The Langurs of Abu: Female and Male Strategies of Reproduction*. Cambridge, Mass.

Blaffer Hrdy, S., and D. B. Hrdy. 1976. "Hierarchical Relations Among Female Hanuman Langurs (Primates: Colobinae, *Presbytis entellus*)," *Science*, 193:913–15.

Blest, A. D. 1963. "Longevity, Palatability and Natural Selection in Five Species of Moth," *Nature*, 197:1183–86.

Chalmers, N. R. and T. E. Rowell. 1971. "Behavior and Female Reproductive Cycle in a Captive Group of Mangabeys," *Folia Primat.*, 14:1–14.

Cohen, Donna, Carl Eisdorfer, and Douglas M. Bowden. 1979. "Cognition," in Douglas M. Bowden, ed., *Aging in Non Human Primates.* New York.

Comfort, A. 1956. *The Biology of Senescence.* New York.

Cummings, Elaine, and William Henry. 1961. *Growing Old: The Process of Disengagement.* New York.

Davis, R. T. 1978. "Old Monkey Behavior," *Experimental Gerontology*, 13:237–50.

Dittus, W. P. J. 1975. "Population Dynamics of the Toque Monkey, *Macaca sinica*," in R. H. Tuttle, ed., *Socioecology and Psychology of Primates.* The Hague.

Drickamer, L. 1974. "A Ten-Year Summary of Reproductive Data for Free-Ranging *Macaca mulatta*," *Folia Primat.*, 21:61–80.

Dunbar, R., and P. Dunbar. 1975. *Social Dynamics of Gelada Baboons.* Basel.

Engle, E. 1938. "The Genital Organs of the Male Gibbon 'Bobby' (*Hylobates Lar*)," *Rep. of the Penrose Research Lab. Zool. Soc. of Philadelphia*, 66(31):23.

Fitts, S. 1976. "Behavioral Stereotype and Social Disengagement: A Descriptive Study of Aging in Nonhuman Primates." Ph.D. diss., Washington State Univ.

Flint, M. 1976. "Does the Chimpanzee Have a Menopause?" Paper presented at the Forty-fifth Annual Meeting of the American Association of Physical Anthropologists, St. Louis.

Goodall, J. van Lawick. 1971. *In the Shadow of Man.* Boston.

Graham, C. E. 1970. "Reproductive Physiology of the Chimpanzee," in G. H. Bourne, ed., *The Chimpanzee*, vol. 3. Basel.

Haldane, J. B. S. 1941. *New Paths in Genetics.* New York.

Hamilton, W. D. 1964. "The Genetical Evolution of Social Behavior, Parts I and II," *J. Theoret. Biol.*, 7:1–51.

———. 1966. "The Moulding of Senescence by Natural Selection," *J. Theoret. Biol.*, 12:12–45.

Hodgen, G. D., A. L. Goodman, A. O'Connor, and D. K. Johnson. 1977. "Menopause in Rhesus Monkeys: Model for Study of Disorders in the Human Climacteric," *Am. J. Obstet. Gynecol.*, 127:581–84.

———. 1979. "Reproductive Function in Aged Female Chimpanzees," *Am. J. Phys. Anthro.*, 50, no. 3:291–300.

Itani, J. 1959. "Paternal Care in the Wild Japanese Monkey, *Macaca fuscata fuscata*," *Primates*, 2, no. 1:61–93.

Iwamoto, T. 1974. "A Bioeconomic Study of a Provisioned Troop of Japanese Monkeys (*Macaca fuscata fuscata*) at Koshima Islet, Miyazaki," *Primates*, 15:241–62.

Jay, P. 1963. "The Social Behavior of the Langur Monkey." Ph.D. diss., Univ. of Chicago.

Kawai, M. 1958. "On the System of Social Ranks in a Natural Troop of Japanese Monkeys, Parts 1 and 2," in S. Altmann, ed., *Japanese Monkeys: A Collection of Translations*. Alberta, 1965.

Koford, C. 1963. "Rank of Mothers and Sons in Bands of Rhesus Monkeys," *Science*, 141:356–57.

Kummer, H. 1971. *Primate Societies: Group Techniques of Ecological Adaptation*. Chicago.

Kurland, J. 1977. *Kin Selection in the Japanese Monkey. Contributions to Primatology*. Basel.

Lill, A. 1974. "Sexual Behavior of the Lek-Forming White Bearded Manakin (*Manacus manacus trinitatis* Hartert)," *Z. Tierpsychol.*, 36:1–36.

Marsden, H. M. 1968. "Agonistic Behavior of Young Rhesus Monkeys After Changes Induced in Social Rank of Their Mothers," *Anim. Behav.*, 16:38–44.

Medawar, P. B. 1952. *An Unsolved Problem in Biology*. London.

Moley, J. F. 1976. "The Essence of Senescence: The Aging Process with Respect to Physiological, Evolutionary, and Behavioral Aspects." Senior Honors Thesis, Harvard Univ.

Ohsawa, H. 1979. "The Local Gelada Population and Environment of the Gich Area," in *Ecological and Sociological Studies of Gelada Baboons. Contributions to Primatology*, 16:3–45.

Partch, Jennifer. 1978. "The Socializing Role of Postreproductive Rhesus Macaque Females." Paper presented at the Forty-seventh Annual Meeting of the American Association of Physical Anthropologists, Toronto.

Pianka, E. R. and W. S. Parker. 1975. "Age Specific Reproductive Tactics," *American Naturalist*, 109:453–63.

Riopelle, A. J. and C. M. Rogers. 1965. "Age Changes in Chimpanzees," in A. M. Schrier, H. F. Harolow, and F. Stollitz, eds., *Behavior of Nonhuman Primates*, vol. 2. New York.

Sade, D. S. 1972. "A Longitudinal Study of Social Behavior of Rhesus Monkeys," in R. H. Tuttle, ed., *The Functional and Evolutionary Biology of the Primates*. Chicago.

Sade, D. S., et al. 1975. "Population Dynamics in Relation to Social Structure on Cayo Santiago." Paper presented at the Forty-fourth Annual Meeting of the American Association of Physical Anthropologists, Denver.

Stearns, S. C. 1976. "Life History Tactics: A Review of the Ideas," *Quar. Review of Biology*, 51, no. 1:3–47.

Van Wagenen, G. 1970. "Menopause in a Subhuman Primate (Abstract)," *Anat. Rec.*, 166:392.

———. 1972. "Vital Statistics from a Breeding Colony: Reproduction and Pregnancy in *Macaca mulatta*," *J. Med. Prim.*, 1:3–28.

Waser, P. M. "Postreproductive Survival and Behavior in a Free-Ranging Female Mangabey," *Folia. primatologica* (in press).

Weismann, August. 1889. *Essays upon Heredity and Kindred Biological Problems*. Oxford.

Williams, G. C. 1957. "Pleiotropy, Natural Selection, and the Evolution of Senescence," *Evolution*, 11:389–411.

Wilson, E. O. 1975. *Sociobiology: The New Synthesis*. Cambridge, Mass.

Biesele and Howell: "The Old People Give You Life"

Biesele, M. 1972. "The Black-Backed Jackal and the Brown Hyena: A !Kung Bushman Folktale," *Botswana Notes and Records*, no. 4:133–34.

———. 1976. "Aspects of !Kung Folklore," in R. B. Lee and I. DeVore, eds., *Kalahari Hunter-Gatherers*. Cambridge, Mass.

Blurton-Jones, N., and M. J. Konner. 1976. "!Kung Knowledge of Animal Behavior," in R. B. Lee and I. DeVore, eds., *Kalahari Hunter-Gatherers*, Cambridge, Mass.

Coale, A. J., and P. Demeny. 1966. *Regional Model Life Tables and Stable Populations*. Princeton, N.J.

Howell, N. 1976. "The Population of the Dobe Area !Kung," in R. B. Lee and I. DeVore, eds., *Kalahari Hunter-Gatherers*. Cambridge, Mass.

———. 1979. *Demography of the Dobe !Kung*. New York.

Katz, R. 1976. "Education for Transcendence: !Kia Healing with the Kalahari !Kung," in R. B. Lee and I. DeVore, eds., *Kalahari Hunter-Gatherers*. Cambridge, Mass.

———. In press. *Boiling Energy!* New Haven, Conn.

Lee, R. 1967. "Trance Cure of the !Kung Bushmen," *Natural History* (Nov.):30–37.

———. 1972a. "!Kung Spatial Organization: An Ecological and Historical Perspective," *Human Ecology*, 1, no. 2:125–47.

———. 1972b. "Work Effort, Group Structure, and Land Use in Contemporary Hunter-Gatherers," in P. J. Ucko et al., eds., *Man, Settlement, and Urbanism*. London.

———. 1979. *The !Kung San: Men, Women, and Work in a Foraging Society*. Cambridge, England.

Marshall, L. 1960. "!Kung Bushman Bands," *Africa*, no. 30:325–55.

———. 1976. *The !Kung of Nyae Nyae*. Cambridge, Mass.

Truswell, A. S., and J. D. L. Hansen. 1976. "Medical Research Among the !Kung," in R. B. Lee and I. DeVore, eds., *Kalahari Hunter-Gatherers*. Cambridge, Mass.

Wiessner, P. 1977. "*Hxaro*: A Regional System of Reciprocity for Reducing Risk Among the !Kung San." Ph.D. diss., Univ. of Michigan.

Sharp: Old Age Among the Chipewyan

Sharp, Henry S. 1973. "The Kinship System of the Black Lake Chipewyan." Ph.D. diss., Duke Univ.

———. 1976. "Man: Wolf: Woman: Dog," *Arctic Anthropology*, 13, no. 1:25–34.

———. 1977. "The Chipewyan Hunting Unit," *American Ethnologist*, 4, no. 2:377–92.

———. 1979. *Chipewyan Marriage*. Museum of Man Mercury Series. Canadian Ethnology Service Paper no. 58. National Museum of Canada, Ottawa.

Van Arsdale: The Elderly Asmat of New Guinea

Bowers, Nancy. 1971. "Demographic Problems in Montane New Guinea," in Steven Polgar, ed., *Culture and Population: A Collection of Current Studies*. Chapel Hill, N.C.

Clark, M. Margaret. 1973. "Contributions of Cultural Anthropology to the Study of the Aged," in L. Nader and T. W. Maretzki, eds., *Cultural Illness and Health: Essays in Human Adaptation*. Washington, D.C.

Eyde, David B. 1967. "Cultural Correlates of Warfare Among the Asmat of Southwest New Guinea." Ph.D. diss., Yale Univ.

Lex, Barbara W. 1977. "Voodoo Death: New Thoughts on an Old Explanation," in David Landy, ed., *Culture, Disease, and Healing: Studies in Medical Anthropology*. New York.

Nag, Moni. 1962. "Factors Affecting Human Fertility in Nonindustrial Societies: A Cross-Cultural Study," *Yale Univ. Publications in Anthropology*, no. 66.

Rappaport, Roy A. 1968. *Pigs for the Ancestors: Ritual in the Ecology of a New Guinea People*. New Haven, Conn.

Sahlins, Marshall D. 1968. "Poor Man, Rich Man, Big Man, Chief: Political Types in Melanesia and Polynesia," in A. P. Vayda, ed., *Peoples and Cultures of the Pacific*. Garden City, N.Y.

Shanas, Ethel. 1975. "Gerontology and the Social and Behavioral Sciences: Where Do We Go from Here?" *The Gerontologist*, 15, no. 6:499–502.

Sowada, Alphonse. 1968. "New Guinea's Fierce Asmat: A Heritage of

Headhunting," in R. L. Breeden, ed., *Vanishing Peoples of the Earth.* Washington, D.C.

Van Amelsvoort, V. F. P. M. 1964. *Early Introduction of Integrated Rural Health into a Primitive Society.* Assen, The Netherlands.

Van Arsdale, Peter W. 1975. *Perspectives on Development in Asmat* (vol. 5 of the *Asmat Sketch Book Series*, ed. F. A. Trenkenschuh). Agats, Irian Jaya.

————. 1978a. "Activity Patterns of Asmat Hunter-Gatherers: A Time Budget Analysis," *Mankind*, 11:453–60.

————. 1978b. "Population Dynamics Among Asmat Hunter-Gatherers of New Guinea: Data, Methods, Comparisons," *Human Ecology*, 6, no. 4:435–67.

Van Arsdale, Peter W., and David E. Gallus. 1974. "The 'Lord of the Earth' Cult Among the Asmat: Prestige, Power, and Politics in a Transitional Society," *Bulletin of Irian Jaya Development* (Irian), 3, no. 2:1–31.

Weiss, Kenneth M. 1973. "Demographic Models for Anthropology," *Memoirs of the Society for American Archaeology*, no. 27 (*American Antiquity*, 38, no. 2, part 2).

Zegwaard, Gerard A. 1971. "Headhunting Practices of the Asmat of West New Guinea," in L. L. Langness and J. C. Weschler, eds., *Melanesia: Readings on a Culture Area.* Scranton. [Orig. 1959.]

Colson and Scudder: Old Age in Gwembe District

Colson, Elizabeth. 1960. *Social Organization of the Gwembe Tonga.* Manchester, Eng.

————. 1971a. *The Social Consequences of Resettlement.* Manchester, Eng.

————. 1971b. "Heroism, Martyrdom, and Courage," in T. O. Beidelman, ed., *The Translation of Culture.* London.

Colson, Elizabeth, and Thayer Scudder. 1976. "New Economic Relationships Between the Gwembe Valley and the Line of Rail," in D. Parkin, ed., *Town and Country in East and Central Africa.* London.

Scudder, Thayer. 1962. *The Ecology of the Gwembe Tonga.* Manchester, Eng.

————. 1971. "Gathering Among African Woodland Savannah Cultivators: A Case Study of the Gwembe Tonga," *Zambian Papers*, no. 5 (Manchester, Eng.).

Scudder, Thayer, and Elizabeth Colson. 1972. "The Kariba Dam Project: Resettlement and Local Initiative," in H. Russell Bernard and Pertti Pelto, eds., *Technology and Social Change.* New York.

Nason: Aging in a Micronesian Community

Athos, Anthony G. 1968. "Time, Space, and Things," in Anthony G. Athos and Robert E. Coffey, eds., *Behavior in Organizations: A Multidimensional View*. Englewood Cliffs, N.J.

Carroll, John B. 1956. *Language, Thought, and Reality: Selected Writings of Benjamin Lee Whorf*. Cambridge, Mass.

Lee, Dorothy. 1959. *Freedom and Culture*. Englewood Cliffs, N.J.

Levy-Bruhl, Lucien. 1966. *How Natives Think*. New York.

Nason, James D. 1970. "Clan and Copra: Modernization on Etal Island, Eastern Caroline Islands." Ph.D. diss., Univ. of Washington.

———. 1974. "Political Change: An Outer Island Perspective," in Daniel T. Hughes and Sherwood G. Lingenfelter, eds., *Political Developments in Micronesia*. Columbus, Ohio.

———. 1975. "The Strength of the Land: Community Perception of Population on Etal Atoll," in Vern Carroll, ed., *Pacific Atoll Populations*. Honolulu.

Shahrani: Aging Among the Kirghiz

CINAM. 1973. "Services for Children Within Regional Development." Provisional report submitted to the Gov't of Afghanistan and UNICEF. Kabul.

Dupree, Louis. 1970. "Population Dynamics in Afghanistan," *American Universities Field Staff Report, South Asia Series*, 14, no. 7.

———. 1971. "Afghanistan," in Harrison Brown and Alan Sweezy, eds., *Population: Perspective 1971*. San Francisco.

Kushkaki, B. 1923. *Rahnuma-i Qataghan wa Badakhshan*. [Guide to Qataghan and Badakhshan.] Kabul.

McClung, J. 1969. *Effects of High Altitude on Human Birth*. Cambridge, Mass.

Shahrani, M. N. 1979. *The Kirghiz and Wakhi of Afghanistan: Adaptation to Closed Frontiers*. Seattle, Wash.

Harrell: Growing Old in Rural Taiwan

Ahern, Emily M. 1973. *The Cult of the Dead in a Chinese Village*. Stanford, Calif.

Baker, Hugh D. R. 1968. *A Chinese Lineage Village: Sheung Shui*. Stanford, Calif.

Cohen, Myron L. 1976. *House United, House Divided: The Chinese Family in Taiwan*. New York.

Fei Hsiao-tung. 1939. *Peasant Life in China.* London.
Gamble, Sidney D. 1968. *Ting Hsien: A North China Rural Community.* Stanford, Calif. (First published 1954.)
Wolf, Margery. 1968. *The House of Lim: A Study of a Chinese Farm Family.* New York.
———. 1970. "Child Training and the Chinese Family," in Maurice Freedman, ed., *Family and Kinship in Chinese Society.* Stanford, Calif.
———. 1972. *Women and the Family in Rural Taiwan.* Stanford, Calif.
Yang, Martin C. 1945. *A Chinese Village: Taitou, Shantung Province.* New York.

Hiebert: Old Age in a South Indian Village

Andhra Pradesh, Government of. 1966. *Census of 1961: District Census Handbook, Mahbubnagar District.* Hyderabad.
Bailey, F. G. 1969. *Stratagems and Spoils: A Social Anthropology of Politics.* New York.
Hiebert, Paul G. 1971. *Konduru: Structure and Integration in a South Indian Village.* Minneapolis, Minn.
Jhā, Gangā-Nātha. 1922. *Manu-Smrti: The Laws of Manu with the Bhāsya of Mēdhātithi.* Calcutta.
Lakshmachari, V. 1951. *Vādārnavanavanēthamanu Vuruseshya Sanvādamu* [The Essence of Vedic Philosophy]. Secunderabad.
———. 1964. *Paramapada Saupāna Mārgamu* [The Path of Ratiocinative Meditation]. Nagarkurnool.
Ryder, Arthur W., trans. 1953. *The Panchatantra.* New Delhi.
Vatuk, Sylvia. 1975. "The Aging Woman in India: Self-Perceptions and Changing Roles," in Alfred De Souza, ed., *Women in Contemporary India.* Delhi.

Amoss: Coast Salish Elders

Achenbaum, W. Andrew, and Peter N. Stearns. 1978. "Old Age and Modernization," *The Gerontologist,* 18, no. 3:307–12.
Amoss, Pamela T. 1978. *Coast Salish Spirit Dancing: The Survival of an Aboriginal Religion.* Seattle, Wash.
———, in press. "The Indian Shaker Church of the Northwest," in *Handbook of North American Indians, Northwest Volume.*
Bagley, Clarence, ed. 1916. "Journal of Occurrences at Nisqually House (1835)," *Washington Historical Quarterly,* 7, no. 2:144–67.
Barnett, Homer. 1955. *The Coast Salish of British Columbia.* Eugene, Ore.
Collins, June M. 1974. *Valley of the Spirits: The Upper Skagit Indian of Western Washington.* Seattle, Wash.

Cowgill, Donald, and Lowell D. Holmes. 1972. *Aging and Modernization.* New York.

Elmendorf, W. W. 1960. *The Structure of Twana Culture with Notes on Yurok Culture.* Pullman, Wash.

Geertz, Clifford. 1966. "Person, Time, and Conduct in Bali: An Essay in Cultural Analysis." Cultural Report Series No. 14, Yale University Southeast Asia Studies. New Haven, Conn.

Haeberlin, Hermann, and Erna Gunther. 1930. "The Indians of Puget Sound," *University of Washington Publications in Anthropology,* 4, no. 1:7–83.

Hess, Thom. 1976. *Puget Salish Dictionary.* Seattle, Wash.

Jilek, Wolfgang. 1974. *Salish Indian Mental Health and Culture Change.* Toronto.

Kew, J. E. M. 1970. "Coast Salish Ceremonial Life: Status and Identity in a Modern Village." Ph.D. diss., Univ. of Wash.

Press, Irwin, and Mike McKool, Jr. 1972. "Social Structure and Status of the Aged: Toward Some Valid Cross-Cultural Generalizations," *Aging and Human Development,* 3:297–306.

Sharp, Lauriston. 1952. "Steel Axes for Stone Age Australians," in Edward H. Spicer, ed., *Human Problems in Technological Change.* New York.

Simmons, Leo W. 1959. "Aging in Modern Society," in *Toward a Better Understanding of the Aging.* New York.

Smith, Marian W. 1940. *The Puyallup Nisqually.* New York.

Spier, Leslie. 1925. "The Distribution of Kinship Systems in North America," *University of Washington Publications in Anthropology,* 1, no. 2:69–88.

Index